The RV Makeover Bible

1st Edition

Jack and Julee Meltzer

DESERT WINDS PRESS
Belfast, Maine
www.desertwindspress.com

Dedicated to Helen Kingsbury for her spirit, her strength, and her precious little tins of pinwheel date cookies.

ISBN: 978-0-9769290-1-7

Printed in the United States of America

Cover photos from left to right: Architectural trimwork and drawer dishwasher (courtesy Monaco Coach Corporation), motorhome photo (courtesy Winnebago Industries, Inc.), and RV interior (courtesy Newell Coach Corporation). Illustrations by Jack Meltzer

Table of Contents

Chapter 1

Introduction

The RV Makeover Bible is the first book to focus entirely on the topic of remodeling, refurbishing, and upgrading recreational vehicles. It's an important book because it helps to define some of the possibilities in terms of improving as well as personalizing an RV.

As a practical matter, The RV Makeover Bible is an "idea" book as opposed to a technical "how to" guide. For detailed information on subjects like flooring, finish carpentry, plumbing, and so on, it's best to refer to books that are specifically devoted to these topics. For that reason, we've listed some of these books at the end of each chapter.

In any case, before continuing, we need to explain why it makes sense to remodel your RV in the first place. Although there are a countless reasons, these are some of the best:

Ten Good Reasons to Remodel your RV

1. Remodeling is the most economical way to upgrade your RV. Remodeling enables you to obtain the features you need and the look you've always wanted at a mere fraction of the cost of a new RV.

2. Remodeling is essentially the process of customizing and decorating an RV to suit your lifestyle, your needs, and your personal tastes. As a practical matter – there's no other way to achieve these crucial goals.

3. Tasteful and competent remodeling adds value to an RV. This added value ultimately results in a higher selling price. In addition, remodeled RVs also tend to sell faster because interested buyers don't want to miss out on a one-of-a-kind model.

4. Remodeled RVs tend to be of a higher quality than those that that haven't. Remodeling, when done properly, is a successful collusion of creativity, quality materials, and workmanship. While some companies claim to accomplish this feat at the factory, it's hard to compete with a proud owner that has all the time in the world to do things right.

5. RV remodeling is extremely enjoyable as well as rewarding. Whether you're changing the style, upgrading furnishings, or adding new features, the process is filled with creativity, anticipation, and excitement.

6. One of the primary differences between a $75,000 RV and a $175,000 RV is the interior. Experienced RVers use skillful interior remodeling and selective upgrades to create a luxuriously customized RV at a fraction of the cost of a new high-end model.

7. Even though high-end RVs cost considerably more than a typical home, many lack even the most basic amenities like dishwashers, garbage disposals, book shelves, desks, and Internet access. For the most part, the only way to obtain these amenities is to install them yourself.

8. Remodeled RVs have significantly more storage space than new models. RV manufacturers don't have the time or the incentive to install closet organizers, drawer dividers, rotating shelves, and pull-out cabinet inserts. But you do.

9. Even though there are more than 2 million full-time RVers, there's no such thing as a special model for full-timers. The only way to obtain an RV that is truly suited for full-timing is to design and perform the modifications yourself.

10. Everyone else is doing it. Today, millions of people routinely remodel and upgrade their RVs. That's why modifications and upgrades represent the single most popular topic of discussion on virtually every RV forum on the Internet.

Chapter 2

Project Planning and Preparations

Some projects can be tackled with very little in the way of planning or groundwork. Unfortunately, RV remodeling isn't one of them. The reasons are numerous but in general – RVs are too confined, too specialized, and too complicated to get away with a casual approach towards remodeling.

So if you want your RV remodeling projects to succeed, you'll have to take the time to develop a good plan. Accordingly, this chapter describes the key decisions you'll need to make and the steps you should take before beginning any RV remodeling or fix-up project.

Identify your True Objectives

When planning a major remodeling project – you should have a pretty good idea of what you're actually trying to achieve. These are some of the more common reasons for remodeling an RV:

- Add more storage capacity
- Make the interior brighter, cheerier, or more colorful
- Upgrade the technology
- Replace or modernize the furnishings or appliances
- Improve the general condition of the RV's interior
- Make the RV more appropriate for a family
- Make the RV more suitable for full-time RVing
- Alter the mood, character, or ambience of the RV
- Change the style of the interior
- Make the RV easier to sell
- Increase the sales price or trade-in value

Brainstorm for Ways to Accomplish your Goals

Brainstorming, when done properly, involves exchanging new ideas without the risk of criticism or disapproval. In other words, arrange to have several open-minded discussions on possible ways to achieve the remodeling goals that you've identified. Be sure to write down any ideas or solutions that you really like.

Window Shop

The top designers in the RV industry spend a lot of time checking out the competition. In fact, that's how they usually get their best ideas. Try to get your hands on everything you can on the subject of interior decorating and home design. Visit your local dealer or go to an RV show. Look through RV brochures, surf the web, go to the library, visit bookstores, check out other people's RVs, and read magazines. The more you see, the greater the likelihood of coming up with a design you like.

Establish a Project Schedule

Before you begin your remodeling project, grab a pad and create a simple schedule. Project schedules serve two functions. First, by arranging your project activities chronologically, you'll know when to order supplies, get materials delivered, rent specialized tools, write checks, and so on. Second, a schedule enables you to see if the project time-frame is actually being met. If it isn't, you can make the necessary adjustments to get it back on track. The following example depicts a two-week schedule for a living room remodeling and upgrade project.

Project Schedule

Date	Task
8/12	Remove furniture & blinds
8/13	Tape windows. prime walls
8/15	Paint walls (2 coats)
8/17	Add decorative border
8/18	Remove carpeting
8/20	Prepare subfloor
8/22	Lay tile flooring
8/24	Install molding & trimwork
8/25	Re-install furniture & blinds
8/26	Clean and inspect RV

A schedule can help you to plan and track project details

Avoid Taking on Multiple Projects

It's often tempting to take on several remodeling tasks at the same time. After all, your tools are out and the disruptions have already begun. However, if you try to juggle multiple projects, you may find yourself facing mounting costs, conflicting priorities, and major delays. In addition, the stress can get pretty intense when your remodeling projects don't exactly go as planned.

Avoid the temptation to juggle more than one project at a time

Create a Project Budget

A budget is the only way to keep an eye on project expenses. At a minimum, estimate the cost for required materials and any skilled labor you might need. Then add 20 percent for unexpected expenses. As the project moves forward, compare your actual expenses to your original estimate. This will tell you if you need to cut costs or secure additional funds.

Project Budget	
Materials	
Lumber	$ 125
Plywood	$ 75
Paint & Varnish	$ 40
Fixtures	$ 550
Hardware	$ 90
Flooring	$ 350
Adhesive	$ 25
Labor	
Contractor	$2200
Assistant	$ 600
Miscellaneous	$ 300
Total	$4355

A budget is the only way to effectively manage and monitor project expenses

Create a Clipping File

Clipping files are used by amateur and professional designers alike as a means of keeping all their project ideas in a single place. An old shoe box or a file folder will do the trick. Clipping files typically contain photos, articles, brochures, sketches, paint swatches, fabric samples, and anything else that may be beneficial to your projects.

Accordion-style file folders are perfect for storing all of your remodeling-related paperwork

Check Out the Online Forums

In the past, local "hobby clubs" used to be the place where people with a common interest conversed, helped one another, compared ideas, quarreled, bragged, and generally had fun. Today, these clubs frequently exist online in the form of Internet forums. Because they're able to attract people from all over the world, you can find useful information (and endless opinions) on virtually any subject imaginable. I'm continually amazed at the level of kindness, cooperation, and support that I've received from total strangers.

Online RV forums can be particularly helpful if you learn how to take advantage of their built-in search capabilities. With selective searching, you'll be able to explore a wide array of relevant subjects that have already been thoroughly investigated. Although there are dozens of RV forums, these are a few of the more popular ones:

- www.rv.net/forum/
- www.irv2.com/
- www.rvusa.com/forum/
- www.rvforum.net/

Approach Warranty-Related Issues Sensibly

Remodeling projects rarely impact a manufacturer's warranty. If you do have any concerns, contact the company. However, don't let blanket threats of warranty-voiding stop you from making beneficial changes to your RV. First of all, you're probably covered anyways. Second, warranties aren't forever, and finally – it's your RV.

Line Up a Reliable Source of Parts

Many projects require specialized parts. Odds are – you won't have them all. That's why it pays to be near a hardware store and a parts dealer when you're doing a project. Then, when you invariably have to go back for something, you won't have to drive too far.

Find a Way to Get the Tools you Need

Many remodeling projects require specialized tools that aren't in the typical toolbox. Therefore, if you're going to undertake a major project, make sure that you can get your hands on the right tools.

It's usually more cost-effective to rent specialized tools only when you need them

Contractor's Tip: Don't purchase an extension ladder, a tile cutter, or any specialized tool for your projects. Places like The Home Depot rent out nearly everything they sell. The lowest rates are for small blocks of time (i.e. 4 hours) so plan ahead. Then rent the item for the duration you'll need it and no more.

Put your Computer to Work

There are several inexpensive interior design applications that can help you with your RV remodeling projects. For example, they can help you to quickly create and visualize any number of different layouts. Once you have a plan you like, the software automatically generates 3-dimensional images that can be colored and enhanced with the click of a mouse. Some examples include Interior Designer® (www.homedesignersoftware.com) or Chief Architect Professional® (www.chiefarchitect.com).

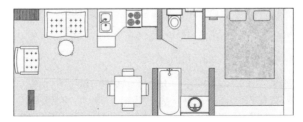

Easy-to-use interior design software enables you to try out different layouts and configurations

Involve the Kids

Children like to help with remodeling tasks. Best of all, when the project is finished, they'll have a sense of accomplishment. Find a way to include them in your projects.

This little guy is responsible for all the computer aided design work

Decide Who's Going to Do the Work

If you're planning a major remodeling project, you'll need to decide who is going to do the work. If you have the skills, the time, and the back, it's generally more satisfying to do your own remodeling. However, there are some projects that are best left to others (see next section). The following questions are specifically designed to help you with this issue.

- Do you have a clear idea of what you want your project to look like?
- Are you willing to research and prepare for each task?
- Do you really have the time to do the project yourself?
- Do you enjoy physical work?
- Do you have the skill, the knowledge, and the talent to do the job?
- Do you have the right tools for the job? If not, can you rent them?
- Is saving money a high priority?

If you answered "yes" to most of these questions, you probably have what it takes to do most projects yourself. Otherwise, ask the service department at your local RV dealer for a list of reliable companies that can handle your specific project.

Hire on the Basis of Competence

If you're planning a major remodeling project, you may want to hire someone to handle the more difficult aspects of the job. However, when you do find someone that seems qualified, try to obtain the following:

- A written estimate that includes material and labor costs. Keep in mind, an estimate is simply a ball-park approximation. A bid, on the other hand, is a formal, legally binding commitment.

- Some references to confirm that they have the experience and the skill to complete the job.

- A written schedule that shows the project commencement date and an estimate of how long the project will take.

- A copy of their insurance policy and/or business license that indicates the level of liability coverage they currently have.

If you hire a professional RV remodeling firm, you'll find that it's generally a collaborative process between you and the firm's design team. You might also meet with product reps to discuss specifications, installation issues, and configuration options. During the life of the project, you'll meet with various participants to compare ideas, discuss design concepts, demonstrate potential layouts, and suggest a myriad of products. The company may also work with the manufacturer of your RV to iron out technical issues. When all is said and done, the process is usually fun, interesting, and worthwhile.

Look for Red Flags

When you're looking for someone to handle your remodeling project, avoid contractors that haven't been in business for long, don't have any references, or won't provide you with a copy of their insurance policy. Likewise, stay away from contractors that claim they have materials (i.e. flooring) that they got cheap and want to pass the savings on to you. In addition, if a company misses appointments, seems disinterested in your project, or pressures you to sign a contract, move on. Remodeling scams generally fall into three categories:

- **Low-Ballers** – They come in with a low bid only to jack up the price once they're entrenched in the remodeling project.

- **Rip-Off Artists** – They'll do anything to get your money and then vanish once they're paid.

- **Shoe-Stringers** – Since they usually have cash-flow problems, these contractors often juggle several jobs at once. As a result, they often take forever to finish a job. In addition, they will often pressure you to pay early.

Leave the Specialized Jobs to the Pros

There are certain projects that should be handled by experienced professionals. One good example is the alteration of an RV to accommodate people with disabilities.

An experienced remodeling firm will begin by meeting with the people that will be using the RV. They'll then design a comprehensive remodeling strategy for the entire RV. For starters, an automated wheelchair lift system may be installed. Bottlenecks are usually eliminated to ensure that someone in a wheelchair can move easily through the RV. The tub is usually removed and replaced with a fully accessible roll-in shower. The toilet and vanity are also reconfigured for barrier-free access. Light switches, monitoring systems, and thermostats are lowered for easy reach. Round door knobs are replaced with lever style handles and assist bars are strategically installed throughout the RV. The faucets are replaced with hands-free automatic models. The kitchen is also re-designed to ensure that every feature can be used easily and safely.

If the disabled individual plans to drive the RV, modifications may also be made to the RV's seat, steering wheel, and braking system. Finally, the entire RV is tested to make sure that everything works exactly as planned. While many projects can be done by a determined do-it-yourselfer, some jobs should be left to the pros. Before you begin any major remodeling project, talk a reputable remodeling company. You have nothing to lose and you may even learn a few things.

On that note, if you're looking for information on RVing with disabilities, start with the following websites.

- www.rvamerica.com/data/rvdisable.htm
- www.handicappedtravelclub.com/
- www.access-able.com/
- www.geocities.com/heartland/9268/access.htm
- www.clockconversions.com/
- www.woodalls.com/outactiv/enjoy/customiz.html

In addition, you may want to participate in some online RV forums. A few of them even have special sections for people with disabilities.

Stand by your Design

Some contractors will try to push you into using certain products, materials, or even colors. They may have business relationships they're trying to leverage or they might simply be overly opinionated. At any rate, stick by your guns and demand that they stay with the program. After all, it's your RV and you're the one that's paying the bills.

Conclusions and Recommendations

Remodeling an RV isn't the same as remodeling a house. Replacement parts can be difficult to find and some products may have to be special ordered. In addition, floors aren't always level, corners aren't always square, hidden utility lines run everywhere, and space is so tight, you'll wonder why you even started the project in the first place.

The key is to anticipate and plan for problems and delays. Give yourself plenty of time and make sure you don't schedule a major project right before a trip. Find out where you can get parts before you begin and don't be afraid to ask for help when things don't go as planned. Online RV forums are a terrific resource for technical advice but it can often take time to get the specific information you need. In summary, when it comes to remodeling RVs, give yourself plenty of breathing room, keep your cool, and have a good time.

Additional Resources

"The Home Remodeling Management Book: How to Plan, Organize, and Manage Your Home Remodeling Project" by Kathryn E. Schmidt

"Home Remodeling Pitfalls and How to Avoid Them: The Definitive and Comprehensive Guide to Successful Home Remodeling Projects!" by Duncan Calder Stephens

"50 Plus One: Tips When Remodeling Your Home" by William Resch

Chapter 3

Obtaining Parts, Products, and Accessories

One of the biggest challenges associated with remodeling projects is the high cost of RV products and materials. In fact, unexpected and excessive expenses are one of the major reasons why some remodeling projects fail. Fortunately, there are several proven ways to keep costs down to a minimum. Here are a few tips from the experts:

Stay Away from One-stop Shopping

The prices for RV parts and products vary considerably. As a result, don't automatically run down to the nearest RV dealer or camping store for everything. Instead, take the time to shop around for the best deals.

Look for Alternatives to RV Products

Some of the specialized products sold in the RV marketplace are short on style and high on price. Check out competitively priced alternatives at discount stores, home supply chains, and of course, the Internet.

Avoid Specialty Stores

Most professional interior decorators are skilled at the fine art of using low-cost objects to make a room look luxurious. That's why many shop at discount home furnishing stores. Lamps can be incredibly expensive at lighting stores but they're routinely discounted at places like Target, Ikea, and The Home Depot. Similarly, framed artwork will cost a mint at an art store. But at places like TJ Max, Costco's, Target, and Wal-Mart, you'll find framed pictures at bargain prices. The trick is to find products that are unique, visually appealing, and affordable.

Think Carefully about Extended Warranties

Surveys consistently suggest that extended warranties on appliances are often a questionable investment. First, the extended warranties are seldom required. Second, in many instances, the companies don't always cover the full cost of the repairs. Ask around before you buy one.

Join Camping World's President's Club®

As the nation's largest retailer of RV-related products and services, Camping World already offers some of the lowest prices around. The

President's Club makes their prices even better. Contact them at 1-800-626-5944 or visit www.campingworld.com.

RV Parts Bargain Basements

If you need a headlight assembly for a 1972 Winnebago Brave, you'll probably find it tucked away in a warehouse somewhere in Elkhart, Indiana. Since a lot of RVs are manufactured there, Elkhart tends to breed RV salvage and surplus dealers. Perhaps you're looking for something a little more recent. A short time ago, we saw two leather-covered captain's chairs for sale at an RV surplus company. They were brand new and made by Flexsteel – a good company. The surplus dealer was asking $450 for both of them!

You can find practically anything you need at an RV salvage and surplus store

So if you're looking for bargains, discontinued products, or hard-to-find RV parts, call some of the RV salvage and surplus dealers listed at the end of this chapter. If they don't have what you're looking for – they probably know who does.

Make Quality a Top Priority

If you try to use the best products and the best installation techniques (whenever remodeling), you'll be able to improve the quality of your RV over time. Plus, when you pay attention to quality, you rarely have to go back later to fix things.

Look on eBay for Parts and Accessories

eBay (www.ebay.com) sells a lot of RV parts. If you do a quick search, you'll find everything from custom RV water tanks and steering stabilizers to back-up cameras and sewer hoses. But the real advantage to eBay is their prices. Many of the products are sold by RV parts surplus stores, overstock dealers, and small manufacturing outfits. As a result, you can find some amazing deals – if you know what you're doing. Here's a quick description of the online auction game.

 How to Buy Products on eBay

Step 1. Register

Before you can buy anything on eBay (www.ebay.com), you must first register. Click on the underlined link that reads '<u>Register</u>' in the upper middle section of the page. Then follow the on-screen directions.

Step 2. Search for products

You can find things on eBay by either browsing through categories or using eBay's search feature. To browse, click on a category in the left-hand column of the eBay home page. To search, click on the open box next to the search button and type in what you are looking for (i.e. RV Water Heaters).

Step 3. Review the items

Take a look at the items listed. Then click on an underlined item to bid on the product or to obtain additional details.

Step 4. Look at the seller's feedback

On the upper right-hand side of the product information page, there's a box titled 'Seller Information'. You'll see the underlined name of the seller and a number that represents the quantity of items they've sold to date. Click on the number and you'll see comments about their past transactions. You can then decide for yourself whether you should do business with them. To be on the safe side, only buy from sellers who have sold at least 10 items.

Step 5. Decide how you want to buy

There are two ways to buy things on eBay. One is to take part in the auction. To bid on an item, click on the button labeled '**BID NOW**'. You'll see a space to place your maximum bid. You may not have to pay that much for the item, but you will need to enter the maximum amount you are willing to pay. When you're done, click on the '**CONFIRM BID**' button. You'll receive an e-mail confirming your bid. The second way to buy things on eBay is to use the "Buy Now" option (if it's available for the item). If you want to avoid the bidding process and you're willing to pay the "Buy Now" price, simply click on the '**BUY NOW**' button and follow the directions. Many people routinely purchase items on eBay this way. If you get really serious about buying things on eBay, get a good book on the subject. Also, do an online search for the keyword "snipeware". This way, you'll be able to see what you're up against.

Step 6. Pay for your item

After you've either won or purchased an item, you'll need to make payment arrangements. Clicking on the '**PAY NOW**' button (on the item page) will enable you to pay with a credit card, bank account, or Pay Pal account. After you pay, the seller will then send you an e-mail that confirms the details of the transaction. Good hunting!

Develop an Eye for Possibilities

A while ago, we were looking for used books at a Goodwill thrift store. We didn't find any books but we did spot an antique solid brass faucet set for less than five dollars. High-quality plumbing fixtures often sell for hundreds of dollars when new. We'll polish it up and install it in our bathroom vanity. Learn to see the potential value of seemingly ordinary things. You'll be amazed at what you can find.

RV Parts and Accessories Dealers

The businesses shown below (listed alphabetically) are not the only places to get RV parts and accessories. However, they're a good place to start.

- Big Discount RV (bigdiscountrv.com)
- Camping World (campingworld.com or 800-626-5944)
- Dyer's RV Supplies (dyersonline.com or 866-713-3429)
- funroads.com
- PPL's RV Parts Superstore (pplmotorhomes.com or 800-755-4775)
- RV Parts Outlet (rvpartsoutlet.com or 866-333-0999)
- rvparts.com (877-600-6000)

Table 1 – RV Salvage and Surplus Dealers

Name	State	City	Phone	Comments
All Rite Exteriors	CA	Hollister	800-262-6541	Collision-repair parts for all types of RV exteriors.
Arizona RV Salvage (azrvinc.com)	AZ	Phoenix	602-272-0301	New/used plumbing, A/C, cooling, lighting, windows, appliances, doors, holding tanks, hubs, rotors, axles, running gears, rear ends
Bill's RV	IN	Elkhart	219-522-1569	RV Salvage yard
Bontrager's Surplus Parts (bontragers.com)	MI	White Pigeon	616-483-7017	Lots of windows, main doors, storage compartment doors, upholstery fabrics, piano hinges
Camper & Recreation Inc. (canvasreplacements.com)	WI	Loyal	800-232-2079 715-255-8142	Will custom fabricate canvas replacement tops for popup campers.
Cinnabar Engineering Inc. (thegmcmotorhomepeople.com)	MI	Sandusky	800-720-2227	All GMC MH parts and publications.
Colaw RV Salvage (colawrvsalvage.com)	MO	Carthage	417-358-4640	Inventory of hundreds of damaged RV's for parts.
Cooper RV Salvage	IN	Elkhart	219-293-3027	All types of parts for all types of RV's.
Dixie Trailer Supply RV Parts	FL	Ft. Lauderdale	305-565-9210	New and hard-to-find trailer and RV parts. 27 yrs. in

Name	State	City	Phone	Comments
& Service				business.
Elkhart Surplus Salvage	IN	Elkhart	219-295-8903	LP tanks, lights, windows, doors, RV furniture
Electrix	KS	Hutchinson	316-669-9966	Custom mfg. of electric wiring harnesses and assemblies, switch panels, clock panels, and misc. electrical devices.
Factory RV Surplus	IN	Elkhart	219-262-3327	
Graber Industries Inc.	MI	Constantine	616-279-5288	Obsolete and new RV parts and supplies. 8 big buildings and acres of outside area.
Gundie's In.	WA	Bellingham	800-444-4344 360-733-5036	Large number of re-built RVs, auto recycling center, appliances, all types of parts for all types of RVs.
Harmony Enterprises	MN	Harmony	507-886-6666	Components for any Harmony roof-lift system. Heco camper canvases for Palimino, Puma, Trade Winds, Winnebago, and many more.
Holiday RV Super Stores Inc.	FL	Orlando	407-351-3096	Specializing in Airstream and Holiday Rambler parts of vintage.
Horn's Sales and Service (hornsrvcenter.com)	WI	Sheboygan	414-564-2381	Parts and accessories for all types of RV's.
Howell's RV Appliance Repair	Ca	El Cajon	619-441-0066	New, used, reconditioned RV appliances.
Huckaby's Recreational Vehicle Salvage (carhuck@swbell.net)	Mo	Holden	816-850-4155	
Icke's RV Surplus	IN	Montpelier	317-728-5668	New/surplus RV parts. Upholstery fabric. UPS nationwide.
Ideal RV & Trailer Supply	CA	Redwood City	415-365-1574	Hard-to-find new/used RV parts.
Inland RV Parts & Service	CA	Corona	800-877-7311	Parts for older Airstream trailers.
IRV Bishko Auto Literature	OH	Novelty	800-544-3312 216-338-4811	Owner's manuals and shop manuals for Dodge chassis motorhomes in the 1970s. Be specific when you call for information.
Isley's RV Service Centers	AZ	Mesa & Glendale	602-834-1234 602-938-4990	Parts and service available for older and current RVs. Specializing in hard-to-find parts, also RV handicap equipment, accessories, and modifications. Mail-order catalog available.
L&M Salvage	IN	Mishawaka	219-256-2606	

Name	State	City	Phone	Comments
Midwest Salvage	IN	Shipshewana	219-825-9822	Lot of reasonably priced RV items from RV manufacturers.
Mobility RV (mobilityrv.com)	IA	Hanlontown	800-933-7742	Winnie/Itasca dealer and mail order parts.
RV Doctor George (rvdoctorgeorge.com)	CA	Sacramento	916-927-7837	
RV Specialist	KS	Augusta	316-775-3098	RV repairs, does re skinning.
RVS Corp. - Recreational Vehicle Services	CA	Morgan Hill	800-821-2266 408-779-3173	Parts available for 1973-76 FMC 2900R; all molds, tooling, dies, fixtures, large parts inventory. Original parts and services and owners manuals.
RV Surplus & Salvage, Inc. (rvsurplussalvage.com)	IN	Elkhart	219-264-5575	Windows, sinks, doors, furniture, paneling.
Salvage Co.	IN	Lakeville	219-784-8954	
Singleton RV Salvage and Sales. (olywa.net/singletonsrv)	WA	Rochester	360-273-9566	Sinks, fridges, stoves, lights, awnings, roof air, propane tanks, axles, body parts, doors, windows, jacks, and more.
State Line Salvage	IN	Middlebury	219-825-7540	Tires, van seats, VCR's, TV's, Drink Trays, Consoles and misc. Van & RV accessories.
Tom's Borderline Bargains (borderline131@aol.com)	MI	Constantine	616-435-5533	Refrigerators, ranges, water heaters, furnaces, paneling, replacement windows, Amish oak, carpet, trim.
Vanderhaags Inc. (www.vanderhaags.com)	IA	Spencer	800-831-5164 712-262-7000	Oshkosh and Winnie surplus parts. New and rebuilt engines, trannies, rear ends, wheels, manifolds and rotors. Installation available.
Walt's RV Surplus	CA	Fontana	909-823-0563	New/Surplus RV parts. Specializing in Fleetwood, as well as National and Cobra RVs.
Warehouse Salvage	IN	Osceola	219-674-9302	Mostly Van items.
Weller Auto	MI	Grand Rapids	616-528-5000	RV gas/diesel drive train parts, used/rebuilt engines, trannies, brakes, rotors, drums, generators, appliances, roof airs, glass, and manuals.
Winnebago Surplus & General Store	IA	Forest City	515-582-6935	

Chapter 4

RV Remodeling and Construction Tips

The previous chapters examined pre-project planning strategies and useful techniques for locating competitively priced parts and accessories. This chapter describes additional methods used by experienced remodelers to ensure that their projects are done properly, on time, and within budget.

Ten Common Remodeling Mistakes

1. Not remodeling because you think it will somehow lower the potential resale value of your RV.

2. Remodeling without a plan, a strategy, or a design theme.

3. Using price, instead of long-term value, to make important purchasing decisions.

4. Making modifications, adding features, and installing accessories that don't fit your lifestyle.

5. Starting a major remodeling project before a big trip.

6. Building more storage capacity before optimizing your existing storage provisions.

7. Failing to take advantage of overlooked or unused areas in your RV.

8. Creating an interior that looks smaller and feels more congested because of clashing styles, dark colors, and conflicting patterns.

9. Spending too much on parts and accessories as a result of one-stop shopping.

10. Believing that it costs a lot of money to create a beautiful RV.

Familiarize yourself with RV Construction Methods

RVs are not like houses. There are no 2 x 4's, utilities are often impossible to access, and the walls are made of sandwiched layers of fiberglass, plywood, insulation, and fiberboard. The furniture is often attached to the walls and specialized fasteners are found nearly everywhere. In addition, several models utilize extruded aluminum framing for structural integrity – complicating the task of securing objects to a wall or adding a window.

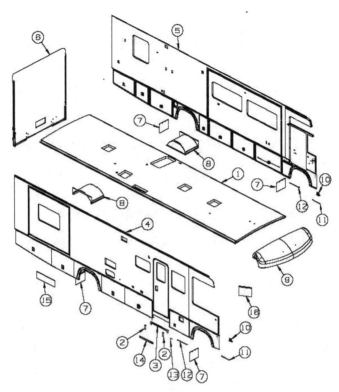

RVs rely on unique materials and proprietary construction techniques (courtesy Winnebago Ind.)

To complicate matters, the products and assembly protocols used by many RV manufacturers seldom adhere to existing design standards. For example, I once began a simple faucet replacement project that turned into a two-day lesson on RV construction techniques. In short, the plastic sink that came with our vanity was so thin – I couldn't use the new drain assembly that came with the replacement faucet. I ended up replacing the entire sink with a ceramic model which meant that a new hole had to be cut into the top of the vanity. Fortunately, I'd been looking for an excuse to buy a cordless jig saw.

Take your Time

RV remodeling projects can be challenging as a result of limited space, specialized construction methods, and unique design requirements. Take the time to think things through and plan carefully before you start. Don't forget the whole reason you bought an RV in the first place – to relax and enjoy spending more time with friends and family.

Get the Specs for your RV

Most RV manufacturers will provide you with construction drawings, utility schematics, and product specifications – if you request them. In fact, Winnebago Industries (www.winnebagoind.com) offer these documents on their websites. These drawings can be extremely helpful as they often reveal important construction details, structural components, and the precise location of concealed utilities. They're also useful for diagnosing problems and making repairs. The following example shows how an RV kitchen was constructed.

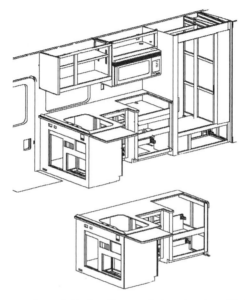

Assembly details are usually available from the manufacturer (courtesy Winnebago Industries)

Stick with the Plan

It's only natural to make small incremental changes to a remodeling project. However, if you're not careful, the project will end up taking three times as long while costing twice as much. Professionals call it "project creep". Successful projects, by definition, are completed in a reasonable timeframe and don't cost more than expected. This should be one of your primary goals.

A plan is meaningless unless it's used as a project roadmap

Stay within your Budget

Your ability to stay within your project budget is crucial – especially over the long-run. If your projects consistently become too expensive, you may be unable to pursue your future remodeling plans. Here are a few ways to keep costs down:

- Make design changes on paper first rather than in your RV.

- Prioritize your remodeling plans. Decide what matters the most and dedicate funds to those specific areas.

- Shop sensibly and avoid one-stop shopping sprees.

- Try to stick with standard sizes and stocked items. Special finishes, unusual fabrics, and custom sizes always cost more.

- Educate yourself about the materials and products you plan on using. When making purchasing decisions, take into account long-term value as well as initial cost.

- Evaluate your purchases and projects from the perspective of need. Forget about status or the latest styles. A year from now, these things won't matter.

- Recycle or refurbish things whenever possible. It's usually a lot cheaper than replacing the item.

- Pay for professional advice. When you're uncertain about some aspect of your project, find an expert and pay them for their input. The savings (from avoiding costly mistakes) can be substantial.

- Save money by doing some of the work yourself (please refer to Chapter 2 for more details).

Make Safety a Priority

If you're using adhesives, paints, thinners, or lacquers, keep the windows open and use your roof vent to discharge the fumes. For large jobs involving volatile chemicals, always wear a canister mask. If you're generating dust from cutting, sanding, removing old carpeting, or working with fiberglass insulation, wear gloves, a dust mask, and safety goggles.

When working with dust or fumes, always wear the correct mask or filter

Watch your Weight

Some remodeling projects can add a substantial amount of weight to your RV. Examples include ceramic tile flooring upgrades, engineered-stone or solid surface countertop installations, and kitchen cabinet replacement projects. Likewise, remodeling projects that create more storage capacity inevitably result in the tendency to carry more stuff. The end result is more weight.

Before you begin a major project, get your RV weighed – preferably at each wheel. This will tell you if you're operating within the RV's specified loading limits. Getting weighed at each wheel will also tell you how the weight is currently distributed. With this information, you can make sure that you aren't creating or compounding a weight-related problem.

Your RV's weight-related specifications will be located in the vehicle's documentation or posted somewhere inside your RV. If you're already exceeding your RV's Gross Vehicle Weight Rating (GVWR), find a way to eliminate some excess baggage. If you're under the manufacturer's specified limits, make sure that your remodeling project won't put you over. The following acronyms are used to classify weight-related limits and specifications.

GVW	Gross Vehicle Weight – The total weight of a fully equipped and loaded RV including passengers, fuel, propane, oil, water, and baggage. The GVW must not exceed the GVWR.
GVWR	Gross Vehicle Weight Rating – The total amount of weight a vehicle can support. The GVWR is determined by the manufacturer and must not be exceeded.
DW	Dry Weight – The weight of an RV without fuel, propane, oil, and water.
UVW	Unloaded Vehicle Weight – The weight of an RV that is full of fuel, propane, oil, and water, plus the driver and any passengers.
CCC	Cargo Carrying Capacity – The maximum permissible weight of all pets, belongings, food, tools, and other supplies that are carried in your RV. The CCC is equal to the GVWR minus the UVW.
GAWR	Gross Axle Weight Rating – The maximum permissible weight that can be carried by an axle with weight that is evenly distributed throughout the RV.
GCWR	Gross Combination Weight Rating – The maximum allowable loaded weight of an RV, including towed vehicles.

Improve the Quality of your RV as you Proceed

When you're working on various projects, use the opportunity to make incremental improvements to your RV. For example:

- Reinforce poorly installed or supported furnishings with brackets, wood strapping, or screws.

- Secure pipes and other plumbing fixtures with strapping and clamps. This will prevent them from developing leaks over time as a result of excessive movement and vibration.

- Replace shoddy parts with higher-quality equivalents. For example, replace rusted screws with stainless steel ones. They'll last forever.

- Install wall anchors whenever you encounter stripped screws.

- Get rid of components that are prone to chronic failure. Day-night blinds (with their weak strings) are a good example.

- Cover susceptible electrical components with a waterproof material to ensure that any leaks nearby don't create problems.

- Install shut-off valves on each water supply pipe. They'll come in handy if you have a leak or a problem with a faucet.

- Plug any holes to the outside to eliminate the infiltration of cold drafts, hungry mice, and nesting insects.

Measure Carefully and Assume Nothing

RV remodeling projects can be full of surprises. Common mistakes include: assuming everything is even and square; making changes that interfere with the movement of slide-outs; leaving too little clearance for cabinet doors to open; and overlooking electrical outlets, floor vents, and hidden utilities. Take your time, measure carefully, and assume nothing.

Get Rid of Needless Stuff

Remodeling an RV is fundamentally different than remodeling a house. In a house, you can take everything out of a room and stash it in the garage or in the basement. In an RV, this isn't an option. As a result, use the remodeling project as an opportunity to get rid of things that you don't really need or use. In the long run, you won't miss the stuff.

Don't Automatically Toss Everything Away

It's often tempting to destroy objects that you're removing or replacing. However, in some cases, you may find that the replacement item doesn't work out. In this case, you may have to put the old one back. If it's been ruined, you're out of luck.

Plywood: The Ultimate Building Material

RV remodeling projects can eat up building materials. Shelving, table tops, cabinets, and built-in furniture all require substantial amounts of wood. Fortunately, there's an abundant supply of inexpensive plywood that can produce great looking results. In addition, most home supply stores will make accurate cuts for you at very reasonable prices. This means that you can bring home pieces that are already sized to fit your specific requirements.

Most hardwood plywood is manufactured according to grading standards established by the American National Standards Institute (ANSI). Hardwood plywood is graded with a letter on the "show" face and a number on the back. The face grades run from A to E and the back panels are graded from 1 to 4. The best plywood grade is A-1. For ½-inch to ¾-inch thicknesses, a typical cabinet grade is A-1 or B-2. For ¼-inch plywood, a typical cabinet grade is A-4.

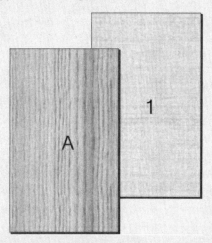

Plywood is graded on both sides. With an A-1 rating, this piece is as good as it gets

Many cabinet makers and amateur remodelers alike consider Baltic Birch Plywood (BBP) to be the ultimate building material. Standard construction grade ½-inch plywood has 5 thick core plies made from inexpensive wood (i.e. poplar) that's soft and weak. On the other hand, ½-inch Baltic Birch Plywood (BBP) is made by gluing together 9 thinner layers of hard wood (birch). In addition, the core voids that are found in standard plywood are not allowed in BBP. Because more plies are used and there are no core voids, BBP is stronger and more stable than standard plywood. Baltic Birch Plywood also has nicer machined edges. Of course, it's also more expensive.

Pre-drill Before Attaching Things

When attaching furnishings or other objects to the walls or floor of an RV, you never know what you're going to run into. I've encountered wood, polystyrene insulation, steel, fiberboard, fiberglass, extruded aluminum, vinyl, plastic, pipes, ductwork, and wiring. When appropriate, use a small nail or an awl to see what you're dealing with. For example, if you encounter aluminum studs (often part of the RV's infrastructure), you'll have to drill a small tap hole and then use sheet metal screws.

> **Anonymous Tip:** RV walls are notoriously thin. As a result, it's very easy to accidentally drill clear through to the outside. Therefore, when drilling into walls – proceed carefully and keep the drill bit as short as possible. To determine the thickness of the walls in your RV, open a window, remove the screen, and measure the width of the window casing. Bear in mind, the casing will be slightly thicker than the wall.

Take your Projects Outside

RV remodeling projects can be particularly challenging because of limited space, uncovered furniture, and exposed carpeting. Fortunately, a number of tasks such as cutting, painting, gluing, and assembling can often be done outside or in a shop. In fact, experienced remodeling shops do much of their work outside the RV.

Use all of the Available Space

In an RV, wall and floor space is always at a premium. As a result, when purchasing or designing furniture, use pieces that fill up all of the available space. For instance, it's better to install a sofa that spans the entire length of a wall than to put in a loveseat that leaves a small, unusable section of wasted space at one end.

Don't Create Attack Corners

An "attack corner" is RV lingo for a physically obtrusive feature that inevitably causes harm to people. A classic example of an attack corner is a TV set that's mounted so low – people constantly hit their head on it. Table tops, counters, and shelving with sharp corners are other notorious examples. While attack corners are one of the consequences of living in a small, confined environment – they can be minimized with careful planning and a good design.

To reduce the risk of attack corners, try to use furniture with rounded corners and soft edges. If you rearrange something, make sure that you haven't inadvertently created a new attack corner. Leave that crucial task to the professionals – the folks that manufacture RVs.

Take Advantage of Unused and Overlooked Areas

Corners in RVs often go unnoticed. Install a small corner shelf or a slender corner table. Similarly, look for wasted space at the upper part of each wall. For example, the area above your RV's doors and windows is often a good place to install a bookshelf.

The unused space above the door in this RV was the perfect place for a bookshelf

Keep your Pets Safe

Remodeling projects frequently involve the use of noisy and dangerous tools. As a result, pets often become frightened. Remodeling projects also tend to result in unsecured access to the outside. Before you begin a project, find some way to keep your pets safe and secure. We often lock our cats and dogs in the bedroom. If necessary, we can also put them in our minivan. If you're taking your RV to a shop for repairs, be sure to let the technicians know about your pets so they don't accidentally let them out. You should always leave a note on the door – just in case.

Conclusions and Recommendations

This chapter describes a number of accepted techniques and proven strategies that are often used by professional remodelers. When looked at individually, some of these suggestions may seem obvious or even trivial. However, as a group, they represent some of the best practices of the top professionals in the business. Consequently, you may want to re-visit these recommendations before starting your next big project.

Chapter 5

RV Utilities

RVs provide much of their comfort and convenience through a series of engineered systems that help to deliver electrical power, fresh water, and LP-gas. In addition, most RVs come with wastewater management and disposal systems that enable its occupants to enjoy the same level of convenience found in a typical home. While this book doesn't go into great detail about these systems, it does examine their potential relevance to the remodeling process.

> **Safety Tip:** Remodeling can sometimes result in an electrical short or a gas leak. As a result, make sure that your RV is fitted with smoke, carbon monoxide, and LP-gas detectors. Likewise, fire extinguishers represent the last line of defense against a fire. Install a few now because once a fire starts, you won't have time to run to the store.

RV Electrical Systems

Most RVs operate on both 120-volt AC and 12-volt DC. In general, the 120-volt AC systems found in an RV are similar to the ones seen in homes. The principal difference is that some RVs have the option of using an AC generator. Fortunately, few remodeling projects require an intimate knowledge of 120-volt electrical systems. For small tasks such as adding or moving a receptacle, check out the books listed at the end of this chapter.

The 12-volt system in an RV is powered by on-board batteries that are kept charged by the vehicle's alternator or a charger/converter device that runs off the RV's 120-volt electrical system. Alternatively, some RVs rely on solar panels and charge controllers to keep their batteries fully charged. In any case, the principal concern when dealing with RV electrical systems is safety. Here are a few suggestions:

Create Dedicated Electrical Lines

Never add a new electrical device to an existing circuit unless the circuit is truly capable of handling the additional amperage. For example, if you're replacing your RV's water pump with a more powerful model, make sure that the existing wiring is capable of handing the increase in current. For technical information about a particular circuit in your RV, contact the manufacturer. Alternatively, you can refer to the electrical schematics for the specific make and model of your RV.

All appliances and accessories will have a specified wattage or amperage rating. If the device has a wattage rating, simply divide it by the number of volts it operates on (12-volt DC or 120-volt AC) to compute the amps. Once you know the amperage, you can then use Table 2 (later in this chapter) to determine the proper wire size.

Never Work on Live Circuits

Always disconnect the power to your RV when working with electricity. This includes both AC and DC systems. AC systems are normally disconnected by pulling the plug to a power pole (assuming that your generator isn't running). DC systems are turned off by either disconnecting your batteries or by tripping a main breaker switch (if the RV has one). Always use a test light to confirm that the power is actually off.

Obtain the Wiring Schematics for your RV

Most RV manufacturers will provide you with detailed electrical schematics if you request them. Wiring diagrams and electrical schematics can be invaluable during a remodeling project because they show the exact location of every electrical component.

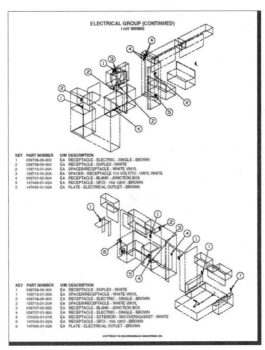

Utility diagrams can help you to understand your RV's electrical system (courtesy Winnebago Ind.)

Always Use Fuses or Circuit Breakers

The fuses and circuit breakers in an RV are designed to cut off the power source in the case of an overload or a short circuit. Without these over-current protection devices (OCPD), your RV's electrical system could overheat, resulting in costly repairs or even a fire. Thus, make sure that all of your electrical circuits include a properly sized fuse or circuit breaker.

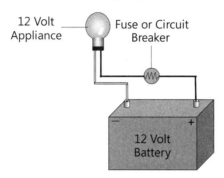

Never install an electrical device without a properly sized fuse or circuit breaker

Protect your RV's Wiring

When you're running wiring through your RV, always use conduit, cable guides, or a secured harness. When installing multiple wires along the same path, use nylon cable ties to keep them together. What's more, when running wire through a hole, always use a plastic or rubber grommet to protect the wiring. Unlike houses, RVs experience significant vibration. Over the long run, this can result in exposed wires, short-circuits, and other dangerous electrical hazards.

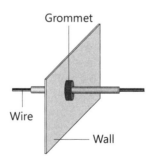

Grommets are designed to prevent short-circuits as a result of damage to the wire's coating

Use the Correct Wire Size

RV electrical circuits generally adhere to the same design and safety standards that are used in homes. These standards are published in the National Electrical Code Handbook. Therefore, whenever installing new wiring or adding a new electrical device – always comply with the guidelines in the code handbook. The following table shows the recommended wire sizes for various loading scenarios.

Table 2 – Wire Size vs. Loading Rate

Maximum Loading (Amps)	Wire Size
6	18
8	16
15	14
20	12
30	10
40	8
55	6

Protect your Electrical Circuits from Moisture

Due to space considerations, many RV manufacturers install circuit breakers in the same cabinet that holds the kitchen sink. Consequently, if a leak develops in the faucet or sink area, you may begin to experience some irregularities that include flickering lights and dead circuits. If you do plan on upgrading your sink or faucet assembly, find some way to protect any electrical components that are installed in the same cabinet.

Use Solderless Terminals

When working on 12-volt systems, try to use solderless terminals for all your connections. They're less prone to failure and they can be quickly disconnected if required. Most hardware store sell inexpensive crimping kits that include a crimper and a set of commonly used terminals.

Tip: Solderless terminals are color-coded to help you match the right terminal to the specific wire size you're working with. If you use the wrong terminal, you may inadvertently create an unreliable or dangerous connection. In addition, when using male and female disconnect terminals (3rd and 4th terminals from the right), make sure they both have the same blade width to ensure a tight fit.

Solderless terminals are designed to help to create a more reliable connection

Use a Test Light or a Multimeter

A simple test light can be invaluable for determining if a circuit is live or not. Similarly, a multimeter that measures voltage, current, and resistance is an indispensable tool for remodeling projects that include electrical modifications. Test lights and multimeters are available in any hardware or electronics store.

> **Caution:** Be sure to follow the directions that come with the meter. If you use the wrong setting, you could permanently damage the meter.

Multimeters are invaluable for testing and analyzing both AC and DC circuits

RV Heating and Air-conditioning Systems

RV Heating Systems

Most RV heating systems are based on an LP-gas driven furnace that relies on a series of 12-volt controls including a thermostat. The one exception is the "all-electric" RV that operates entirely on AC power. The heating systems in these motorhomes are strictly 120-volt AC and therefore do not use LP-gas.

LP-gas furnaces are often serviced from the outside (courtesy Suburban Manufacturing Co.)

Since LP-gas furnaces need to be vented, they tend to be installed against an outer wall. The heated air from the furnace is distributed via ductwork that is installed beneath the RV's floor. Floor vents are usually located in strategic places to evenly distribute the heated air.

RV Air Conditioning Systems

Virtually all RV air conditioning systems rely on 120-volt AC power. While most air conditioning units are installed on the roof, a few are located in the basement of the RV. Basement models are always ducted. In most cases, they use the same ductwork that is connected to the RV's furnace. Roof-mounted air conditioners may or may not be ducted. The roof-mounted models that are ducted rely on a network of piping that's located inside the RV's roof lining. The roof-mounted models that aren't ducted discharge cool air directly into the room (from the unit).

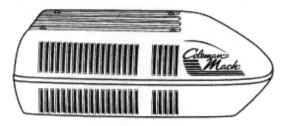

Typical RV roof-mounted air conditioner unit

System Modifications

If your goal is to heat or cool an area that isn't receiving enough (or any) treated air, look for simple solutions. Modifying the ductwork in an RV is a major endeavor as the systems are usually installed while the unit was being built. As a result, access to the ductwork is next to impossible. Some RVers have been able to improve the circulation of air in their RVs by hanging small 4-inch electronic fans in the doorways. Some of these fans include a variable speed control so they can be operated at very low rpm's (making them very quiet). The key is to install the fan in the right place.

RV Plumbing Systems

The plumbing systems in RVs are pretty straightforward. However, here are a few tips from the experts:

Disconnect and Drain Everything

RV freshwater systems normally operate under pressure from either a local water supply or from an on-board 12-volt water pump. Even if the water supply is disconnected or the pump is turned off, your water pipes can still contain significant volumes of pressurized water, As a result, before performing any plumbing modifications, always drain your pipes. It isn't necessary to blow out the water lines but you should open all available drainage valves. Likewise, you may want to open the pressure relief valve on your water heater.

Find a Good Supply of Pipe Fittings

The water supply in most RVs consists of ½-inch O.D. polybutylene (PB), PVC, or cross-linked polyethylene (PEX) pipe. There are special fittings that are normally used with each type of piping.

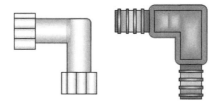

The flared cone-and nut fitting is on the left and the brass fitting is on the right

The most common are plastic compression type fittings, otherwise known as a flared cone-and nut fittings. These fitting are essentially pushed on, hand-tightened, and given a full turn using pliers.

The second type is a brass fitting that requires the use of a separate crimp ring. To connect brass fittings, you need to use a special crimping tool. A crimper normally costs around $100 but you can rent one for a few dollars a day. PEX piping and brass fittings offer a level of reliability and strength that is generally only found in soldered copper.

> **Plumber's Tip:** Most RVs use ½-inch (O.D.) polybutylene (PB) piping and plastic quick-connect style fittings. When you're installing new plumbing fixtures, you might want to upgrade some of the fittings as well. Go to a good plumbing supply store and check out Shark Bite® push-fit fittings. These well made adapters enable you to mix and match PB, PVC, PEX, and copper pipe. As a result, you'll be able to take advantage of high-quality brass fittings and valves. Alternatively, ask your local RV parts dealer about Flair-it® universal transition fittings.

Shark Bite® push-fit fittings enable you to upgrade your RV's plumbing system to copper and brass

Wastewater drainage systems in RVs usually consist of a network of PVC, ABS, or HDPE piping. Elbows, couplings, and fittings are connected with special adhesives. Pipes should always be properly supported to minimize unrestrained movement and chronic vibration (both of which can result in leaks). Regardless of which type of drainage piping you use – make sure that you have a few of the more commonly used fittings on hand when preparing for changes to your RV's plumbing. In addition, keep a can of cleaner and adhesive on hand.

LP Gas Systems

LP-gas is extremely volatile as well as flammable. As a result, always observe the following rules when working with LP-gas:

Turn the Gas Off before you Begin

I realize that this point seems obvious. However, each year, hundreds of people are injured or killed because they failed to disconnect the LP-gas supply before working on or near the gas lines.

Deal with Leaks Immediately

If you detect an LP-gas leak, take the following steps immediately:

- Extinguish any flames
- Avoid touching or operating any electrical switches
- Turn off the gas supply at the tank
- Open windows and doors to clear the air
- Vacate the RV until the leak is corrected
- Have the system tested and correct any leaks

Test for Leaks

Check the connection with a leak-detection solution or an electronic gas detector whenever you connect an LP device (such as a cooktop). If there's evidence of gas, tighten the fittings and re-test.

Additional Resources

"RV Electrical Systems: A Basic Guide to Troubleshooting, Repairing and Improvement" by Bill and Jan Moeller

"RV Repair and Maintenance Manual, 4th Edition" by Bob Livingston

"The RV Handbook: Essential How-To Guide for the RV Owner" by Bill Estes

Chapter 6

Creating an RV Remodeling Strategy

To some degree, interior remodeling is a balancing act designed to create an environment that is both easy to live in and pleasing to look at. To make an RV easier to live in, this chapter includes some important design principles along with a list of desirable attributes that regularly appear in well-designed RVs.

The second goal (making an RV pleasing to look at) is addressed with a discussion on the role of color along with a detailed listing of design themes that are frequently used by professional decorators.

Design your RV for the Way you Live

 When you're designing changes and modifications to your RV, be sure they make sense for your particular lifestyle. For example, if you're a full-time RVer or you travel with children, select designs that offer practicality and convenience over stylishness and flash.

Likewise, if your plans entail being on the road much of the time, focus your efforts on creating a level of convenience and comfort that doesn't require much set-up. In this case, look for changes and improvements that make it easy to come and go from each campground.

First Take Care of the Important Things

When planning your RV remodeling projects, focus on addressing functional requirements before addressing aesthetic concerns. For example, if you need more storage capacity in your kitchen, solve that problem first before you put in a new floor or paint the walls. Your first priority should always be to make your RV comfortable, functional, and safe. Once that is done, you can then focus on improving the way your RV looks and feels.

Always Optimize the Space you Already Have

Before designing ways to create more storage capacity, take steps to improve the space you already have. Otherwise, you may be creating more storage space than you actually need. RVs tend to have a lot of storage capacity that isn't being utilized or organized effectively. It could be a cupboard, a closet, a drawer, or a wardrobe. Optimizing the existing storage space in an RV typically involves the following:

- Use adjustable shelves to accommodate a wide range of contents.

- Take advantage of bins and baskets to organize stored items. Use transparent containers and labels to make things easier to find.

- Use dividers, shelves, and non-slip liners to keep things in-place.

- Make sure that the most commonly used items are easy to reach.

- Eliminate clutter (i.e. rarely used, unused, or redundant items).

- Install small shelves and utensil racks on the inside of the cupboard doors to squeeze in some more storage capacity.

- Organize things by category or by the way they're actually used (i.e. baking goods, office supplies, or commonly used utensils).

- Take advantage of slide-out and pull-out technology to make it easier to access items that are stored inside cabinets and cupboards.

- Use flexible silicone bakeware that can be stuffed into small spaces.

- Install cup hooks to hang things like mugs, utensils, and pots.

Do your Own Thing

RV manufacturers tend to select interior styles that they believe will help them sell RVs. Consequently, many RV interiors are fairly conservative, somewhat predictable, and relatively unexciting. Correspondingly, in order to justify the steep price, high-end RVs have a tendency to be loaded with glitzy embellishments and extravagant designs that look great in a brochure but are impractical to live with. The principal idea behind effective remodeling is to make your RV the way you want it to be.

Avoid the "contemporary-catalog" Look

Contemporary-catalog is a humorous term to describe the predictable and unexciting appearance you get when you purchase all of your interior accessories from an RV accessories catalog. For decorations and some furniture – try to stick with traditional home furnishing stores. You'll have a greater selection plus you may find some real bargains.

Maintain Some Design Consistency

In a house, it's perfectly acceptable (and often desirable) to choose a different design strategy for each room. However, when remodeling the main area of an RV, utilize a consistent design theme as it helps to create the illusion of more space. That's why most RV manufacturers use similar colors and fabrics throughout the interior.

Take Advantage of Adaptable Furnishings

Whenever possible, use furniture that can be folded, stacked, deflated, and put away when it's not needed. Similarly, look for furniture that can be adapted to fulfill multiple functions such as a couch that can fold out into an extra bed or a foot stool that provides some additional storage.

Design Storage Solutions for Specific Items

A common RV remodeling mistake is to build nonspecific storage provisions without actually knowing what you're going to use it for. Invariably, the new space ends up becoming a magnet for miscellaneous belongings and orphaned objects (i.e. a big junk drawer). Before you begin, decide exactly what you need the space for. Then create a customized storage solution that efficiently solves that particular problem.

Enjoy Yourself

This book describes a number of remodeling ideas that entail building pieces of furniture and other useful accessories. Don't get too hung up on the construction details. Some people will use exotic hardwoods, specialized fittings, and expert construction techniques. On the other hand, many people will make the most of whatever materials and techniques they can muster up. Bear in mind, remodeling isn't a race or a contest. It's a way to enjoy yourself while making your RV more comfortable, functional, and appealing.

A Dozen Features that are Nice to Have

RVs are a personal thing. Some people like the versatility of a lightweight trailer while others wouldn't be caught dead in anything less than a forty-five foot bus conversion. At any rate, there are a number of features and traits that are nice to have in any RV. Some of these features are only possible in larger motorhomes or fifth wheels while others are viable in any RV. Nevertheless, keep this wish-list in mind when you're planning your next remodeling project.

1) An Accessible Bathroom

Some RVs have "private" bathrooms that are located in the rear of the bedroom. The concept is similar to the master bedroom that is often found in houses. However, in a real house, there is usually more than one bathroom. In an RV, this design means that everyone has to parade through your bedroom to use the toilet. At two in the morning, this can be very annoying. Chapter 14 focuses on RV bathrooms.

2) Flexible Wardrobes

When it comes to closets and wardrobes, most RV manufacturers build a box, install a closet rod, throw on a door, and call it good. That works fine if everything you own fits on a coat hanger. However, with some adjustable shelving and a few bins – wardrobes and closets can be easily configured to meet the storage needs of everything and everyone.

3) Easy to Maintain Floors

Regardless of the type of flooring you prefer – the key is maintainability. If the floors in your RV are hard to keep clean and difficult to maintain, you've got the wrong flooring. For ease of maintenance, look into vinyl tile, linoleum, or plastic-laminate wood. For a good compromise, consider carpeting in the living room area and tile (or linoleum) in the kitchen and bathroom areas. In heavy traffic areas, use a carpet or vinyl runner for extra protection. Check out Chapter 7 for further information.

Tiled kitchen floors are attractive and easy to maintain (courtesy Monaco Coach Corporation)

4) An Adjustable Television Set

Most RVs come with televisions that are mounted inside a cabinet. As a result, people have to twist their bodies, turn sideways, or move their chairs to get a good view (assuming the chair even moves). It makes a lot more sense to have a television that can be adjusted for the viewer. A good choice is a flat-screen television attached to a flexible TV mount that can be extended, rotated, and tilted in all directions. You can find them in good appliance stores or on the Internet.

An adjustable television mount can make your TV viewable from numerous angles and locations

5) An Island Style Bed

An "island style bed" is not an exotic bed that's designed by primitive islanders for ritualistic purposes. Instead, it's a bed that can be accessed from three sides. Beds that have two sides against a wall can be a real challenge when changing the sheets. Furthermore, when two people are sleeping in the bed, the person against the wall not only has less wiggle room – they also have to find some way to get up without climbing over their partner.

If you have the room, an island-style bed is the way to go (courtesy Monaco Coach Corporation)

6) Separate Vanity and Toilet

When a bathroom vanity is in the same room as the toilet, both fixtures are tied up when either one is being used. When they're separate, one person can brush their teeth while the other uses the toilet. This may sound trivial but in a one-bathroom dwelling – issues like this matter.

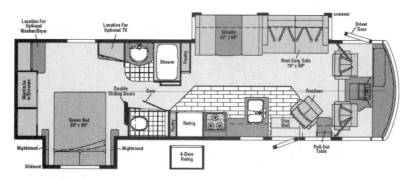

This highly functional floor-plan has a separate toilet and vanity (courtesy Winnebago Industries)

7) A Flip-up Kitchen Countertop Extension

RV kitchens are frequently short on useful workspace. A large drop-leaf countertop extension can provide badly needed surface area whenever you need it. You can make your own using plywood and hardware from your RV dealer. Alternatively, IKEA (www.IKEA-usa.com) sells a wood drop-leaf table (called the NORBO®) that can be adapted to serve as a countertop extension. It cost around $30 plus shipping. Please see Chapter 12 for details.

This homemade drop-leaf countertop extension provides a sturdy place to work when you need it

8) Well-designed Food Pantries

The best RV kitchens have pull-out food pantries that are specifically designed for canned goods, spices, and other commonly stored items. Look for adjustable, display-style shelves that are removable for easy cleaning. Take a look at Chapter 12 for additional insight.

This kitchen includes a well designed pantry in a convenient place (courtesy Monaco Coach Corp.)

9) A Dedicated Workspace

Most RV manufacturers haven't yet addressed the fact that RVers need a dedicated place to work. A few RVs have token desks but they usually don't offer enough surface area for serious use. Plus, many of these desks are located in the bedroom rendering them useless for those that work after hours.

This charming little workstation sits inside a bedroom slide-out

Genuine work areas should have enough surface area for a laptop PC as well as a printer. They should also have enough space for a real office chair with wheels. Chapter 11 provides some additional suggestions.

10) Real Doors

Privacy is no less important simply because you're staying in an RV. Accordingly, bathroom and bedroom doors should be solid and capable of being locked. Likewise, in toy haulers, there should be a solid door separating the living quarters from the "garage" to keep fumes (and toys) out of the living quarters.

11) A Re-Configurable Dining Area

Removing a fixed dinette and replacing it with a free-standing set of table and chairs is one of the most commonly performed remodeling projects. Unfortunately, some manufacturers make this task a great deal harder than it should be. Nevertheless, it's still worth the effort for those that want the flexibility and breathing room of a free-standing table and set of chairs. Chapter 13 describes several dining area remodeling ideas.

12) Lots of Windows

RVs are largely about experiencing the great outdoors. Windows help to bring the outside in. They also make an RV seem brighter, bigger, and more cheerful. Many RVers install extra windows in their RV. Ask your dealer for a list of companies that sell RV windows.

When it comes to RVing, you can't have too many windows (courtesy Monaco Coach Corp.)

Working with Color

Any remodeling guide would be incomplete if it didn't include a discussion on the importance of color. In truth, the potential impact of color is so significant – it can literally make or break a remodeling strategy. Imagine for a moment, an RV that has bright pink walls and florescent green colored furniture. Then imagine that you're the salesperson that has to sell that RV. What do you suppose the reaction would be of each potential customer that walked into the RV? The point is that color should be one of the first decisions you make when designing a remodeling strategy. That's where a color wheel comes in.

Using a Color Wheel

Nearly all interior decorators and designers use something known as a color wheel to help them create successful remodeling proposals. Within a color wheel, colors are divided into three categories: 1) primary; 2) secondary; and 3) tertiary.

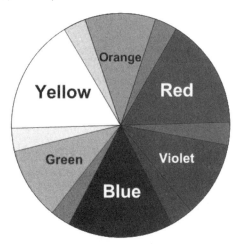

Color wheels are often used for selecting color schemes

The primary colors are red, blue, and yellow. When you mix two primary colors – you create a secondary color. The secondary colors are orange, green, and violet. When a primary color is mixed with an adjacent secondary color, you get six tertiary colors including: red-orange; red-violet; yellow-green; yellow-orange; blue-green; and blue-violet.

Any color can be lightened with white to create a tint or darkened with black to create a shade. In most cases, designers work with two colors. However, a third color can create a greater sense of depth in a room. If you want to produce a more subtle look, use colors that are similar in tone. For maximum visual impact, use high-contrast colors.

Choosing a Color Scheme

Color schemes are essentially visual strategies based on the controlled use of specific colors. There are four widely used color schemes:

Analogous   Analogous color schemes take advantage of adjacent colors on the color wheel. An example would be violet, blue-violet, and blue. Analogous color schemes tend to be soothing because the colors don't visually conflict with each other.

Complementary   Complementary color schemes use two colors that are opposite one another on the color wheel. An example would be violet and yellow. When complementary colors are used together, they tend to make each one appear brighter and more intense. Thus, complimentary color schemes are highly effective at livening up an area that seems bland and muted.

Monochromatic   Monochromatic color schemes incorporate a single color and a neutral color. An example would be blue-green and cream. Monochromatic color schemes often rely on texture and patterns to make the area look more visually interesting. Monochromatic color schemes are very effective in an RV because they tend to make an area seem larger and less cluttered.

Triadic   Triadic color schemes use three colors evenly spaced from each other on the color wheel. An example would be red, yellow, and blue. Triadic color schemes can often make a room seem more cheerful and uplifting. However, this strategy can be tricky when used in small areas, like an RV.

The actual process of picking a color scheme for your RV depends on your design objectives and the medium you're dealing with (i.e. walls, furniture, or flooring). Many people look through decorating books or magazines to find a color scheme they really like. This is a good approach if you understand the role that color plays in each medium. If you don't, you may find that your RV looks a lot different than the picture in the magazine. Remember, color can make or break a remodeling strategy. As a result, take your time, learn about color, and bring plenty of paint swatches back to your RV. Be sure to view the swatches at night time too.

Selecting a Design Theme

Design themes are essentially predefined remodeling road maps. While they aren't mandatory, design themes can help to characterize the type of style you might be looking for. When you're thinking about a possible design theme in your RV, try to answer the following questions:

- What are the primary uses of this part of the RV?
- What routine activities are performed here?
- What other things would you like to do?
- What do you like and dislike about this area?
- What kind of mood or emotion are you trying to evoke?
- How can you design this area to create this mood?

The answers to these questions can help you to fashion a design theme for your RV. Here are a few popular design themes to get you started:

Cabin Style

Cabin style conjures up images of a log cabin in a beautiful wooded or lakeside setting. Walls are typically covered in high-gloss knotty pine paneling. Furniture tends to be simple and practical. Examples include Hitchcock chairs, Adirondacks, old rockers, painted wicker, antique coffee tables with checkerboard tops, twig furniture, old leather, and other primitive style furnishings. Fabrics and window dressings should take advantage of gingham, plaid, checks, and other traditional patterns.

Cabin style should generate a feeling of the beautiful outdoors – away from civilization

Varnished or painted wood floors are a must in conjunction with braided, hand-hooked, Navajo, or rag rugs. Lighting should include oil-style lamps, wrought-iron fixtures, wagon wheel lights, wall sconces, birch bark shades, and other primitive style fixtures. The right decorations are critical and should include objects like antlers, snow shoes, hunting pictures, mounted fish, baskets, taxidermy, stone crocks and old mason jars, fishing accessories, old books, rifles, and animal hides. In general, the cabin style is warm, casual, and fun.

Country Style

Country themes are intended to create a feeling of simplified rural life at its best. The furniture should be practical and relatively simple (i.e. Windsor or wicker chairs). Floors are bare wood or painted slate blue, beige, brick red, or gray. Braided rugs, rag rugs, and old oriental rugs are essential. Window dressings should be simple but elegant. Egg shell or pastel colored curtains and valances made of lace, linen, or muslin are ideal. Patchwork designs prevail as do stenciled motifs and primitive artwork.

Country style offers a relaxed and casual look – perfect for an RV

Wainscoting (stained or painted) is classic country. The remaining exposed walls are usually white or cream. Lighting fixtures, wall sconces, and candle holders should be made of polished brass or wrought iron. Decorative items should include baskets, folk art, old maps, simple glazed pottery, dried flowers, and wooden bowls. The key to the country style is simplicity and practical elegance.

Southwestern Style

Southwestern style, also known as Santa Fe, is growing in popularity due to its clean, natural look. Spanish and Native American influences result in the extensive use of Navajo rugs, rough hewn furniture, brightly colored textiles, and terracotta dishware and pottery. Floors are usually made of polished terracotta (i.e. vinyl tiles or vinyl sheet flooring). The walls can take advantage of special painting techniques to mimic adobe or stucco.

For the windows, consider natural fiber shades, wood mini blinds, or simple curtains with a Native American motif.

Native American pottery is a key component of the Southwestern style (snowwowl.com)

Decorations and artwork should portray Spanish and Native American culture with Indian pottery, Navajo weavings, hand-made baskets, beaded accessories, colorful wall hangings, and katsina dolls. The selective use of rough-hewn stained wood is also classic Santa Fe. The secret to this style is to take advantage of the natural materials and earth-tones that were used by the early inhabitants of the Southwest. For color and texture, use Native American pieces and rugs throughout.

Western Style

Western themes are designed to represent the rugged images shown in popular westerns and traditional cowboy films. Walls are typically painted in muted colors or covered in rough planking (i.e. barn board). Curtains are simple white or ivory linen. Lamps mimic candle or kerosene types and are typically made of wrought iron or carved wood. Tables are primitive and covered with a simple tablecloth. Chairs are made of unpainted wood with leather or rattan seats. Rag rugs, braided rugs, or Indian style rugs are appropriate. Old trunks and crates can serve as small tables or seating.

Fitting decorations include guns, statues of horses, cowboys, and Indians, kerosene style lamps, old bottles, wrought iron candle holders, and other western memorabilia. Wall-mounted decorations could include rifles, old maps, wanted posters, barbed wire or hand-cut nails mounted in a frame, cowboy hats, mounted animals, antlers, old signs, whips, farm tools, belts, and other similar items.

French Country Style

French country, also known as French provincial, is one of the more formal styles still used today. Typical colors include bright pink, blue, white, yellow, and red. Walls are often white washed or color washed in pale tones of gold, rose, apricot, peach, and ocher.

French country is a very formal style with bold textures and bright colors

Floors are often done in terracotta tile or patterned carpeting. The furniture is solidly made in both light and dark woods. Upholstery fabrics are often detailed with vivid patterns and floral designs. Drapes should be formal with bold colors and vivid patterns. Fabric-covered cornices are a must. Kitchen sinks often have a tiled backsplash. Decorations should be formal such as cut crystal, floral designed dishware, and gold and silver anything. The key to French country is the liberal use of color, texture, and unrestrained elegance.

Modern Style

Modern is an increasingly popular style due to its generous use of bright colors, unique shapes, and minimalist décor. Virtually any color combination is suitable but popular colors include orange, turquoise, gray, yellow, pink, and black. Floors should be wood or colorful tile. Furniture is clean looking and makes use of bright colors, light woods, molded plastic, stainless steel, and unique designs. For the windows, consider using thin colorful mini blinds or brightly colored honeycomb shades. Track lighting and modern looking wall-mounted fixtures should create a brightly lit environment. Decorations typically include modern art, avant-garde statues, simple ceramic vases, and futuristic artwork made from odd materials. Because of its clean look and colorful furnishings, the modern style is highly suitable for an RV.

Shaker Style

The Shaker sect, founded in the late 1700s, had thousands of members by the first half of the 19th century. Their highly recognizable (and mimicked) style is characterized by beautifully crafted unpainted furniture with tapered legs, dovetail joints, slender features, and clean lines (see photo). Wall-mounted pegs, installed at chest-level, were used for hanging chairs, brooms, mirrors, baskets, and anything else that could be kept off the floor. Shaker crafts and decorations are well-designed and functional, including stacked oval boxes, hand tools, seed boxes, and simple toys.

Due to its slender style and light features, Shaker style furniture works well in an RV

Floors consisted of unpainted wood and the walls were a combination of bead-board wainscoting and white-washed plaster. Architectural trimwork and molding was simple but prevalent. Rugs were scarce. Their artwork frequently depicted people involved in agricultural activities and religious celebration. Windows were covered in simple cotton curtains. An RV done in Shaker style would be nothing short of stunning.

Sports Style (tailgate style)

Sports based themes offer unlimited possibilities due to the fact that each team has its own unique color scheme and logo. Some RVers tile the floor in the team colors and include the team logo into the design. The walls could display posters, pennants, action photos, balls, bats, jerseys, and other elements of the game.

This beautifully remodeled RV incorporates a racing car theme (courtesy Eric Rupert)

Furniture can be upholstered in fabric that matches the team colors and incorporates the team's logo. Furnishings should be colorful, fun, and entertaining including score cards, memorabilia, beer ads, and other traditional symbols of the sport.

Brando Theater Seating® by Palliser with sports logo

Coastal Style

Coastal themes, if done properly, should convey the relaxed feeling of a country home or guest cottage on the ocean. Walls are typically painted in high gloss white or light pastels. Wall stencils are a nice touch, especially if the design includes shells, sea-horses, and other marine symbols. Curtains are made of light cotton, lace, or linen. Delicate patterns are okay but avoid dark colors. Floors should be wood. Oriental and braided rugs are classic coastal.

Framed coastal maps are perfect for this style

White bead-board wainscoting with chair rail molding is a common element. Wall pegs are appropriate as are plate rails, decorative mirrors, and small wall-mounted shelves. Table legs should be painted white. The tops can be made of unpainted wood or painted metal. Wicker furniture is ideal, especially when painted white of dark green. Adirondack chairs are also a nice touch. Decorative items including sea shells, sand dollars, starfish, and coral should be used tastefully. Dried flowers and colorful dishes can also help to create a homey, coastal feel. Popular colors include shades of blue, green, white, and sand.

Remodeling an RV for Full-Time Use

Full-time RVing requires determination, flexibility, and operational efficiency. If you plan on living in your RV for extended periods of time, consider some of these modifications:

Windows, Floors, and Furnishings

Fabric covered window cornices look terrific in the showroom but they block valuable light and collect dust like a magnet. Likewise, day-night blinds have a tendency to self-destruct with full-time use. Remove the cornices altogether and replace the day-night blinds with something more practical like fabric shades, simple curtains, or honeycomb blinds.

For the floors, consider linoleum, vinyl tile, or plastic-laminate wood. If you want carpeting, find something with exceptional durability, good dirt-hiding characteristics, and StainMaster® treatment. Similarly, choose furniture that's durable, easy to keep clean, and extremely comfortable. Install shelving in unused or overlooked areas (i.e. above the door). Mount your TV on a flexible support so you can change the angle to accommodate various viewing scenarios. Use small, wall-mounted directional lamps to illuminate areas that need the most light. Stay away from florescent lighting and fixtures that emit excessive glare.

The Kitchen and Dining Areas

Install a flip-up countertop extension to provide enough surface area for serious cooking. Use every square inch of wall space for storing knives, utensils, and measuring cups. Install a stainless steel sink and a faucet with a built-in sprayer. Bring a slow cooker and a small electric heater to minimize propane use. Efficient use of space and impeccable organization is the key. For added flexibility and comfort – consider replacing your booth-style dinette with a table and set of chairs. Look for a table that can be extended and chairs that can be folded or stacked.

The Bathroom

Cram in shelving, cabinets, hooks, and racks to create additional storage. Design ways to store things without having to pack and unpack every time you move. A porcelain toilet and sink are a must for full-time use.

The Bedroom

Use shelving, bins, hooks, and rods to make your closets more useful. Buy the best mattress you can afford. Use layers of light bedding instead of heavy blankets and install washable fabric curtains (they're easier to launder). To control the level of light, use room darkening shades.

1950's Style

In the 1950s, recreational vehicles were starting to become progressively more popular. Fortunately, if you're willing to spend time at antique shows and flea markets, you can still find lots of authentic accessories from that era. A suitably styled 1950's RV would contain naugahyde-upholstered furniture, white enameled appliances, yellow walls, Formica® countertops with metal edges, café-style checkered curtains, varnished wood cabinets, and solid color tile floors. Classic 1950's accessories include floral tablecloths, colorful throw pillows, animated salt and pepper shakers, plastic wall clocks, enameled bread boxes, aluminum tumblers, and colorful rugs. Furnishings were frequently colorful and modern looking. Popular colors included turquoise, yellow, orange, and red. Check out *Silver Palaces* by Douglas Keister. It's loaded with great pictures of older Airstreams – many from the 1950s.

If you play your cards right, you could be cruising down Route 66 in a 1950's style RV

1960's Style

The 1960s has become a legitimate style in its own right due to the era's unique colors, vivid textures, and distinctive fashions. For fabrics, look for Indian prints, tie-dye, paisley, embroidered cotton, dyed burlap, colorful bandanas, and blue denim. Decorations could include lava lamps, black lights, incense burners, candles, bead doorways, dried flowers, 1960's era posters, water pipes, American flags, peace signs, and bells mounted on leather belts.

In terms of furnishings, mix and match to your heart's desire but avoid formal or conservative pieces. 1960's era furnishings were commonly improvised. Seating often consisted of bean bags, recycled recliners, and old sofas. Look for produce boxes, wire-spool coffee tables, cinderblock and pine plank shelving, and brightly painted tables. Area rugs should be simple but colorful. Colors should be vivid and daring such as purple, florescent pink, turquoise, raspberry, and bright blue.

Conclusions and Recommendations

RVs that have been successfully remodeled have two fundamental characteristics that distinguish them from those found on the lot. The first is that they've benefited from incremental improvements as a result of being lived in. In other words, the owners have systematically made changes and improvements that make the RV nicer to live in. There's plenty of storage, everything has its place, there's room to move around, it's easy to maintain, and the furnishings are appropriate for the available space and their lifestyle.

The second distinction is that successfully remodeled RVs look nicer. The interior colors and patterns complement each other, decorations are used tastefully and sensibly, there's lots of light, the mood is comforting and pleasing, and the window dressings are attractive as well as functional. Regardless of personal preferences, budgetary restraints, or the type of RV you have – these are the qualities that define a successfully remodeled RV.

Additional Resources

"Decorative Style: The Most Original and Comprehensive Sourcebook of Styles, Treatments, Techniques" by Kevin McCloud

"Decorating Basics: Styles, Colors, Furnishings" (Better Homes & Gardens by Better Homes and Gardens Books and Linda Hallam)

"Nell Hill's Decorating Secrets: Easy and Inspiring Ways to Bring Style into Your Home" by Mary Carol Garrity

"Silver Palaces" by Douglas Keister

"Small House, Big Style" (Better Homes & Gardens) by Better Homes and Gardens Books and Paula Marshall

Chapter 7

RV Flooring

The impact that floors can have on both the character and appearance of a room is indisputable. In addition, as the residential remodeling market continues to flourish, there are more flooring options available than ever before. This may explain why RV flooring upgrades are consistently one of the most commonly performed remodeling activities.

Fortunately, the actual process of replacing the flooring in an RV is pretty straightforward (for most flooring types). Accordingly, this task is commonly done by do-it-yourselfers – with surprisingly good results. To help you make a decision regarding the floors in your RV, this chapter covers the repair, selection, and installation of a wide range of flooring types. The following table summarizes the advantages, shortcomings, and average cost (including installation) of each major flooring type. Of course, the prices shown will be considerably lower if you take advantage of sales and do the installation yourself.

Table 3 – Description of Major Flooring Types

Flooring	Advantages	Drawbacks	Cost (installed)
Carpeting	Inexpensive; never slippery; warm feel; mutes noise; available in numerous colors, patterns, and textures.	Must be vacuumed frequently; stains easily; must be cleaned occasionally; not as durable as other flooring types; relatively difficult to install.	$3 to $5 ft^2
Solid Wood	Available in several wood types and tones; durable and relatively stain resistant; easy to maintain; can be refinished several times.	Expensive. Difficult to install; Can warp; Slippery when wet; prone to water damage, warping, and scratches; requires occasional refinishing.	$6 to $13 ft^2
Engineered Wood	Easier to install than solid wood; Easy to maintain; Will not warp; Durable; Water/stain resistant.	Can only be refinished once; slippery when wet.	$5 to $10 ft^2
Plastic-Laminate Wood	Easier to install than solid wood; easy to maintain; extremely durable; water and stain resistant.	Can not be refinished; slippery when wet.Slippery	$4 to $9 ft^2
Parquet Tile	Easy to install; lightweight. Relatively inexpensive.	Not as durable as other wood flooring. Difficult to cut.	$3 to $9 ft^2
Vinyl Tile	Inexpensive; light weight; easy to install; easy to maintain and repair; available in many colors and patterns; durable; .water/stain resistant.	Can be slippery when wet.	$3 to $8 ft^2

Flooring	Advantages	Drawbacks	Cost (installed)
Linoleum	Inexpensive; durable; available in lots of colors and patterns; light weight; easy to maintain; water/stain resistant.	Relatively difficult to install; difficult to repair; slippery when wet.	$4 to $9 ft^2
Ceramic Tile	Easy to maintain; durable (except for cracking); available in lots of colors and patterns; water/stain resistant.	Expensive; difficult to install; heavy, prone to cracking; slippery when wet; can feel cold; requires occasional sealing and grout maintenance.	$8 to $15 ft^2
Cork	Lightweight; easy to install; mutes noise; excellent insulating qualities; inexpensive; can be installed over most flooring types.	Stains easily; inconvenient to clean; not as durable as other flooring types; Fades if exposed to direct sunlight; Swells if it gets very wet.	$5 to $10 ft^2

Repairing Damaged Floors

While replacing or upgrading your RV's flooring, you should always check to see if the underlying floor is in good condition. While RV floors usually require minimal attention, you may encounter small holes, splitting, cracking, and water damage. Most cracks and holes can be filled with a commercial floor patch. However, if your RV has been subjected to major flooding or a long-term moisture problem, there may be some serious damage to the underlying floor. If the damage has compromised the integrity of the subfloor (i.e. sections are sinking, buckling, or spongy), you'll need to repair the damage before installing any type of flooring.

Eliminate the Leak before you Start

Water damaged floors don't happen overnight. They're almost always the result of a long-term (and frequently undiscovered) problem. Consequently, before you begin making repairs, make sure that you've identified and eliminated the source of the moisture. Otherwise, your repairs could actually make matters worse by creating a new pathway to the RV's subflooring and underlying frame.

The process of repairing a damaged floor requires some understanding of how RV floors are constructed. In most cases, RV floors consist of two layers of plywood or some other type of wood-based composite. The bottom layer (the subfloor) is usually bolted to the RV's chassis and supported by wood or steel floor joists and cross members. The top layer (the one you see when you peel back the tile or carpeting) is generally glued, nailed, or stapled to the underlying subfloor. Both layers must be in good condition before you can install any type of flooring.

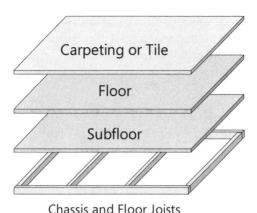

Chassis and Floor Joists

The flooring in most RVs consists of layers of plywood or particleboard

If a significant portion of the floor has been damaged by long-term flooding, you should contact the manufacturer to locate a qualified dealer that can properly assess the damage. If the extent of the damage is significant, you could be facing major expenses and substantial delays while the flooring is being repaired or replaced. Regrettably, it's not something that you can put off because it could affect the integrity as well as the safety of your RV. On the other hand, if the damage is contained within a manageable area, you may be able to make the repairs yourself.

When making flooring repairs, you'll first need to determine the extent of the damage. If the floor is carpeted, tiled, or covered in linoleum, carefully remove enough to examine the underlying floor. If the top layer is saturated, use a chisel to assess the condition of the subfloor. On the other hand, you can drill ⅝-inch holes to visually inspect the condition of the underlying subfloor. Keep in mind, these inspection holes will have to be filled when you're done.

A circular saw with the blade depth adjusted properly is a good tool for removing damaged flooring

The repair process generally entails cutting out the damaged area and filling it with a snug fitting replacement piece of the same thickness. If only the top layer is damaged, use a circular saw to make a cut down to the subfloor. Carefully adjust the depth of the blade so that it only `cuts the top sheet. You may also need to use a sharp wood chisel to cut away pieces that are close to walls, cabinets, or bathroom fixtures. If the damaged flooring extends beneath a cabinet, toilet, or sink, you'll need to first remove these fixtures before you begin making the repairs. If there's mold present, use a solution consisting of three parts water to one part household bleach. Let it dry completely before continuing.

If possible, use the piece you removed as a template for cutting the replacement piece. Make sure that the replacement piece is exactly the same thickness at the original flooring. Then use glue and flat head screws to secure the new piece in place. The screws must be counter-sunk so they don't interfere with the installation of the flooring. Use floor patch to fill any gaps and sand the area until it's smooth.

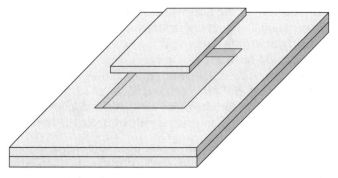

The replacement piece of flooring is glued and screwed onto the underlying sub-floor

If the subfloor is damaged as well, you'll have to cut out pieces from both layers in the same fashion. However, when replacing a section of damaged subflooring, first cut out a larger piece of the top layer. Then cut out and remove a smaller section of the damaged section of the underlying floor. This way, when it comes time to replace the upper piece, you'll have the added support of the undamaged section of the subfloor.

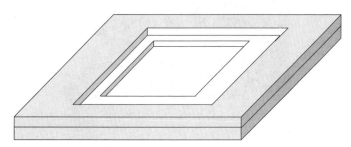

When removing a piece of subflooring, first cut out a larger section of the top piece

However, here's where things can sometimes get a little complicated. In a perfect world, you would cut out a piece of subflooring that just happens to be above some floor joists or cross members. That way, the replacement pieces would be sufficiently supported. However, in the real world, you may find yourself staring through a hole in the floor with no supporting members in sight. In this case, you'll have to fabricate your own support. The process generally entails securing new cross-members to the RV's existing floor joists.

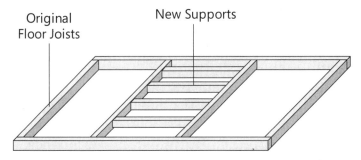

Original
Floor Joists

New Supports

New cross members may have to be added to support the replacement flooring

The actual details will depend on your situation. However, use bolts, brackets, screws, or whatever it takes to create a strong support grid. You can then secure the replacement piece of subflooring to the newly constructed cross-members. When you're done, patch and sand the area. If done properly, your new floor will be at least as solid as the original.

Carpeting

There's a reason why most RVs come with carpeting. It's inexpensive and easy to install. It's available in thousands of colors, textures, and patterns. It reduces noise. It looks good, and it's nice to walk on.

At the same time, carpeting has some major shortcomings – especially in an RV. Carpeting requires frequent vacuuming. It stains easily and it tends to look shabby after a while. Last but not least, too many RV manufacturers have a habit of installing poor quality carpeting that is visually unexciting, old-fashioned looking, and difficult to keep clean. As a result, many RVers end up replacing their carpeting much sooner than they expected.

> **Remodeler's Tip:** If you plan on replacing or removing your carpeting because it's dingy looking, rent a carpet steamer or have it professionally cleaned. You may be surprised at how good it looks. If that doesn't help much, consider having it professionally dyed in a darker color. It might buy you some time.

Routine Carpet Care

Stain resistant technology, such as StainMaster® from DuPont, is now a commonly requested feature in carpeting installations. While the need for spot removers and elbow grease will never be eliminated, removing spots is markedly easier because treated carpets tend to prevent the soaking that results in permanent staining. Even if your RV's carpeting is stain resistant, it will still need to be cleaned periodically. Instead of renting a machine or calling a carpet cleaning service, consider purchasing a carpet cleaner from a discount store. They're inexpensive and do a respectable job.

How to Repair Damaged Carpeting

If you have a sizable section of carpeting that's permanently stained or damaged, there are some techniques for repairing the problem area. The first step is to find a piece of carpet that will match your existing carpet. There are a number of ways to accomplish this task.

- Contact the manufacturer or dealer to see if they have any remnants of the carpeting that was used in your model.

- Call RV salvage dealers to see if they have any models on the lot with your exact carpeting. See Chapter 3 for a listing of RV salvage and surplus dealers.

- Take a piece of carpeting from a closet, under the bed, beneath a cabinet, or under permanently installed furnishings. Only remove what you need since you may be back for more later on.

- Go to a carpet store and look for the best match. Then use the piece from the store to swap out a matching piece somewhere else in your RV (where it won't show).

To repair the carpet, take a lid from a can and nail it to the floor (over the damaged area). With a utility knife, cut around the lid into the carpet. Remove the lid and take out the damaged piece of carpeting. Use the same lid to cut a circular piece of matching carpeting.

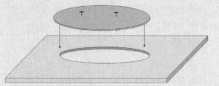

Apply some seam cement to the edge of the replacement piece (to keep it from fraying). Place a piece of double-sided tape into the hole and insert the round piece of matching carpeting. Then put some heavy books on top to keep the piece down. In an hour, remove the books.

Removing Small Stains

Small stains can be fixed with a tuft setter – a special tool that's designed to replace damaged carpet fibers with new ones.

A tuft setter is specifically designed to repair small sections of damaged carpeting

To use a tuft setter, prepare the area by cutting away the damaged pile (with scissors) and wetting the exposed area with latex cement. Obtain some matching carpet fibers from another area of your RV and fold a fiber into the notch of the tuft setter. Then, punch the setter into the exposed area with a few taps of a hammer. Repeat this process until the pile is slightly taller than the rest of the carpet. Finally, use scissors to trim the new pile to the right length.

Here are some proven ways to chemically remove carpet stains. Trichloroethane is available at stores that sell carpet cleaning products. As with all stains, the longer they stay, the harder they are to get rid of.

Table 4 – Carpet Stain Removal Solutions

Stain	Removal Method
Blood	Water, then detergent
Butter	Trichloroethane, then ammonia
Chocolate or Ketchup	Detergent, then ammonia
Coffee or Wine	Detergent, then vinegar
Crayon	Trichloroethane, then detergent
Egg or Ice Cream	Detergent, then ammonia, then vinegar
Grease, Oil or Mayonnaise	Trichloroethane, then detergent
Lipstick or Shoe Polish	Trichloroethane, then detergent, then ammonia, then vinegar
Oil Paint	Trichloroethane
Latex Paint	Detergent
Candle Wax	Place paper towel over wax and use hot iron to soak it up
Tea	Detergent, then vinegar, then trichloroethane
Urine	Vinegar, then ammonia, then vinegar, then detergent

Installing Carpeting

Fortunately, most carpeting upgrade projects are both manageable and affordable. In fact, some carpeting shops can replace the carpet in an RV in less than a day. Then again, if you have the time, the determination, and a good carpeting manual, you should be able to perform the task yourself. On that note, this section is designed for people that plan on doing most of the work themselves.

Carpet Squares – Quick and Easy Carpeting

If you want wall-to-wall carpeting without all the hassle, check out carpet squares. As the name implies, they come in squares and are installed like pieces of vinyl tile. No padding is required and the squares are simply attached using peel-off adhesive strips. Residential carpet squares cost anywhere from $1.50 to $9 per ft^2, depending on the quality. You can find them at The Home Depot, Lowes, and most carpeting stores. To learn more, visit www.interfaceflor.com or www.millikencarpet.com.

Install High-Quality Carpeting

Premium carpeting looks better and lasts longer. It's easier to maintain because it's more resistant to dirt and grime. Added to the fact that RV floors tend to take a beating – you can see why it makes sense to buy the best carpeting you can find.

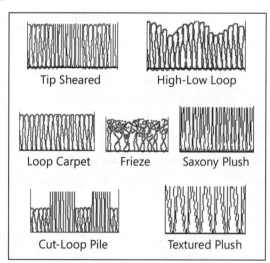

This diagram shows the seven most commonly installed carpeting types

In general, look for heavier pile weights, twisted yarn, and high-density pile. It will provide greater durability and a nicer feel. Similarly, cut-loop pile combines the qualities of both cut-pile and loop-pile carpets. It's very durable and it takes on a somewhat sculptured pattern that helps to conceal footprints. Try to consider long-term value (instead of price) when making your decision.

Pick a Practical Color and Pattern

Unless you want everyone to take off their shoes when they enter your RV, stick with something practical. Carpeting with a distinct pattern can pull a room together – yet solid colors traditionally make a room look bigger. On the other hand, solid colors, especially ones that are very dark or very light, tend to show everything.

Carpeting with a strong pattern will dominate practically any room

Choose something with good dirt-hiding qualities that is also attractive, colorful, and stylish. Avoid very dark and very light colors – especially if they're a large part of the pattern.

Alternatively, you might also want to consider installing the same type of commercial carpeting that's used in offices and retail shops. This rugged carpeting is specifically designed to hide dirt, resist staining, and hold up under heavy foot-traffic. At the carpet store, ask to see their line of commercial carpeting. You may be pleasantly surprised.

Choose a Color Strategy

In terms of selecting the color of a carpet, there are two basic design strategies. The first is to treat the color of the carpet as the major influence on the overall appearance of your RV. In other words, you intentionally choose the color and the pattern as a means of shaping the room's theme.

The second strategy is to pick a color that essentially matches the established colors that already exist in your RV. This option basically treats the carpet as a complementary addition to the room's existing décor. If your RV's interior already has a dominant color theme, consider using a neutral colored carpet with good dirt-hiding qualities. If the interior is generally lacking in color (i.e. all the furniture is ivory colored), consider going with the first strategy by choosing a bold color with good dirt-hiding qualities.

This carpeting complements the existing décor (courtesy Monaco Coach Corporation)

Use the Right Padding

The padding that goes under the carpet is designed to reduce wear, provide cushioning, and hide imperfections in the subfloor. Carpet padding is available in rubber, foam, and urethane. Most people tend to use padding that's either too soft or too thick. The current favorite for durability and cushioning is flat rubber (with a density rating of 19 to 22 lb.). Stay away from bonded urethane foam as it contains butylated hydroxyl toluene (BHT), a potentially toxic substance. Regular urethane foam is okay. Carpet stores typically buy padding in bulk so don't let them push you into using theirs (unless it's suitable).

Determine your Actual Material Requirements

After you measure the square footage of your RV, convert the figure to square yards by dividing the number of square feet by nine. Then add 10 percent to cover mistakes and trimming losses. If your goal is to prevent seams, purchase a rectangular piece of carpeting that will cover the entire area. Alternatively, make sure that any seams are concealed underneath the furnishings.

Some RVs have vertical surfaces that are carpeted along with the rest of the room. These surfaces are typically located in stairwells, inside the cockpit, and around the engine compartment. If you are going to carpet these areas, make sure that you purchase enough carpeting. Some RVers take their engine compartment (dog house) covers to a carpet store to have them professionally carpeted.

In most RVs, the carpeting extends into others areas besides the floor

Remove the Old Carpeting

The carpeting in most RVs has been stapled to the floor. Consequently, removing it typically entails tearing it away with your hands. Some people use locking pliers to grab hold of the carpet. At any rate, be sure to wear safety glasses and gloves because staples and other debris will be flying everywhere. Many RVs are carpeted before the cabinets and counters are installed. This means you'll have to use a utility knife to cut the carpeting around counters and other fixtures. If you cut carefully, you may be able to use the old carpet as a template for the new one.

Get the Subfloor Ready

The subfloor in most RVs consists of plywood or some other type of wood-based composite. When it's exposed – look for holes, weak spots, depressions, or moisture. Holes must be filled with floor patch and sunken areas should be filled with a floor-leveling compound and sanded smooth. In short, before you can install any type of flooring, the subfloor must be solid, level, perfectly dry, and free of debris.

Prepare the Underlay

Some professional carpet installers use something called tackless strips. Tackless strips are wood or metal strips attached to the floor near the walls. They contain multiple rows of pins on which the carpet backing is stretched and secured (see diagram). They're called "tackless" because they eliminate the need for carpet tacks. However, some installers avoid the use of tackless strips in RVs because of the small areas involved. Instead, they use conventional $7/8$-inch carpet tacks or staples.

If you do use tackless strips, cut them to fit each wall and nail them around the perimeter of the room. The pointed pins on the strips should always point towards the wall. The strips should meet each other at the corners without any gaps. Use wood spacers to maintain a gap between the wall and the tackless strips. The width of the wood spacer (and the gap) should be equal to roughly two thirds of the thickness of the carpet.

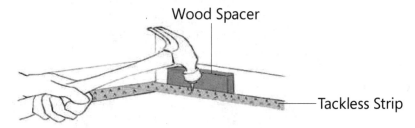

Wood Spacer

Tackless Strip

Tackless strips enable carpeting to be secured without the use of staples or carpet tacks

Put Down the Padding

Cut the padding in strips the length of the area to be carpeted. Then lay out the padding with the "waffle" side facing up. Staple it every 6 inches along the edge of the room – just inside the outer perimeter of the room. If you aren't using tackless strips, leave a ¼-inch gap between the padding and the wall. When you're done, the edges of the padding should butt together to form even seams without overlapping. Finally, cover all of the seams with duct tape.

Lay the Carpeting

Cut the carpet so that you have about four extra inches on all sides. If you're installing a carpet that's in separate sections, be sure to match any patterns or designs. Likewise, make sure that the carpet's pile runs in the same direction. After measuring carefully, flip over the excess carpet and use a utility knife to trim it to size. Use a cutting board and a straight edge to guide the cuts (always cut from the backside). The carpet should still overlap the edges a little on all sides to allow for final fitting and trimming.

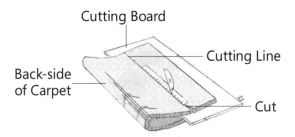

Cutting Board

Cutting Line

Back-side of Carpet

Cut

A cutting board, straight edge, and utility knife are essential for making accurate cuts

After the seams are cut and trimmed, insert strips of adhesive seaming tape underneath any adjoining pieces of carpet. The adhesive side of the tape should be facing upward and the seams butted together. Use a carpet iron to melt the adhesive on the seaming tape by pressing firmly on the iron. Once the adhesive has melted, push the carpet over the seam and seal it with a rolling pin.

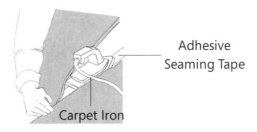

A carpet iron and seaming tape are used for joining separate pieces of carpet

Secure the Carpeting

To ensure a tight fit at the walls and corners, you'll need to use a specialized carpeting tool known as a knee kicker. You can rent them from tool centers, home supply outlets, and carpeting stores.

A knee kicker is designed to produce a snug fit along the walls

Starting in one corner, hook the carpet on to a tackless strip. Next, dig the teeth of the knee kicker into the carpet roughly one inch from the wall. Then "knee" the cushioned end of the knee kicker to shove the carpet forward onto the tackless strip. If you aren't using tackless strips, secure the carpeting to the floor with ⅞-inch carpet tacks or staples.

To finish the job, you may also need to rent a carpet stretcher. Carpet stretchers are used for stretching carpet to the opposite wall, once one corner is already secured (see photo). Because carpet stretchers are typically used for long sections of carpeting (greater than 10 feet), their use in an RV is generally limited to stretching the carpet length-wise.

Carpet stretchers are used for stretching long sections of carpeting

To use the stretcher, you place the base at the corner where the carpet is already attached. A piece of scrap padding is used to protect the wall. The teeth of the stretcher are then pushed into the carpet at the opposite wall, around 6 inches from the edge. When you press a lever on the stretcher, it pulls the carpet towards the opposite corner where it's then secured using tackless strips, tacks, or staples. You essentially work your way around the room using the stretcher to create a snug fit. Most carpeting installation guides include a diagram that shows the proper sequence for using a carpet stretcher. After the carpet is secured at the edges, use a sharp carpet-trimming knife to remove any excess flooring.

Dealing with Slide-outs

Arguably, slide-outs represent the single greatest improvement ever made to a recreational vehicle. With the touch of a button, you can increase your living space without affecting the external dimensions or drivability of your RV. However, slide-outs can often complicate the installation of certain flooring materials, including carpeting.

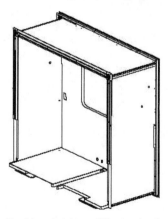

Installing carpeting in an RV with slide-outs takes a little planning (courtesy Winnebago Industries)

Specifically, the installation of a new carpet, if not done properly, can interfere with the normal movement of the slide-out – resulting in damage to the carpet or the slide-out itself. That's why some RV remodeling shops tilt or even remove the slide-outs before they install any flooring. For these reasons, some people believe that you should always hire a professional to carpet an RV with slide-outs. That being said, many do-it-yourselfers have found a couple of tricks for getting around the potential problems associated with slide-out rooms.

> **Note:** The methods described in this section do not apply to flush-floor type slide-outs (example shown in photo on page 72). Flush floor slide-outs usually incorporate proprietary edging solutions that must be properly removed and reinstalled when the flooring is altered in any way.

Both methods require that the slide-out be extended to its maximum position before you start. The first technique entails making a cut where the front edge of the slide-out and the floor intersect. The old carpet is then removed up to that point. The new carpet is then put down and secured with glue, staples, adhesive seaming tape, or tacks. The old carpet is simply left in place (underneath the extended slide-out). The following diagram illustrates this technique.

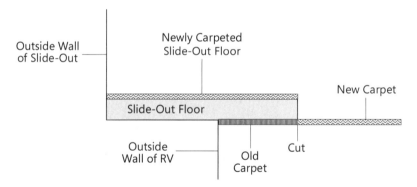

Butting method for re-carpeting an RV with slide-outs

In the second approach, the old carpet is cut approximately one inch from the edge of the slide-out. The new carpet is then tucked under the old carpet. After that, the two overlapping layers are secured to the floor with staples or tacks. However, with this technique, a thin strip of the old carpeting will still show. Thus, this method should only be used if the old and new carpeting are reasonably similar in appearance. It's also only suitable if the overlapping section of the carpets is flat enough to ensure that the slide-out doesn't bind when moving in and out.

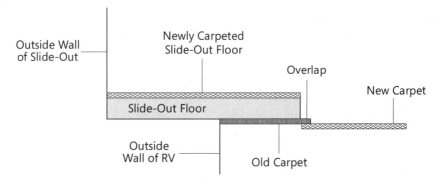

Overlapping method for re-carpeting an RV with slide-outs

Carpeting a Slide-out Room Floor

There are two different techniques for carpeting the floor of a typical (raised) slide-out room. The first method entails using a strip of half-round wood molding to create a "nose" along the front edge of the slide-out. The nose is carpeted along with the rest of the slide-out floor – producing a rounded and more finished appearance. This same technique is frequently used when carpeting stairs.

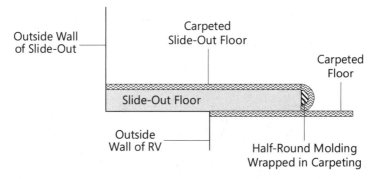

This carpeting technique results in a more finished appearance

When using this approach, first cut a piece of carpeting that is a little wider and approximately 10 inches deeper than the slide-out floor. Then attach the front edge of the carpeting to the strip of half-round molding with carpet glue and staples. The half-round molding (with the rug attached) is then secured to the front edge of the slide-out using screws. You may have to drill holes and use sheet metal screws since many slide-out floors are constructed of extruded aluminum.

With the front edge secure, stretch the carpeting towards the rear of the slide-out room. You may want to rent a knee kicker to ensure a snug fit. When the carpeting is stretched as tight as possible – use carpet tacks or staples to attach it to the floor. Finally, use a utility knife to trim away any excess carpeting along the walls of the slide-out. For a more finished appearance, install quarter-round or cove molding along the back and sides of the slide-out room.

The second method looks a little less polished when it's finished but it's a lot easier to pull off than the first technique. In addition, this method can be used for most flooring types including carpeting, tile, wood, and linoleum. With this approach, the carpeting is first measured carefully and then secured to the floor. Once secured, a piece of metal or wood edging is used to protect the exposed edge of the flooring. As with the first technique, you might want to install wood molding to conceal any gaps or seams.

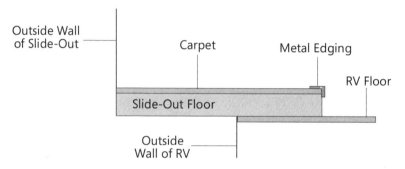

This approach is more straightforward and thus can be used for any type of flooring

Solid Wood Flooring

If your objective is to install something other than carpeting, it's hard to beat the warmth and elegance of solid wood. Available in numerous varieties, tones, and finishes, real wood defines the standard for beautiful floors everywhere.

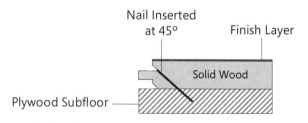

Profile of solid wood flooring nailed to a plywood subfloor

However, in an RV, real wood has some serious shortcomings. Besides being comparatively expensive and difficult to install, real wood lacks the durability and water resistance of man-made alternatives. In fact, some RVers have actually seen their beautiful wood floors warp after accidentally leaving the ceiling vent open in a rain storm. Fortunately, there are some good alternatives to solid wood including engineered-wood and plastic-laminate flooring (i.e. Pergo®). In any case, here are a few guidelines to follow:

Measure the Floor

Determine how much flooring you'll need in total by breaking your floor space into rectangles. Total up the square footage of each section and then purchase 10 percent more flooring than you calculated.

Acclimate the Flooring

It's essential that you keep all new flooring in unopened cartons for a minimum of 72 hours in the same area it will be installed in. This will enable the flooring to become acclimated to your RV's current temperature range and humidity level. If you ignore this step, you may find that the flooring shrinks or buckles after it has been installed.

Installing Solid Wood Flooring

¾-inch solid wood flooring is normally installed with nails that are driven into the RV's subfloor. Thinner planks are usually stapled or glued. If the flooring does require nailing, be sure to rent a manual or pneumatic floor nailer. Never use a hammer and nails unless you want to create a lot of expensive kindling.

Engineered-Wood Flooring

A good alternative to real wood is something called engineered-wood flooring. Engineered-wood flooring utilizes a thin veneer of real pre-finished wood over structural plywood.

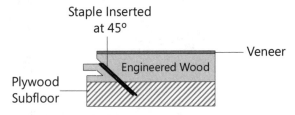

Profile of engineered-wood flooring stapled to a plywood subfloor

Engineered-wood flooring costs about the same as solid wood, but it's easier to install and more resistant to wear and tear. Best of all, engineered-wood flooring is highly moisture resistant when compared to solid wood – making it more suitable for RVs. Furthermore, with its tight-fitting tongue-and-groove joints, engineered-wood can be quickly installed and stapled using a floor stapler. With real wood, each piece must be precisely nailed to the subfloor using a specialized nailing tool.

In terms of maintainability, real wood can be refinished numerous times whereas engineered-wood flooring can be lightly sanded and varnished only once or twice, depending on the thickness of the veneer. However, engineered-wood is considerably more durable than real wood, reducing the significance of this minor shortcoming. Here are some other facts about engineered-wood flooring.

Determine the Installation Method

The width of the engineered-wood flooring can determine the method of installation. Planks up to 3 inches wide are usually stapled. Wider planks are either glued down or "floated" (i.e. held down by their own weight).

Cover the Subfloor

For engineered-wood flooring, you have to first cover the subfloor with roofing felt (tar paper) or rosin (kraft) paper. The paper is overlapped a few inches at the seams and secured with staples every 12 to 18 inches. Use short staples to ensure that they go in all the way.

Use a Flooring Stapler

When installing engineered-wood flooring, be sure to rent a flooring stapler. The stapler must be adjusted so that the staples end up slightly below the wood's surface. If the staples stick out a little, you won't be able to insert the next piece of flooring. If they go in too far, they may not hold the boards adequately. The last few boards will need to be face-nailed because flooring staplers can't operate close to a wall.

Plastic-Laminate Wood Flooring

Plastic-laminate flooring (i.e. Pergo®) consists of a fiberboard core that's covered with a graphic image (the pattern layer) and a highly durable clear substance (the wear layer). Compared to solid wood, plastic-laminate flooring is easier to install, more durable, and less expensive.

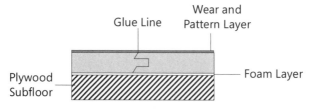

Profile of plastic-laminate wood flooring (thickness is 0.39-inch) on top of a plywood subfloor

Plastic-laminate flooring also tends to look better longer than real wood flooring – especially in areas with lots of foot traffic. Furthermore, plastic-laminate flooring is virtually impervious to spills, stains, and moisture. As a result, it's an excellent candidate for RVers that stay in rainy places. The one disadvantage of plastic-laminate flooring is the fact that it cannot be refinished once the clear wear layer becomes worn or damaged. However, with its exceptional durability, this is rarely an issue.

Plastic-laminate flooring is easy to install (courtesy Pergo, Inc.)

The process of installing engineered-wood or plastic-laminate flooring varies depending upon the specific product. For a professional looking installation, always follow the directions provided by the manufacturer. Here are some other issues to keep in mind:

Use a Foam Underlayment

Plastic-laminate flooring is installed over a foam layer to provide cushioning and reduce noise. To simplify the installation process, products such as Pergo Prodigy® come with a foam layer already attached. If you decide to use a separate foam layer, be sure to follow the manufacturer's instructions.

Leave Room for Expansion

Plastic-laminate flooring must have room to expand. Consequently, always leave a ¼-inch gap between the wall and the flooring.

Apply the Right Glue

Plastic-laminate flooring is normally glued together at each joint and held in place by its own weight (hence the term "floating floor"). The flooring sits on a foam layer that is sometimes glued to the RV's subfloor. In this scenario, be sure to use the brand of glue that is recommended by the flooring manufacturer. Using another brand could affect the integrity of the installation and possibly void the warranty.

Use Templates

When installing plastic-laminate flooring (or any type of flooring) around odd-shaped fixtures, floor ducts, architectural trimwork, or cabinets, carefully trim a piece of cardboard to create an accurate template. Then use the template to trim the flooring for a snug, professional-looking fit.

Take Advantage of Transition Molding

Flooring manufacturers sell a variety of moldings and transition technologies that can simplify the installation process. They include:

- **End Molding** – Used to transition plastic-laminate flooring to existing flooring, door thresholds, and sliding doors.

- **T-Molding** – For joining two areas of plastic-laminate flooring at archways and doorways.

- **Hard Surface Reducer** – For transitioning plastic-laminate flooring to a lower hard surface floor such as tile, linoleum, vinyl, or wood.

- **Carpet Reducer** – For transitioning plastic-laminate flooring to carpeting.

- **Stair Nosing** – For finishing stair edges and other step-down applications.

Parquet Tile Flooring

Parquet tiles are essentially a compromise between wood flooring and vinyl tiles. It provides the warmth and beauty of wood along with the ease of installation of tile. Most parquet tiles come in 12-inch squares in thicknesses ranging from $5/16$-inch to $3/4$-inch. In terms of installing parquet flooring, you'll need to create a set of perpendicular layout lines as you would with any tile job. You should then make a trial run with the tiles to get accustomed to their tongue and groove design.

When you're ready, adhesive is applied (with a notched trowel) to a manageable area of floor. Be sure to give the adhesive plenty of time to set (become tacky). The first tile is usually placed in the corner of the intersection of the layout lines. The tiles that go along the edge of the room are finally trimmed to fit. To accommodate natural expansion, leave a $3/8$-inch gap between the perimeter tiles and the wall. When you're done with each section, use a flooring roller to press the tiles into the adhesive. Then stay off the tiles for at least 24 hours.

Parquet flooring combines the warmth and beauty of wood with the simplified installation of tile

> **Contractor's Tip:** Never use a carbide-tipped saw blade to cut
> parquet tiles. The manufacturer installs a corrugated metal strip in the
> back of each tile to hold the strips of wood together. If you use a
> carbide blade, you'll damage both the tiles and the blade. Plus, tiny
> pieces of metal will fly everywhere. The best tool for cutting parquet is
> a saber saw. Be sure to apply a strip of masking tape over the cut line
> to minimize splintering.

With a beautiful new wood floor, Randy has a lot to smile about (www.rvliving.com)

Wood Flooring – Handling the Problem Areas

Entrance-ways and driver's areas can be highly problematic when installing wood flooring. For the most part, you have three options. The first is to leave these challenging areas alone. If the existing flooring is in good condition, this may be the most sensible option.

The second option is to use a different type of flooring for the driver's area and entrance-way. Carpeting or vinyl tile is much easier to cut and install than wood. Carpeting also helps to reduce noise. On the other hand, if you want the look of wood (in these areas) without all the work, consider installing vinyl tile or sheet flooring that mimics wood. Look for a pattern and a shade that closely matches the wood flooring that you're installing in the remainder of the RV. Traffic-Master Allure® is one example of a "wood" flooring product that goes down without any glue. The realistic-looking flexible planks cost around $50 for 21 square feet.

This elegant wood floor is actually made of vinyl sheet flooring

The last option is to cover these areas in the same wood material that you're using for the rest of your RV. However, this requires some serious cabinetry skills and access to good cutting tools. The task usually entails using wood trim and architectural molding to conceal seams. Keep in mind – these areas normally take a beating from heavy foot traffic and hard use. If you do use wood, make sure that it's fastened securely. Otherwise, you could be creating a wood masterpiece that requires never-ending maintenance.

Vinyl Tile Flooring

One of the best flooring options for an RV is vinyl tile (also known as resilient tile). The installation is manageable for do-it-yourselfers. It's reasonably priced. It's very durable, and it's easy to maintain. Furthermore, because tile is available in a broad range of patterns and colors, it can dramatically improve the appearance of any RV. Besides the usual colors and patterns, you can now purchase vinyl tile that very successfully emulates wood, stone, terracotta, brick, ceramic, marble, granite, and more. If you've always wanted a ceramic tile floor, consider installing vinyl tile instead. It's a respectable looking substitute without all the weight, maintenance, cracking, and expense.

If you don't mind the traditional look of resilient tile, you might want to check out something called commercial-grade vinyl composition tile (VCT). A good example is Armstrong's Excelon®. Packaged 45 pieces to a box (⅛-inch thick) in one foot squares, Excelon® is installed with a commercially available adhesive. There are other (more expensive) types of vinyl tile that use peel-back style adhesives, but they lack the exceptional durability and maintainability of VCT. In any case, when installing vinyl tile, be sure to follow the suggestions described here.

Take some Samples Home and Order some Extra Tiles

Before you make a major investment in any type of flooring, see what it will actually look like in your RV. If a tile store won't give you some samples, go to another store. Put the pieces on the floor and see how they look in different lighting scenarios. When ordering tile, always purchase a few extra pieces (known as "attic stock"). They'll typically be used to replace tiles that become damaged during the installation process. Plus, you'll inevitably have to replace tiles that wear out over time.

Decide on a Color Strategy

With tile (and carpeting), you have two basic color strategies. The first is to treat the color and the pattern as the leading influence on the overall look of your RV. In other words, the flooring effectively drives the overall appearance of the area – like the floor in the following photo.

The second strategy is to select a color and a pattern that complements the area's existing color scheme. This approach essentially treats the flooring as a matching accessory to the room's existing décor. For example, if your RV's primary color scheme is green, consider using a neutral color tile with a green colored pattern that provided good dirt-hiding qualities. On the other hand, if your RV's interior is somewhat muted (i.e. the walls and the furniture are neutral), select a unique color and pattern that delivers the overall appearance you want.

This eye-catching VCT floor is perfect for the RV's racing car theme (courtesy of Eric Rupert)

Be Prepared to Tile Vertical Surfaces

Unlike a house, many RVs have vertical surfaces that are often tiled. These areas may include entranceways, portions of the cockpit, and the engine cover (in some motorhomes). When you're ready to install a new tile floor – decide how you want to tackle these areas as well.

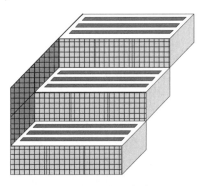

In many RVs, the walls and step risers in the entry-way are tiled

Let the Tile Acclimate

As with all flooring materials, store the tiles in the same area that you'll be installing them in for at least 72 hours. This will enable the tiles to become acclimated to the current temperature range and humidity levels inside your RV.

Read the Directions

Even though there are a number of good books on installing tile flooring, always refer to the manufacturer's directions. For instance, some products require you to leave a small gap between the tile and the wall (to allow for expansion). On the other hand, other products state that the tile should fit tightly against the wall.

 # How to Remove Old Vinyl Tile

Removing old vinyl tile is basically a process of starting with the weak tiles (the ones that come off easily) and moving on to the stubborn ones. Look for seams that enable you to slip in a wide-blade putty knife. Self-adhesive tiles should come off easily while glued tiles may take more work. After you've removed the easiest ones, use a flooring scraper to pry off the remaining tiles. Be sure to keep the angle of the scraper low to the floor to prevent the blade from digging in to the underlying floor. Wear goggles and gloves since bits of debris tend to fly everywhere.

Finally, for those persistent tiles that still won't let go, use a heat gun to soften the adhesive. Keep the gun roughly 5 inches from the tile and move it back and forth. Then use the wide-blade putty knife to scrape the tile off the floor. Be sure to clean the blade of your putty knife while the adhesive is still soft.

Prepare the Subfloor

Before you begin, examine the underlying floor carefully. Holes and sunken areas should be filled with a floor-leveling compound and sanded smooth. Weak spots must be located and fixed. To sum up, the subfloor must be dry, solid, level, and impeccably clean before you can install any type of resilient flooring.

Read the Instructions

Allow the adhesive to set (become suitably tacky) according to the manufacturer's directions. In most cases, the adhesive should be tacky, but not wet. You'll also need to purchase some solvent to clean up any squeeze-out (the adhesive that invariably oozes out between the tiles).

Each brand of adhesive has a specific set (waiting) time (courtesy Parabond Products)

For a Perfect Fit, use Layout Lines

You should never install vinyl tile without first carefully drawing a set of perpendicular layout lines on the subfloor. Be sure to make the layout lines dark enough to be seen through the adhesive. If the tile is hard to cut, soften it with a hair dryer or a heat gun.

Use a Notched Trowel

Vinyl tile (including VCT) requires the use of a specialized notched trowel. If you use a regular trowel, you may put down too much (or too little) adhesive.

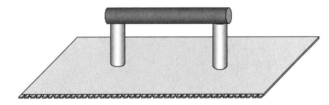

A notched trowel is specifically designed to apply the correct amount of adhesive

Rent a Floor Roller

Floor rollers serve two purposes. First, they push the tile into the adhesive, resulting in a stronger bond. Second, they help to produce a more level looking installation.

Install Cove Base Molding

Cove base molding is one of the tricks used by vinyl flooring professionals to create a more polished looking installation. The molding also helps to keep the edge pieces from coming up over time.

Vinyl cove base molding delivers a more finished looking installation (courtesy of easy2.com)

Vinyl cove base molding is easy to work with and comes in a wide range of colors. Although it's available in either rolls or strips, go with the rolls as you'll have fewer seams. The vinyl molding is attached to the base of the wall with an adhesive that is applied to the molding, not the wall. To prevent squeeze-out, keep the adhesive approximately half an inch from the top of the molding. Corners are best handled by using a utility knife to miter each piece for a seamless fit. Use duct tape to hold the pieces in place while the adhesive dries.

While not as durable as vinyl, wood cove base molding is also a good choice. However, wood is generally more work since it has to be sealed or painted. Wood molding should be attached to the wall with screws (especially in an RV). For a professional looking fit, cut the corners at a 45° angle using a miter box and saw. On the other hand, a butt joint is more than adequate in most situations.

Order some Extra Tiles

When ordering tile, always purchase a few extra pieces (known as "attic stock"). They'll typically be used to replace tiles that become damaged during the installation process. Plus, you'll inevitably have to replace tiles that wear out over time.

Vinyl Sheet Flooring

Vinyl sheet flooring consists of the same material that's used in high-quality resilient tile. The principal difference is that it's manufactured and installed in sheets. Most vinyl flooring is ⅛-inch thick and has a tough coating for durability and tear resistance. Like tile, vinyl sheet flooring is available in a wide range of colors, patterns, and textures. As a result, it can effectively mimic everything from hardwood to polished marble. We have vinyl sheet flooring in our kitchen that looks a lot like real wood.

One key distinction between vinyl sheet flooring and tile occurs during the initial trimming. When cutting tiles, you simply grab another tile if you make a mistake. With vinyl sheet flooring, trimming errors can ruin an entire piece.

Vinyl sheet flooring is attractive, reasonably priced, durable, and very easy to maintain

Vinyl sheet flooring is normally installed in one of two ways. The first technique, known as a full-adhesive installation, involves applying an adhesive to the entire surface being covered. The second method, known as a loose-lay or perimeter installation, entails using staples or an adhesive at the edges of the room only. The adhesive can either be double-sided tape or a commercial adhesive applied with a trowel. If everything else is done properly, both methods are equally acceptable. Here are a few tips worth noting:

Use your Old Carpet as a Template

If you're replacing a carpeted floor with vinyl sheet flooring, you might be able to use the old carpet as an accurate template. However, the old carpet must be free of tacks, major tears, and defects. In short, the old carpet must be capable of lying perfectly flat.

Make a Good Template

The most critical step in the installation of vinyl sheet flooring is the creation of an accurate template. Professionals like to use rosin or kraft paper because it's durable and lays flat. Use a utility knife to trim out any bubbles or waves in the paper. Then cover the holes with masking tape. The tape will stick to the underlying floor, effectively keeping the paper template in place.

Use Scrap Paper to Create Highly Detailed Templates

When you encounter odd shaped objects such as door jambs, cabinets, or plumbing, first cut the template paper so that it goes around the object, leaving a one or two-inch gap. The paper should fit loosely around the odd-shaped object but snugly against the wall, as shown below.

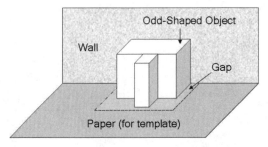

Although there's a gap around the object, the template paper is snug against the wall

Then, use small sheets of paper and masking tape to completely fill the gap around the object. The tape keeps the sheets of paper together and securely attached to the template paper. The result will be a very accurate paper template.

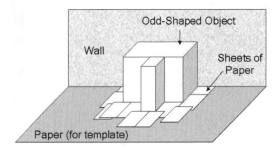

Pieces of scrap paper are placed against the object and taped down, creating an accurate template

Use the Template to Get a Perfect Fit

When the template is finished, tape it to the top side of the vinyl sheeting. With a marker, trace the outline of the template onto the vinyl sheet flooring. Carefully cut the vinyl along the outline with a metal straightedge and a sharp utility knife. Be sure to protect the underlying floor.

> **Installer's Tip:** Test a small piece of vinyl flooring to make sure that the template lines can actually be cleaned off. Also, if the vinyl flooring is difficult to cut, use a heat gun or a hair dryer to soften it up.

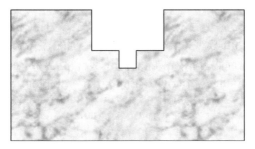

The end result is a section of vinyl sheet flooring with a very accurate cut-out

How to Remove Old Vinyl Sheet Flooring

The process of removing old vinyl sheet flooring will depend on how the flooring was installed originally. If it was a perimeter installation (only secured along the edges), you're in luck. In this case, use a utility knife to first cut around the perimeter of the area. Then cut the freed section into strips for easy removal. To remove the flooring that's still attached along the edges, use a wide-blade putty knife. For sections that won't come off, use a heat gun to soften the adhesive. Hold the heat gun approximately 5 inches from the floor and keep it moving continually. Then use a putty knife to peel back the remaining pieces of flooring. Be sure to clean the putty knife blade quickly with a rag (while the adhesive is still soft).

If your RV is older than ten years, the vinyl flooring was probably put down using a full-adhesive installation. Start by using a utility knife to cut the flooring into strips. Then use a putty knife to determine if any of the strips can be pulled up by hand. Finally, use a flooring scraper to scrape off the remaining flooring. The angle of the scraper blade must be kept low to the floor to prevent the sharp blade from digging into the underlying floor. Be sure to wear goggles and gloves as it's a messy job.

For those stubborn sections that still won't let go, spray on a mixture of warm water and dishwashing detergent. This will often help to separate the flooring from its felt backing. Better yet, hire someone else to remove the old flooring. As you can see – you won't be missing much.

Before Gluing, Check the Fit

Assuming that the underlying floor is solid, smooth, and clean – lay out the vinyl sheet flooring to check the fit. The flooring should fit tightly against the walls. Make any last minute adjustments with a utility knife. With a full-adhesive installation, roll up half of the flooring and apply the glue to the exposed floor. When the glue is ready, unfurl the flooring. Use a flooring roller to smooth it out and remove any air bubbles. Larger bubbles can be eliminated by making a tiny cut and releasing the trapped air. Be sure to use the adhesive that's recommended by the manufacturer.

For a perimeter installation, use staples or an adhesive to secure the vinyl flooring along the edges. If you're using staples, staple it every 2 inches. Before it's attached, make sure that the flooring is pulled tight against the wall. For seams, always use a strip of adhesive. When you're done, use a hand roller or a rolling pin to press the flooring onto the adhesive. Clean up any squeeze-out with a rag that's damp with solvent. Finally, install cove base molding or wood trim to conceal the staples.

Apply Adhesive around Obstacles

Regardless of which installation method you use, always apply some adhesive around obstacles such as pipes, door thresholds, and floor vents. Otherwise, these areas will constantly peel and tear.

Use Transition Strips

If the vinyl flooring has been installed with other types of flooring (i.e. carpeting), you'll need to use transition strips. Available in several widths and colors, transition strips protect the edges of each flooring type while producing a cleaner, more professional looking installation.

Ceramic Tile Flooring

Of all the flooring options, ceramic tile represents one of the most challenging. It's difficult to install. It's heavy. It has a tendency to crack, and it's usually slippery when wet. These disadvantages are compounded by the fact that RVs are rough on everything, including flooring. Yet, with all of these shortcomings – ceramic tile is still one of the most beautiful and desirable flooring options available today. As a result, it's frequently found in many high-end motorhomes.

In any case, ceramic tile flooring should only be considered if the drawbacks are clearly understood and the installation is done properly. If you plan on installing the tile yourself, be sure to pay close attention to the installation directions provided by the manufacturer. Here are a few other suggestions regarding the installation of ceramic tile in an RV.

This ceramic tile floor is striking and easy to maintain (courtesy Newell Coach Corporation)

Check Out the Corners

Ceramic tile is very difficult to install in RVs that aren't perfectly square. Check the corners in your RV using a carpenter's square. If the corners are square, the installation job will be a lot easier. If they aren't, plan on using lots of baseboard molding to conceal the gaps.

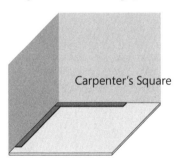

A carpenter's square can be used to quickly assess the shape of your RV's corners

Use a Flexible Membrane Liner

The primary reason ceramic tile is difficult to install and maintain relates to its brittleness and subsequent tendency to crack. Most professionals install ceramic tile on top of a thinset mortar base. However, in an RV, you should consider putting down a flexible membrane liner in order to reduce the probability of cracking. The membrane liner is normally attached to the floor with a peel-back adhesive. The A thinset mortar with a liquid latex additive can then be applied on top of the flexible membrane liner. This strategy will help to reduce the likelihood of cracking that typically occurs as a result of vibration, flexing, or shock.

Install Smaller Tiles

Because of normal flexing, large ceramic tiles tend to crack more often than smaller ones. Consequently, you may want to consider using 6-inch or 12-inch tiles instead of the larger 18-inch ones.

Leave Room for Expansion e

The larger the tile squares, the greater the likelihood of cracking. As a result, you may want to consider using 6 inch tiles instead of 12 inch ones.Be sure to leave room for expansion at the perimeter of the room. Although the manufacturer will typically specify the gap size, make it a little wider. You can then use baseboard molding to conceal the gaps.

Likewise, to minimize cracking, you should allow the tiles to move and flex as much as possible. While traditional grout isn't designed to flex, there are specific products that exhibit a certain degree of elasticity. Ask about them at your local home supply or hardware store.

Cork Flooring

Manufactured in numerous colors, cork flooring is available in either planks or tiles. It's light, attractive, easy to install, comfortable to walk on, and offers excellent sound insulation. Its downside relates to the fact that cork tends to fade in direct sunlight and it can swell up when exposed to high levels of moisture.

In terms of the installation, cork can be glued down or floated. Some companies now sell cork flooring with a specially designed tongue and groove, moisture-resistant inner core for easier installations. Most cork floors come with a vinyl finish layer to protect the surface and make cleaning easier. Some RVers have had great success with cork flooring.

Mixed Flooring

Most RV floors are covered with a mixture of carpeting and vinyl sheet flooring (or tile). The carpeting is typically installed in the living room and bedroom while the vinyl is installed in the kitchen and bath. As this strategy seems to represent the best of both worlds, you may want to consider it for your RV. If you do, you'll need to become familiar with the specialized transitioning techniques and associated products that are used with mixed flooring installations. Ask the people at your local home supply store for assistance.

Conclusions and Recommendations

Although there is a vast selection of available floor coverings, your choice should be primarily based on your lifestyle and your tastes. If you want the elegant look of wood, it's hard to beat the ease-of-installation and durability of plastic-laminate wood flooring. If you're looking for more color, vinyl tile or vinyl sheet flooring is durable, attractive, easy to install, and a breeze to keep clean. If you want the best of both worlds, use carpeting in the living room and bedroom, and tile in the kitchen and bathroom. There has to be some reason why this combination appears in the vast majority of RVs sold today. The following table compares the positive qualities of each flooring type.

Table 5 – Flooring Type vs. Features

Flooring Type	Easy to Install	Easy to Maintain	Durable	H_2O–Stain Resistant	Provides Color	Mutes Sound	Light Weight
Carpeting	✓				✓	✓	✓
Wood		✓					
Engineered Wood	✓	✓	✓	✓			
Plastic-Laminate Wood	✓	✓	✓	✓			
Parquet Tile		✓	✓	✓			
Resilient Tile	✓	✓	✓	✓	✓		✓
Vinyl Sheet		✓	✓	✓	✓		✓
Ceramic Tile		✓		✓	✓		
Cork	✓	✓			✓	✓	✓

Additional Resources

"Flooring Basics" by Rick Peters, Sterling Publishing Company, Inc., New York, NY

"The Flooring Handbook: The Complete Guide to Choosing and Installing Floors" by Dennis Jeffries

"The Complete Guide to Flooring" (Black & Decker) by the editors of Creative Publishing International

"Flooring 1–2–3: Expert Advice on Design, Installation, and Repair" (Home Depot 1–2–3) by John Holms

"Guide to Floor and Carpeting Installation and Repair" (McGraw–Hill paperbacks home improvement series)

"Carpeting Simplified (Easi-Bild Simplified Directions)" by Donald R. Brann

"Lowes Complete Tile and Flooring" (Lowe's Home Improvement) by Barbara Finwall and Nancy Javier

Chapter 8

RV Walls

The vast majority of RVs come with institutional looking walls due to the industry's long-standing use of vinyl-coated wallboard. The mottled pattern is allegedly suitable for any style of interior but in truth – it looks more like something you might find in a Wal-Mart restroom. Fortunately, this ubiquitous wall covering can be painted, wall papered, stenciled, or even paneled with excellent results.

RV Wall Construction

RV walls are typically constructed by sandwiching layers of modern building materials. The outside layer is usually made of aluminum or gel-coat fiberglass, depending upon the manufacturer and the model. Next is a sheet of low-grade ⅛-inch plywood, known as Luan wood backing. Structural support is provided by aluminum, steel, or wood framing. In between the framing is insulation – typically polystyrene foam or fiberglass batting. The interior walls, as a rule, consist of vinyl-coated wallboard.

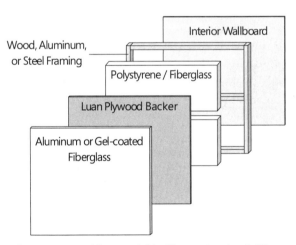

Most RV walls are constructed from sandwiched layers of modern building materials

RV manufacturers that specialize in "all-season" models often use additional layers of Luan wood backing and thicker insulation. However, the majority of RV walls are less than 2½ inches thick in total. As a result, the R-value (insulating value) of a typical RV wall is usually less than R-10. The R-value of a modern home is usually between R-15 and R-28.

Repairing Damaged Walls

Before you begin any project involving the walls in your RV, examine them to ensure that they're free of any noticeable scratches, dents, or holes. Scratches can be filled with spackle or a drywall compound. Holes and gaps should be filled with acrylic or siliconized acrylic caulk. When the patching compound is dry, smooth it out with 200-grit sandpaper. Then wipe the area with a damp rag to remove any residual dust.

> **Contractor's Tip:** To determine the thickness of the walls in your RV, open a window, remove the screen, and measure the depth of the window casing. The wall will be slightly thinner than the casing.

If a large section of interior wallboard is damaged, you may have to resort to other repair strategies. The actual technique you use will depend on the extent of the damage and the wall's construction. In any case, you'll have to obtain a piece of wallboard that is of the same thickness as the original wallboard.

If the walls in your RV are filled with a solid insulating material such as polystyrene foam (i.e. Styrofoam®), use a utility knife to remove the damaged piece of wallboard. A new piece can be cut using the removed piece as a template. Apply a commercial adhesive (i.e. contact cement) and insert the replacement piece into the hole. The polystyrene foam insulation inside the wall should serve as a solid backing. After the adhesive is dry, use patching compound to fill any gaps. Use sandpaper to smooth out the rough spots and then wipe the area clean with a damp rag to remove any remaining plaster dust.

If the wall is hollow or uses fiberglass batting as an insulating material, the task may be more complicated due to the lack of a solid backing inside the wall. Fortunately, you can now purchase drywall repair kits that are specifically designed for hollow walls.

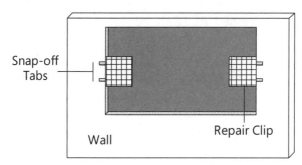

Drywall repair kits come with clips that are specifically designed for repairing hollow walls

The kits include a set of special repair clips that are slipped onto each side of the damaged area. The clips are recessed which enables you to insert a piece of wallboard into the hole. The piece of wallboard is then held in place with screws that go through the wallboard and into the grid portion of the repair clips. The small clips that initially held the repair clips in place snap off, eliminating any evidence of the underlying repair clips. Finally, any remaining seams are filled with a patching compound and sanded smooth.

Constructing New Walls

Some remodeling projects entail the construction of a new interior wall. For instance, a small section of wall may be required to help support a countertop, a built-in computing area, or a new shower stall. The following diagram shows the basic components of an interior wall.

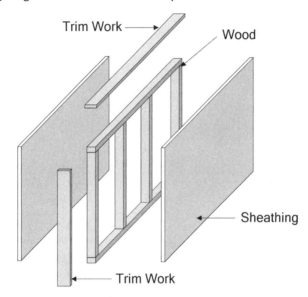

Wall additions are typically built from stock lumber and wallboard sheathing

The wall is first sized and framed from pieces of stock lumber. The width of the lumber depends on the final wall thickness you're seeking. If the wall needs to act as a barrier to sound or heat, consider inserting fiberglass insulation inside the framing. The wall is then attached to the floor or the wall before it's sheathed. The easiest approach involves drilling holes in the wood framing and using screws to secure the new wall in place.

Once the wall is framed and secured, cover it with some type of sheathing. Options include wallboard, wood paneling, plywood, or sheetrock. The exposed edges of the new wall may have to be covered, depending on how the wall is being used. Stained and varnished trim is my particular favorite.

Using Anchors

Anchors are used for attaching things to a wall when screws, nails, adhesives, or other fasteners won't work. In an RV, where the walls and doors are frequently hollow, wall anchors are a blessing. To help you choose the right kind, here's a brief description of each type:

> **Contractor's Tip:** If you encounter wood when attaching something to the wall in your RV, drill a small hole and use wood screws. If you run into aluminum framing, use self-tapping sheet metal screws instead. Otherwise, use one of the anchors described here.

Winged Plastic Anchors

Designed for hollow walls, doors, and cabinetry, small winged plastic anchors are ideal for most RVs. On the other hand, if the walls are insulated with polystyrene foam, you may have to use plastic expansion or threaded drywall anchors (described ahead).

Winged Plastic Anchor

To install a winged plastic anchor, first drill a hole in the wall. Then fold the wings towards each other and push the anchor into the hole. Winged plastic anchors come with a pointed tool that is used for pushing the center of the wings out so that they properly expand inside the wall. If you miss this step, the anchor won't expand properly. If you don't have the special tool, simply insert a small screwdriver or a nail into the screw hole. When you install a screw into a winged plastic anchor, the wings pull firmly against the inside of the wall. To remove a winged plastic anchor, turn a screw slightly into the head of the anchor. Then use a pair of pliers to pull it straight out.

Plastic Expansion Anchors

Plastic expansion anchors are extremely popular because they are inexpensive, easy to install, and available in a wide range of sizes. Plastic expansion anchors are designed to be used in a solid wall, such as plaster or concrete. If they're used in a hollow wall like the type normally used in RVs, their holding ability will be severely compromised. In general, the more heavily ribbed they are, the greater the gripping strength. Plastic expansion anchors are appropriate when the load is light and the force on the anchor is primarily perpendicular to the wall. When greater holding force is required, use more than one anchor.

Plastic Expansion Anchors

To install a plastic anchor, first make a hole using a drill or an awl. Then hammer (or press) the anchor into the hole until it's perfectly flush with the surface. The hole should be slightly smaller than the thickest part of the anchor. To remove a plastic anchor from the wall, turn a screw slightly into the head of the anchor. Then pull it straight out with pliers.

Threaded Drywall Anchors

Threaded drywall anchors are often referred to as EZ Anchors® or Zip-Its®. They utilize large threads which are capable of gripping securely into drywall. Most threaded drywall anchors use #6 or #8 sheet metal screws. Designed for solid walls, threaded drywall anchors are roughly twice as strong as plastic expansion anchors.

Threaded Drywall Anchors

Although threaded drywall anchors are considered to be self-starting, they go in a lot easier when you use an awl or a punch to create a starter hole. The anchor is then screwed into the wall with a Philip's head screwdriver until the head is flush against the surface of the wall. To remove a threaded drywall anchor, turn a screw slightly into the head of the anchor. Then use a pair of pliers to pull it straight out.

Threaded Drywall Toggles

Like winged plastic anchors, threaded drywall toggles are designed to be used in hollow walls. However, threaded drywall toggles are preferred when greater strength is required. They are installed the same way as threaded drywall anchors. However, with a threaded drywall toggle, a small arm swings out as the screw is tightened. When installed properly, threaded drywall toggles are very reliable.

Threaded Drywall Toggle

> **Warning:** Threaded drywall toggles are often difficult or impossible to remove. Some people simply pound them in a little with a hammer and use spackling compound to hide the dent. In any case, you won't be able to insert anything in the same location.

Molly Bolts

Molly bolts combine ease of installation with considerable holding power. In fact, some of the larger molly bolts can support over 50 lbs. There are two types of molly bolts – regular and drive. Drive molly bolts (shown on left) are designed to be hammered into a wall, like a nail. Regular molly bolts (on the right) are pushed into a pre-drilled hole like a plastic expansion anchor. However, since drive molly bolts tend to get damaged when they're hammered in, it's better to drill a hole for both types.

Molly Bolts

To install a molly bolt – first drill a hole in the wall that is the same diameter as the molly. Then use a hammer to tap the molly into the hole until its head is flush with the wall. Then turn the bolt that comes with the molly clockwise (↻) until you feel strong resistance and the top of the molly is slightly sunken into the wall. Professionals that install molly bolts all the time use a special tool called a "molly setter".

> **Warning:** Molly bolts are extremely difficult to remove. Since they are already recessed, remove the screw and use spackling compound to cover the rest. However, you won't be able to insert anything in the same location.

Toggle Bolts

Due to their superior strength, toggle bolts are frequently used for installing heavy objects like kitchen cabinets, wardrobes, bunk beds, and floor to ceiling book shelves.

Toggle Bolt

Toggle bolts are measured by their length as well as the diameter of the machine screw. To install a toggle bolt, you'll need to first drill a hole in the desired location. The following table shows which drill bit to use for various sized toggle bolts.

Table 6 – Toggle Bolt Size vs. Drill Bit Size Required

Toggle Bolt Size	Drill Bit Needed
⅛ inch	⅜ inch
³⁄₁₆ inch	½ inch
¼ inch	⅝ inch
⁵⁄₁₆ inch	⅞ inch
⅜ inch	⅞ inch
½ inch	1¼ inch

When you're ready to mount the object, push the machine screw through a hole that's been drilled in the object. Then thread the toggle onto the bolt far enough so that the threads prevent the toggle from turning sideways. This step will ensure that the toggle opens properly inside the wall. Place the object into position and push the toggle through the hole in the wall until you hear the toggle snap open. As you tighten the bolt, pull on the object to keep the toggle's wings from rotating. Before the toggle is fully tightened, carefully position the object. Then tighten the bolt while being careful not to over tighten. To remove a toggle, simply remove the bolt. The wing will then drop inside the wall.

Paint and Stencils

The easiest way to improve the appearance of the walls in your RV is to paint them. When we painted the walls in the main living area of our RV, we were astonished at the transformation. If you decide to paint your walls, here are a few things to keep in mind:

Prepare the Walls

Before painting, fix any cracks, scratches, or holes as described previously. In addition, the walls should be clean and free of mildew or mold. Use warm water and detergent to clean the walls. For mildew, use a solution consisting of three parts water to one part bleach. Finally, use a sponge and cold water to remove any remaining bleach or detergent.

Use Painter's Tape Sparingly

Blue painter's tape is great stuff but most professionals use it sparingly. The reason is that it takes a lot of time and patience to properly apply and remove. Moreover, in some situations, paint seeps into the gap between the tape and the surface, producing a ragged appearance. Your best bet is to paint slowly and carefully when painting next to window frames, cabinets, and other unmovable objects. Also, consider using a beveled brush that is designed for painting trimwork. It can give you more control in tight situations.

Buy Good Paint

Since there's very little wall space in an RV, you won't use a lot of paint. As a result, get the best paint you can find. High quality paint goes on easier, covers better, looks nicer, and is more durable. Consumer's Reports frequently rates paint so check out their guide or sign up for a subscription to their website. Whatever you do, stay away from cheap paint. Just trust me on this one.

Use the Right Finish

Paints generally come in four finishes: flat; satin; semi-gloss; and high-gloss. For surfaces that require occasional cleaning, use a gloss or semi-gloss paint. For rough surfaces, go with a satin finish because it's better at hiding defects. As a general rule, use a satin finish for walls and a semi-gloss or high-gloss for trimwork, cabinets, and doors. In areas with high levels of moisture (like a bathroom), always use high-gloss paint.

Use the Right Tools

RVs are too small and too crowded to consider spraying as a feasible option. However, with a good quality paint and professional-grade tools, you'll be surprised at the results. In terms of which way to start, everybody has their own approach. I like to begin with a roller because it minimizes the amount of brush work I have to do. If I start with a brush,

I'm never certain how close I can get with a roller. As a result, I end up painting more of the wall than is necessary.

> **Painter's Tip:** For latex or water-based paints, always use brushes with synthetic bristles and paint rollers with synthetic covers.

For large sections, always use a paint roller with a smooth cover. For painting next to cabinets, windows, and other fixtures, use a variety of tools including brushes, a small roller, and a trim pad. Trim pad painters are a very quick and efficient way to paint next to any straight object. However, you must keep the small rollers free of paint. As a result, check them each time you add paint and remove any paint with a clean cloth.

Trim pads are indispensable when painting next to cabinets, windows, and doors

Select your Colors Carefully

When picking a color for the walls, choose carefully. Light colors tend to give the illusion of more space whereas dark colors have the opposite effect. Look at remodeling books for ideas and bring paint swatches into the RV to see how they appear at night as well as during the day. Before making a final decision, paint a small section of wall with the actual color that you've selected. Then see how it looks over the next few days. This technique is used by most professional decorators.

Paint for the Future

If you're planning to replace your carpeting or get some new furniture, select a paint color (for the walls) that will complement these planned changes. Otherwise, you may find that the color you pick today limits your future possibilities.

Use Color to Create the Illusion of Space

In an RV, use similar colors in two adjoining areas to make it appear like one larger area. Likewise, visually broaden narrow areas by using lighter tones on the longer walls and darker tones on the shorter ones –

effectively drawing them in. You can also open up small areas in your RV by using pale shades. For contrast, use brightly colored furniture and accessories. Similarly, use accent colors to emphasize slide-out frames, fancy trimwork, and other interesting features in your RV. The contrast will make them stand out more.

Light colored furniture and walls make this RV feel roomier (courtesy Monaco Coach Corporation)

Decorative Stenciling

Stenciling is the process of using decorative designs and repeating patterns to embellish the appearance of an object. In an RV, the effect can be dramatic. Pre-cut stencils can be found on the Internet and in craft stores. If you don't see a design you like, try combining two different patterns.

To stencil a wall, use a carpenter's level to apply a horizontal strip of blue painter's tape. Then apply spray adhesive to the back of the stencil. When it becomes tacky – press the stencil into position using the painter's tape as a guide. When applying the paint, make sure that the stencil brush is nearly dry. Lightly dab the stencil brush into each cutout while being careful not to move the brush sideways.

Stenciling requires the use of a special brush (with very little paint on it)

When you're done with that section, carefully remove and clean the stencil. Then apply more adhesive and continue stenciling across the wall. For multi-color stencils, simply apply one color at a time. In other words, after the first color has dried – start from the beginning with the next color.

Thousands of pre-cut stencils, like this beauty, are available at craft stores as well as on the Web

Specialized Painting Techniques

There are several specialized painting techniques that can give your RV a uniquely stylish appearance. Some are strictly decorative like sponging, dragging, color-washing, and ragging while others are designed to mimic traditional materials like stucco, marble, and wood. Most of these techniques are relatively easy to master. In general, a base coat is first applied to the wall. Then a glaze consisting of watered-down latex paint is applied in various ways to produce the desired effect. When using these techniques in a high-moisture area, such as a bathroom, apply a protective coat of polyurethane. In spite of their simplicity, specialized painting methods can have a dramatic effect on the appearance of any RV.

Wall Paper and Decorative Borders

While few people think of wallpaper when remodeling an RV, most RVs are delivered with vinyl-coated walls. As a practical matter, wallpaper offers several important advantages including durability, moisture resistance, and attractiveness. With its unique patterns, colors, and textures, wallpaper can provide a whole new dimension to an otherwise nondescript wall.

The same can be said of decorative borders. When used creatively, they add a level of style and elegance that defies their simplicity and easy installation. That's the principal reason why you'll find decorative borders in most RVs. Unfortunately, the decorative borders found in most RVs are relatively conventional and unexciting. In any event, when it comes to using wallpaper and decorative borders in an RV, here are a few issues to keep in mind:

Don't Compromise on the Quality

You won't have to buy a lot of wallpaper to cover an entire RV. As a result, stay away from bargain wallpaper. Typically made of thin, vinyl-coated paper, cheap wallpaper tears easily and cannot be washed. Instead, look for pre-pasted (paper-backed) vinyl wallpaper. Vinyl wallpaper is easy to install, it's completely washable, and it doesn't tear. Fabric-backed vinyl wallpaper is another excellent choice but it's rarely pre-pasted. Expanded vinyl is an interesting option if you're looking for a three-dimensional look. It's available in a wide array of interesting textures and styles including stucco, granite, marble, and brick.

Avoid Bold Patterned Wallpaper

In an RV, stay away from wallpaper that has a strong pattern or a distinctive motif since each piece will have to be properly matched and aligned. Instead, choose wallpaper with a subtle design that can be applied to small areas without any special matching requirements.

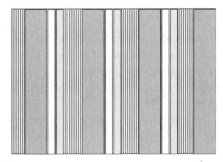

In an RV, trying to properly match a bold wallpaper pattern like this one is next to impossible

Use a Vinyl-to-Vinyl Primer

Most of the interior walls in an RV are coated with a vinyl covering. If yours are, apply a vinyl-to-vinyl primer to ensure adequate drying of the wallpaper adhesive. Give the primer 24 hours to dry before hanging the wallpaper. Similarly, use a paste activator. It will ensure that the wallpaper doesn't become unglued and fall down. Ask the folks at the paint and wallpaper store for advice on your particular situation.

Ask for Help

Hanging wallpaper isn't difficult. As a result, most people can do a respectable job with a little practice. However, there are a few paper-hanging tricks and specialized tools that can make things go a lot easier. Look for some free booklets or brochures from your local home supply store. Most bookstores also carry several how-to guides. Also, see if you can find someone who has wall-papered before to help you get started.

Hanging wallpaper in an RV isn't hard but it does take a little practice and some special tools

The Hidden World of Exotic Remodeling Materials

There are specialty stores that sell amazing products that can transform even the most modest RV into a stunning showcase. You'll find molded ceiling tiles that resemble old-fashioned tin, Egyptian wallpaper, Roman columns, hand-painted decorative borders, beautiful trimwork, and custom wood paneling that's ready to install. And the cost of these treasures? As they say...if you have to ask.

Exotic wallpaper will transform any RV (courtesy burtwallpapers.com)

Fancy Molding, Architectural Trimwork, and Ceiling Materials

- www.cumberlandwoodcraft.com
- www.decoratorssupply.com
- www.mbossinc.com
- www.thetinman.com
- www.mccoymillwork.com
- www.elitemouldings.com
- www.maple-grove.com
- www.focalpointap.com

Designer Wallpaper, Wall Coverings, and Wainscoting

- www.adelphipaperhangings.com
- www.bradbury.com
- www.brewsterwallcovering.com
- www.burrows.com
- www.burtwallpapers.com
- www.carterandco.com
- www.charlesrupert.com
- www.mason-wolf.com

Use the Right Tools

Wallpapering is one of those tasks that tend to get easier as you progress through a room. However, it always goes a lot better if you have the right tools. Fortunately, wallpapering tools are inexpensive and readily available at any hardware or home supply store. These are the basics:

- Wallpaper tray – to wet pre-pasted paper
- Bucket and sponge – to smooth out the wallpaper
- Tape measure and carpenter's square – to measure and cut
- Wallpaper brush – to apply primers, activators, and paste
- Seam rollers – to press the seams tightly against the wall
- Level and straightedge – to ensure that the paper is hung properly
- Wide-blade putty knife – various tasks
- Utility knife and scissors – to cut and trim the wallpaper

> **Contractor's Tip:** Professional paper hangers change the blades on their utility knives every few hours. A sharp blade will save time, minimize tearing, and help to produce a cleaner looking installation.

Using Decorative Borders

Available in many colors, patterns, and widths, decorative borders can be found at any good home supply or paint store. In an RV, borders are usually applied along the middle of the wall because of the presence of cabinets. Tape the border on first to see how it will look.

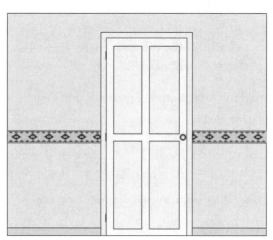

In an RV, decorative borders look best if they're installed along the mid-section of a wall

Since decorative borders are highly effective at drawing together separate walls, use it sparingly to avoid a closed in appearance. In general, use borders that are less than 4 inches wide. Heavier borders tend to make small rooms appear even smaller.

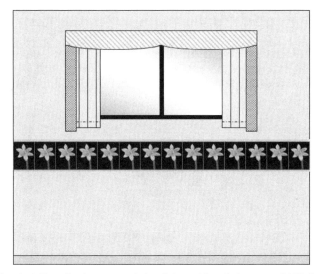

When installing a border near a window, intersect the window or go right below it

Because of their relatively small size and simple furnishings, bathrooms are the perfect candidate for the creative use of decorative borders. Likewise, consider installing a row or two of decorative ceramic tile along the middle of the wall. Be sure to add a length of chair rail, wood trim, or quarter-round cap tile on top of the tile. In addition to providing a more polished look, this step will minimize chipping.

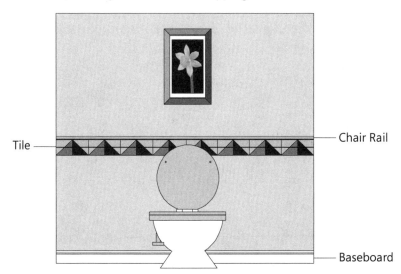

A strip of colorful ceramic tile can add a touch of elegance to any bathroom

Wainscoting

Bead-Board Wainscoting

The classic wainscoting seen in older homes was originally constructed of tongue and groove planks known as bead-board. It was usually bordered by a chair rail at the top and a baseboard at the bottom. The wainscoting was then stained and varnished or painted with high-gloss paint.

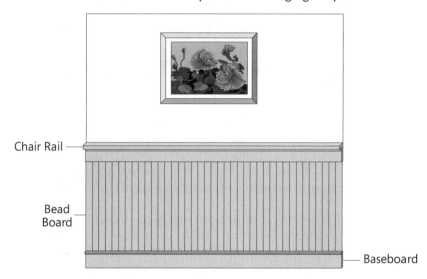

Traditional bead-board wainscoting is durable, attractive, and easy to install

Fortunately, installing wainscoting in an RV is easy. We put prefabricated wainscoting panels in our living room slide-out with excellent results.

This slide-out room was covered in bead-board wainscoting

The (48″x 30″) panels were installed using screws and a commercial wood paneling adhesive. You can also find wainscoting kits at home supply stores. The kits contain connecting sections of pre-primed (white) ¼-inch particleboard along with enough chair rail and baseboard to create a 6-foot section of bead-board wainscoting. All you do is measure the width of the wall, make the appropriate cuts, and attach everything with screws, nails, or an adhesive. If you want unpainted wainscoting (to stain and varnish), look for bead-board planks at a lumber yard or at your local home supply store.

Stained and varnished bead-board wainscoting provides a very traditional look

Modified Frame and Panel Wainscoting

The term "wood paneling" tends to conjure up images of the now defunct wall covering that was installed virtually everywhere in the 1960's and 70's. Today however, wood paneling has taken on a whole new image. Built from beautiful hardwoods and architectural trimwork, wood paneling is now seen in million dollar yachts, executive offices, and luxury motorhomes. If you're looking for the natural beauty of wood without the tackiness of paneling – consider installing modified frame and panel wainscoting.

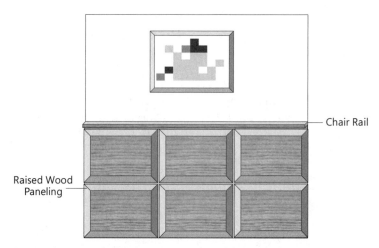

Modified frame and panel wainscoting will make any RV look and feel more luxurious

The foundation typically consists of a one-side finished piece of ¼-inch plywood. The details are added using architectural molding and wood trim. The entire panel can then be painted, stained, lacquered, or simply treated with wood finishing oil. The visual impact modified frame and panel wainscoting can have on an RV is extraordinary.

By matching the wood wainscoting to the cabinets, this RV has a very solid appearance

Wallpaper Wainscoting

Wallpaper hung in conjunction with a chair rail can produce a very elegant look for extremely little effort.

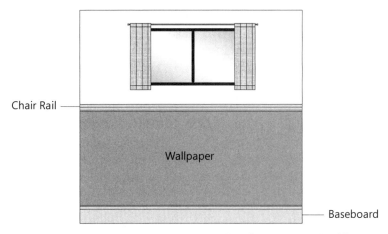

This simulated wainscoting was created with wallpaper and wood molding

Wallpaper is first hung along the lower section of a wall (approximately 30 inches high). A section of chair rail is then attached along the top of the wallpaper. As a general rule, the wallpaper should be darker than the color of the remaining wall. For a more polished look, install a section of baseboard at the bottom of the wall. The chair rail and the baseboard should have the same type of finish.

Tiled Wainscoting

Ceramic tile, applied half-way up the wall, can make a bathroom feel more elegant without overwhelming it. Transition the area between the tiled section and the upper wall with some type of architectural molding. It will look surprisingly good.

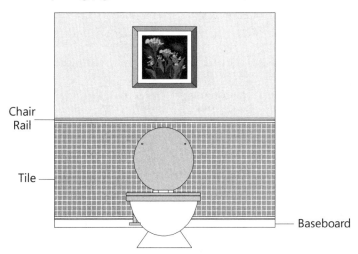

Colorful ceramic tile wainscoting is perfect for high-moisture areas like bathrooms

When tiling large areas – choose smaller tiles that have a subtle pattern. Large tiles with a bold design tend to make the bathroom appear smaller and more congested. In addition, for better light dispersion and easier maintenance, choose a light colored tile with a high-gloss finish.

Mirrors

If you look at the interior of any new RV, you'll invariably see the creative use of wall-mounted mirrors. The reason for their popularity has to do with the fact that mirrored surfaces have an unmatched ability to make any room seem larger and brighter. Mirrors come in a wide variety of sizes, shapes, and styles, including ones that are tinted, beveled, etched, and stenciled. You can install them on doors, ceilings, around counters, behind shelves, and anywhere else you can think of. Be sure to use a high quality mounting system such as a holding lip (see below) along with a set of mounting clips. Some RV manufacturers rely on a hidden bracket to attach their mirrors to the wall. To remove them, you generally use a special tool that's available at the RV dealership.

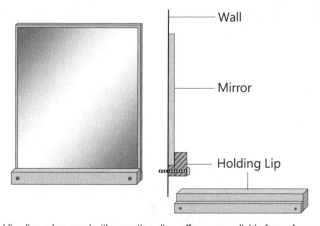

Holding lips, when used with mounting clips, offer a very reliable form of support

> **Designer's Tip:** Don't install a mirror that inadvertently reflects a cluttered or private area (i.e. the toilet) in your RV. Similarly, don't put up a mirror that could generate intense levels of light. For example, a mirror that is installed opposite a large window could produce intolerable reflections (and too much heat) on sunny days. Experiment a little before permanently installing any large mirror.

Trompe l'oeil

Trompe l'oeil (pronounced trum-ploy´) is an age-old style of artwork that is essentially designed to create a realistic illusion using a two-dimensional image.

Stunning Trompe l'oeil murals, like this one, can be used to create the illusion of space

Sometimes appearing in large murals, Trompe l'oeil artwork often depicts ornate doorways, windows with ocean views, elaborate village scenes, and romantic images of rural life. The real value of this ancient art-form lies in its ability to successfully create the illusion of distance and space.

This Trompe l'oeil mural can create a beautiful view no matter where you are

Trompe l'oeil can be used very effectively in an RV to make an area appear more spacious as well as more interesting. Fortunately, you don't have to hire a renaissance artist to enjoy this unique art form. Ready to install prints are sold on the Internet at reasonable prices. For example, visit www.berlinwallpaper.com and select Trompe l'oeil from the product directory. Trompe l'oeil prints are usually put up without frames in order to help sustain the illusion they create.

Decorative Molding and Trimwork

One subtle but important difference between regular RVs and high-end luxury models is the creative use of architectural trimwork and decorative molding. The reason is very simple. Architectural trimwork is capable of delivering a measure of elegance and quality that is difficult to achieve in any other way. For the creative RVer, it provides a cost-effective way to dramatically alter the appearance of your RV without altering its basic structure or floor plan. The following tips are designed to get you started:

Use the Right Material

A good home supply or lumber store will have a large selection of molding and trimwork. Molding is typically available in wood, polyurethane (plastic), medium-density fiberboard (MDF), and flexible vinyl. Wood is a good choice if you're trying to match the existing woodwork in your RV. If you plan on painting the molding, consider MDF. Because it comes primed, it can usually be covered with a single coat of paint. If you're dealing with curved surfaces, use flexible vinyl. It conforms to virtually any shape and can easily be painted. Polyurethane molding is a popular choice because it's inexpensive, white, easy to cut, and extremely lightweight. As a result, it can often be installed using a commercial adhesive (instead of nails or screws).

Balance the Molding and Trim to the Job

Molding and trimwork come in a wide array of shapes and sizes. Select a type that is appropriate to both the task and the overall look you're seeking. There are also numerous ready-to-use architectural accessories that can greatly enhance your trimwork projects. For small trim jobs (like framing a mirror), use a thinner, less ornate type of molding. Conversely, to add some elegance to a row of kitchen cabinets, install some highly decorative crown molding. The trick is to enhance an object without overpowering it.

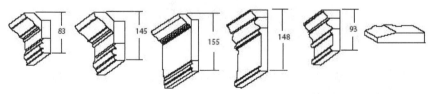

RV manufacturers rely on molding to add elegance and style (courtesy Winnebago Industries)

For similar projects, always use the same type of molding. For example, if you plan to add decorative molding to each of your cabinets, be sure to use the same type throughout your RV. The result will be a cleaner and more professional looking installation. Accessories, like the rosette shown below, are typically used to accent the corners of doors, windows, and slide-out rooms. If you look closely, you'll find them in many RVs.

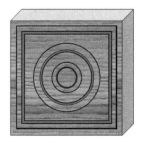

Wood accessories, like this rosette, can add a polished look to any architectural trim project

Use Colors Carefully

In an RV, heavy, dark colored trim will often make an area seem boxed-in and confined. When you're painting picture frames, chair rails, door frames, and baseboards, select a color that is relatively close to the color of the wall. This will help to make the room look bigger by creating large, uninterrupted blocks of color.

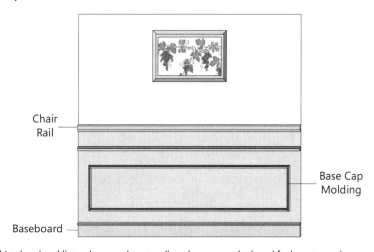

Light colored molding, when used on a wall, makes a room look and feel more spacious

Get a Miter Box and Saw

Miter boxes are essential for cutting molding at the right angle. Use a clamp to hold the molding in place when making difficult cuts. When joining separate pieces of molding, there are three commonly used techniques. For corners, use either a bevel joint or a butt joint. The bevel joint is more formal and thus should be used when the joint is noticeable. The 45° cut is used for connecting straight sections of molding.

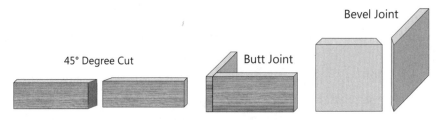

When joining sections of molding, use one of these three techniques

Some Good Trimwork and Molding Projects

From a remodeling perspective, there's no limit to the types of things that can be done with molding and architectural trimwork. The following projects are frequently used in RVs.

- Install crown molding to conceal the seam between built-in cabinets and the ceiling. This not only adds stylishness, it also creates a more built-in appearance.

- Use quarter-round or crown molding to improve the intersection between the walls and the ceiling.

- Install wood trim around doors and windows to provide a more luxurious look.

The woodwork surrounding this slide-out is extraordinary (courtesy Monaco Coach Corporation)

- Add a chair rail, picture rail, or plate rail to a wall.

- Use hardwood molding to enhance the appearance of a mirror.

- Install crown molding along the front edge of a slide-out and place a string of hidden rope lighting behind it.

- Use baseboard, cove molding to conceal the joint between the floors and the walls.

- Use architectural trim to frame your windows. Attach the trim to the walls with screws.

- Use pieces of polished wood to enhance the appearance of your vehicle's dashboard.

Conclusions and Recommendations

What you ultimately do with your walls could have a profound impact on the overall appearance of your RV. If you're looking for the most impact for the least effort, consider using paint or wallpaper along with stenciling or a decorative border. From there, the choice is yours. For elegance and polish, wainscoting is unbeatable. The easiest way to install wainscoting is to use wallpaper and a strip of molding. For maximum stylishness, consider using specialized painting techniques in conjunction with Trompe l'oeil artwork. Last but not least, incorporate some fancy trimwork into your plans. Luxury coach makers have been using the stuff for years as a dependable way to add style and elegance. Start small until you get the hang of it.

Additional Resources

"Ortho's All About Painting and Wallpapering" by Ortho Books, Brian Santos

"Home Remodeling Guide to Paneling, Painting & Wallpapering" by Sunset

"Wallpapering in a Weekend" by Anthony Evans

"Step-By-Step Interior Painting" (Do-It-Yourself Decorating) by Julian Cassell, Peter Parham

"Black & Decker: The Complete Guide to Painting & Decorating" (Black & Decker Home Improvement Library)

"1001 Ideas for Trimwork by Wayne Kalyn" (Creative Homeowner, 2006)

"Trim Idea Book" by Mary Ellen Polson

"The New Decorating with Architectural Trimwork" by Jay Silber

Chapter 9

RV Ceilings

A while ago, we were inside a 1986 Country Coach Motorhome that belongs to some friends of ours. Their RV is a striking example of a solidly built and well-designed motorcoach. The cabinets are built from solid cherry, the counters are made of polished marble, and the floors are covered in large squares of imported Italian tile. It also has a dishwasher, an ice maker, and a four-burner stove with a built-in grill and electric rotisserie. Yet, the one feature that seemed the most luxurious was the ceiling. It was made of beautifully stitched panels of soft, supple leather!

If you look closely at most high-end motorhomes, you'll notice that the ceiling has received a significant amount of attention (see example below). The rationale for this strategy relates to the fact that a properly designed ceiling can help to make an RV appear much larger and taller than it actually is. Of course, lavishly designed ceilings also help to justify the price of these well-appointed motorhomes.

The ceiling in this RV plays a major role in the room's appearance (courtesy Newell Coach Corp.)

RV Ceilings Design Considerations

From a fashion perspective, a well-designed and executed ceiling remodeling project can produce dramatic results. On the other hand, a poorly designed project can be disastrous. Accordingly, when it comes to giving your ceiling a facelift – it's best to defer to the design experts. Here are a few tricks used by RV design professionals:

Raise your Ceilings using Color

If your RV's ceiling is dark, create the illusion of more height by painting it a lighter color than the rest of the room. Neutral colors or pale pastels work best.

Use a Consistent Design Theme

Make sure that the remodeling strategy you select fits in with the rest of the furnishings. If the design is fundamentally different from the surrounding décor, it's apt to appear unnatural and out of place. For example, if you plan on using wood trim to accent your ceiling lights, be sure to use a stain that matches the existing woodwork.

The trim around the ceiling light fixture matches the cabinets (courtesy Monaco Coach Corp.)

Lights and Mirrors

The basic idea, when remodeling a ceiling, is to use an approach that creates the illusion of more space. That's why manufacturers of high-end coaches frequently use lights and mirrors in their ceiling designs. The simple ceiling fixture shown below is one example. Pay a visit to your local RV dealer or go to a show. When you find a ceiling design you like, take a few pictures, make a sketch, or get a brochure. When you go back home, you can design your own version.

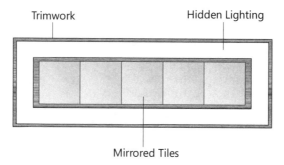

Trimwork   Hidden Lighting

Mirrored Tiles

High-end motorhomes use ceiling fixtures with mirrors and lights to create the illusion of space

Project: Stylish Ceiling Light Fixture

Various versions of this ceiling light are often used in high-end motorhomes. The fixture below is constructed from a piece of finished hardwood along with some wood strapping. The width of the board should be approximately 6 inches. The length is a matter of preference. The lights are mounted evenly on the board, every 12 to 18 inches. The wiring is hidden inside the frame (between the board and the ceiling).

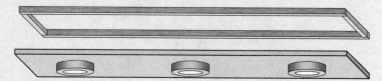

This ceiling light can be sized to run the entire length of your RV's living room

The lights are small halogen fixtures known as "puck" lights. They're available in packs of two or more at most home supply stores. The wiring is specifically designed to snap into each fixture. Then, the last light in the string is connected to a low-voltage transformer which is connected to a nearby power source. The board is attached to the ceiling with recessed screws that are concealed with wood plugs. Use anchors to ensure that the screws hold firmly.

Roof Vents, Skylights, and Ceiling Fans

If you're looking for additional light and fresh air, consider installing a roof vent or a ceiling fan. The choice should be made on the basis of what you're trying to accomplish. Roof vents are generally intended for exchanging air whereas ceiling fans are primarily designed for moving air. In addition, ceiling fans add a touch of elegance to a room whereas roof vents are largely functional.

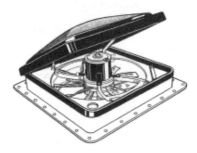

Most RV roof vents are designed to fit in any 14" x 14" opening (courtesy FanTastic Vent Corp.)

Because roof vents provide some added light, their presence can have a significant impact on the look and feel of your RV. Roof vents also come with a number of handy features including rain-detectors, thermostatic controls, and 3-speed reversible fans. Most vents require a standard 14"x14" opening but they take up less than half an inch of head-room. Ceiling fans, on the other hand, require at least six inches of head-room. Both roof vents and ceiling fans need access to a 12-volt power source.

The blades of this fan are available in several materials and colors (courtesy www.cetsolar.com)

If you're looking for a significant increase in light, consider installing a skylight. Commonly located in bathrooms, skylights are relatively easy to install since there's no moving parts or electricity to deal with.

Furthermore, the companies that make RV skylights have done a good job at making them leak-proof.

> **Installer's Tip:** Before installing a roof vent or a skylight, contact the manufacturer to see if there are any obstructions (inside the roof) that you should be aware of (i.e. AC ductwork). If there is – ask them to suggest an alternative location.

Conclusions and Recommendations

You have two basic options when it comes to RV ceilings. The first is to leave them alone. Ceilings are tricky. If you don't adhere to narrowly-defined design conventions, you could inadvertently make your RV feel smaller and more cluttered. The second option is to carefully and tastefully use lighting, mirrors, and quality materials to add depth and style to your RV's interior. Start by looking at high-end RVs. When you find a ceiling design you really like, see if there's some way to design a simplified version. You may be on your way towards creating a beautiful addition to your RV's interior.

Additional Resources

Some manufacturers of high-end ceiling materials:

www.abbingdon.com	www.cumberlandwoodcraft.com
www.acpideas.com	www.decoratorssupply.com
www.bradbury.com	www.mbossinc.com
www.ceilingsmagnifique.com	www.thetinman.com

"Building & Finishing Walls & Ceilings" (Black & Decker) by Creative Publishing international, Phil Schmidt

"Ceilings" by Everett J. Mohatt

Chapter 10

RV Windows

Window dressing modifications consistently rate as one of the most popular RV remodeling projects. One probable reason relates to the fact that most RVs have lots of windows. Consequently, their impact on the appearance of an RV is considerable.

Another likely explanation for all this window remodeling could be the RV industry's long-standing preference for conservative styles and unexciting solutions. In fact, a recent visit to an RV show in Phoenix, Arizona confirmed that when it comes to windows, it's business as usual. Model after model included the same fabric-covered cornices and day-night blinds that have been used for decades – even though there are some excellent alternatives. Accordingly, this chapter describes a wide array of window-related remodeling options.

The Parts of an RV Window

Other than their size and shape, most RV windows are basically the same. The primary distinctions relate to the way they open (sliding vs. louvered) and the number of panes they have (single or double-glazed). The following illustration shows the individual components of a typical sliding RV window (courtesy Winnebago Industries).

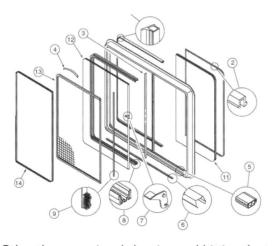

2	Vinyl Glazing
3	Glass Weather-Stripping
4	Screen Clip
5	Slide-Stop
6	Screen Spacer
7	Latch Assembly
8	Channel-Run
9	Screen Weather-Stripping
11	Glass Pane (stationary)
12	Glass Pane (sliding)
13	Screen Assembly
14	Retainer Trim

Other than occasional cleaning and hitting the tracks up with a little silicone spray, most RV windows are maintenance free. Sometimes, clips and other small parts will break from fatigue. However, these items can be ordered by most RV parts dealers. Dirty window screens should be removed and cleaned with a soft brush and some soap and water. It's best to do this task outdoors with a hose (to rinse off the soap). In a pinch, a quick vacuuming with a soft brush attachment will suffice.

If the screening is damaged, you'll have to replace it. Luckily, it's pretty easy to fix a damaged screen. You can find screen repair kits at most hardware stores. They contain everything you need including some black plastic screening, several feet of vinyl spline, and a special screen repair tool. Alternatively, you can have the screen repaired at any hardware store that fixes screens.

Project: Replacing a Damaged Window Screen

1. Remove the screen from the window.
2. Place it on a surface that's big enough to support the entire screen.
3. Pull the vinyl spline out of the groove and remove the screening.
4. Cut a new piece of screening (add an extra 2 inches on all sides).
5. Cut a piece of vinyl spline long enough to go all away around.
6. Lay the piece of screening on top of the frame.
7. Use the screen repair tool to press the vinyl spline into the groove.

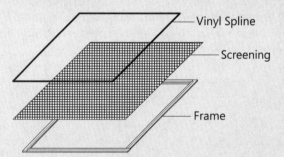

Vinyl Spline

Screening

Frame

8. Work your way around the frame, making sure the screening is tight.
9. Use a sharp utility knife to trim away any excess screen material.
10. Place the screen back into the window casing.

Installing a New Window

Installing an extra window in an RV can provide a number of valuable benefits. These include more light, better ventilation, and an improved sense of spaciousness. For example, we know of one couple that installed a small louvered window in their bathroom. The new window not only supplied additional light and ventilation, it also eliminated the "boxed in" feel of the old bathroom.

RV windows are available in virtually any shape, size, and type

The actual process of installing a new window is relatively straightforward. However, it's imperative that you have the new window on hand before you start. This way, you'll be able to verify the actual dimensions before making any cuts. Use a level and a carpenter's square to ensure that the window will be perfectly level. Your RV must be properly leveled before you begin.

> **Remodeler's Tip:** Before cutting a hole in the side of your RV, contact the dealer or the manufacturer to identify any potential complications. These could include the presence of hidden utilities, supporting frame members, or high stress points. Stud finders are of no use since most RVs are framed in wood or aluminum.

The opening is initiated with a starter hole and finished with a skill saw (with a fine tooth blade). After the opening has been cut, you'll need to glue in pieces of wood as shown in the following illustration.

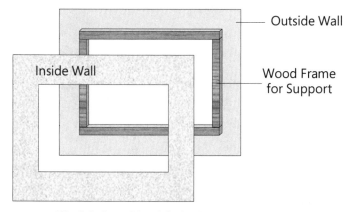

Wood trim is used for reinforcing the new window opening

The wood trim provides additional support around the new opening. If the wall is filled with polystyrene foam insulation, you'll have to use a sharp knife to remove just enough to insert the pieces of wood. The thickness of the wood pieces must match the space between the interior and exterior walls. Likewise, the length of each piece must be carefully measured so as to ensure a good fit. The top and bottom pieces are inserted first. Then, slip in the two side pieces. When the wood pieces are inserted, they must be carefully positioned so they don't interfere with the installation of the window. Use clamps to hold the wood pieces in place and check the fit before tightening the clamps completely. Let the adhesive dry completely before removing the clamps. Wipe off any excess adhesive so it doesn't run down the side of your RV.

Install the window according to the directions provided by the manufacturer. Use high-grade flexible caulking to seal the window and check the action of any moving parts before tightening all the mounting screws.

Tinting Windows

If you plan on spending the majority of your time in a warm climate, you might want to look into tinting some of your windows. While most RV side windows are slightly tinted at the factory, it isn't enough to make much of a difference. Fortunately, there are companies that manufacture and sell high-grade tinting film that can be applied to the inside of your RV's windows. The material is designed to cut glare, reduce heat build-up, and lower your cooling costs. Best of all, it can be easily removed at any time. The tinting usually comes in a roll and is applied with the help of a soapy solution and a rubber squeegee. Contact the parts department of your local RV dealer or do a search on the Internet for available tinting products.

Double-Glazed Windows

If you're shopping for new windows – you might want to check out double-glazed windows. Because they have superior insulating characteristics, they tend to reduce the level of condensation that builds up on the glass in cold weather. In hot weather, double-glazed windows can also reduce the load on your RV's air conditioner.

However, the one drawback to double-glazed windows (besides the cost) has to do with the way they're designed. The space between the panes of glass is typically filled with a special gas that helps to inhibit the transfer of heat. If the gas escapes for any reason, the insulating value of the double-glazed window is severely compromised. Double-glazed windows in houses tend to last for decades. But in a moving vehicle, the windows are continually subjected to bumps and vibration as an RV moves down the road. This vibration, over time, often results in leaks in the seal between the two panes, effectively releasing the gas. In some cases, the effect is minimal except to reduce the window's insulating value. However, in other cases, the windows often become cloudy as a result of moisture getting trapped between the two panes. In a few cases, people in areas with humid or rainy climates have been unable to see out their windows.

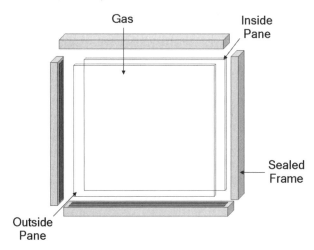

Double-glazed windows are filled with a special gas that lowers the transmission of heat

This is the primary reason why companies are reluctant to offer long-term warranties for RV-installed double-glazed windows. For now, look closely at the product warranty. See if the company will install new ones if there's a moisture problem. If not, you may be in for an expensive ordeal. Hopefully, manufacturers will be able to come up with a more durable design for these highly desirable windows.

Window Treatments

Window treatment options for an RV are essentially the same as they are for a house with one significant distinction – RV window treatments must usually be custom ordered because of their unique sizes. The good news is that there's a vast selection of commercially available window treatments that can be custom made to fit virtually any window. Additionally, if you're handy with a sewing machine, there's an endless supply of attractive fabrics that can be fashioned into curtains, blinds, drapes, valances, and more.

With respect to choosing a suitable window treatment, RV windows generally operate under the same principles that apply to windows in a house. However, there are a few unique issues to keep in mind.

Adaptability is the Key

Because houses don't move, you always know what your lighting and privacy requirements are. But in an RV, you never know which way the sun will be shining. Similarly, your need for privacy could change at every new campgrounds and site you stay at. What this all means is that the best window solutions for an RV are the ones that can easily accommodate changing situations. We'll get into the practical aspects of this requirement later on in this chapter.

Let the Light In

Light is the secret to making a room (or an RV) look bigger than it really is. Therefore, to maximize the level of light, try to keep the window treatments from covering much of the glass. This is particularly important with older RVs that tend to have fewer windows to begin with. If your RV's windows are fitted with cornices (fabric-covered boxes), consider taking them out. Cornices tend to block significant amounts of light and therefore will make any RV seems darker and smaller than it really is. Likewise, if you have curtains that extend into your window's viewing area (during the day), use curtain ties to keep them away from the glass.

Use Window Awnings

If you frequently RV in places that are warm, consider getting some window awnings. They can greatly reduce the need for air conditioning. This is a real plus when you're dry camping or boondocking.

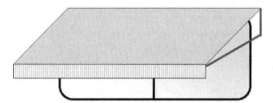

Along with an air conditioner, window awnings are the best way to keep cool in hot weather

More importantly, window awnings help to keep your RV cooler without the need for heavy, room-darkening shades and blinds. As a result, they enable you to focus more on the visual aspects when selecting window dressings for your RV. Here's a run-down on some of the more popular window treatment options for an RV:

Curtains and Drapes

One of the easiest ways to spice up the windows in your RV is to install curtains or drapes. If you know how to sew, you can take advantage of the vast selection of fabrics that are available. If not, there are many places that sell custom curtains and blinds including J.C. Penny, Sears and Roebuck, The Curtain Shop, and Bed, Bath & Beyond. Here are a few tips:

- If your RV has small windows, expand them visually by installing extra long rods and over-sized drapes that extend beyond the window frame.

- To give the illusion of greater space, match the fabric color to the walls.

- When selecting curtain rods, look for ones that can be firmly attached to their mounting brackets. Also, be sure to use screws (not nails) when securing the mounting brackets to the wall. Otherwise, you may find your curtains on the floor whenever you drive on rough roads.

- Use plain, patterned, or crinkled sheers for sheer curtains or drapery panels.

- If you're looking for a little more privacy, consider semi-sheers such as light-weight linen or lace panels.

- For an elegant appearance, try chintz – a durable variety of polished cotton.

- Simple valances made of gathered or pleated fabric can be very attractive.

- Try putting up window swags. Swags are sweeping folds of fabric that extends from one upper corner of the window to another. For a stylish and sophisticated look, construct swags using soft, supple sateen, antique satin, or shantung.

- For a casual or natural look, consider cotton or linen prints (including tea dyed).

- For an old world appearance, search for Toile type fabrics that depict a country scene on a light colored background.

- For excellent insulating qualities and a formal appearance, consider using lightweight velvet for your drapes.

- When privacy is crucial as well as a casual appearance, consider using cotton duck, canvas, or ticking for roman shades, simple panels, and flat valances.

- For a formal and highly thematic look, check out jacquards. These heavy, tone-on-tone drapery fabrics include damask, brocade, and tapestry.

- Select crisp, plain fabrics for a sleek look and use curtain clips, ties, or loops whenever possible.

Homemade Curtains

Curtains and drapes come in a wide range of materials, styles, and colors. If you or someone you know is handy with a sewing machine, visit a fabric store to really expand your options. Most stores have a local person that can create virtually anything out of fabric. If not, they'll usually have a bulletin board that contains the business cards of local people that sew for a living. We've seen some striking curtains (as well as wedding dresses) that were constructed from fabrics that came off the remnant table. If you're looking for ideas, consider using fabric that supports a specific design theme. Examples include:

- Nature Scenes
- Patriotic Themes
- Animal Prints
- Country Lace
- Tie Dye

- Plaid or Madras
- Nautical Themes
- Checkered Café Style
- Modern
- Sports Themes

Window Cornices

Many RVs arrive from the manufacturer with ornate fabric-covered enclosures, known as window cornices or valances. The rationale for these decorative additions is to add a touch of elegance while covering the "unsightly" aspects of your windows and blinds.

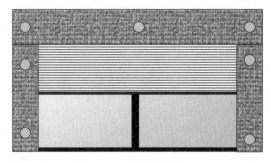

Many RVs come with fabric-covered cornices and pleated day-night blinds

However, these enclosures achieve this dubious objective at a fairly high cost. First, they reduce the viewing area of each window while blocking valuable light. Second, they often get in the way of the operation of the window locks as well as the blinds. Third, cornices, by way of their bulky appearance, violate one of the primary principles of decorating small spaces. As a result, most RV interiors seem darker and smaller looking than they should be. If you have any doubts about this last point, check out an RV without these enclosures (on a sunny day). After seeing the difference in other RVs, we eventually removed ours. Our RV instantly became brighter, cheerier, and more spacious looking.

Adding a New Window Cornice

Regardless of their shortcomings, some window cornices, if properly designed, can be quite attractive. You can either make your own or purchase ready-to-install cornices from companies that specialize in high-end window treatments.

This attractive window cornice was made from a kit (cornicekits.com)

Constructing your own Window Cornices

There are basically two ways to go when building a window cornice. The first is to make them out of wood (like the one shown here). If I were skilled in woodworking, I'd go with this option.

This attractive window cornice was built with stained pine and crown molding

The second choice is to mimic the cornices that are installed in most RVs. These are usually made of double-sided stiffener that's covered with foam and upholstery fabric. Available at most fabric stores, double-sided stiffener is a flexible but rigid material that comes with a peel-off type adhesive (on one or both sides). As a result, you can attach fabric directly to the stiffener without using any glue. In addition, the stiffener is thin and flexible so it can be trimmed and curved if required.

Most RV window cornices are made of double-sided stiffener, upholstery foam, and fabric

You'll need to attach small strips of wood (see diagram) as a means of securing the front panel to the sides. You can also cover the top of the cornice with another piece of stiffener, if desired. If you want to create a full-frame cornice like the ones used in many RVs, extend the sides and the front so that it looks something like this:

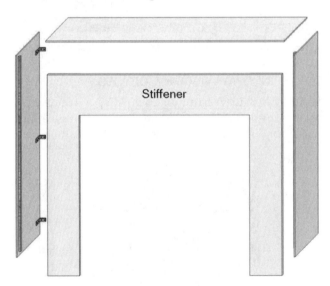

Full-frame cornices have a U-shaped front panel and extended sides (note the corner brackets)

In terms of a design, it's simply a matter of your imagination. The fabric you select will be crucial as well as any enhancements that you make to the front and side panels. Most RV manufacturers insert pieces of foam under the fabric to give the cornice more body. They also tend to use upholstery fabric and accessories that match the RV's existing furniture. As shown by these three examples, the front panel can be cut into any shape you want. It can also be bowed.

Pennant Style   Arch Style   Classic Style

Purchasing Pre-Made Window Cornices

If you're interested in ready-to-install cornices, check out some of the companies that specialize in high-end window treatments. One good example is Smith+Noble Windoware® (www.smithnoble.com or 866-298-2664). They have one of the largest selections of window treatments on the web (in addition to a great catalog). Their products are extremely well made and attractive, as can be seen in the following photo. When ordering cornices, you'll be required to specify the outside width as well as the inside clearance depth. The inside clearance depth is required because the cornice must be deep enough to clear any additional window treatments or molding.

This window cornice is made of beautifully finished hardwood (courtesy Smith+Noble)

Removing an Existing Window Cornice

For various reasons, you may choose to remove the cornices that came with your RV. As mentioned previously, we took ours off a while ago and subsequently replaced the original day-night blinds with fabric covered honeycomb shades (discussed later on). Our RV's interior now looks noticeably brighter, more colorful, and more modern looking.

This window was originally covered in a bulky full-frame cornice and pleated day-night blinds

The process of removing a window cornice will vary depending on the manufacturer. However, these directions should give you enough insight to complete the task.

Remove the Blinds

Before you can remove the cornice, you'll first need to take down the blinds. In most cases, the blinds are secured with snap-on brackets that are attached to the underside of the cornice. To release the blinds, pry open the clips that keep them in place. The clips are usually hidden between the top rail of the blind and the underside of the cornice. If you can't figure out how to release yours, call your local dealer or the manufacturer for assistance. If you have day-night blinds, you'll also have to remove the posts that keep the blind's strings taut.

Remove the Cornice

Cornices are usually attached to the wall (and to any adjoining cabinets) with screws. Our cornices were secured with so many screws – they probably could've withstood a nuclear blast. In some cases, screws were hidden underneath the fabric, suggesting that the cornices were upholstered after they were installed. Use a utility knife to cut away enough material to expose the screws. Since you'll probably miss a few screws, you may have to tug on the cornice to find out where the remaining ones are. You'll also have to remove the brackets that held the blinds in place (be sure to save them). When the cornice is finally removed, fill in all the holes with spackling compound.

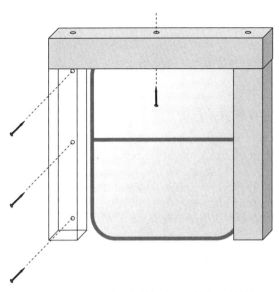

Window cornices are often held in place with lots of hidden screws

Re-install the Blinds

If you're going to install the original blinds (without the enclosure), you'll have to re-use the mounting brackets that held them up. If you have storage cabinets above the window, you can simply secure the mounting brackets to the underside of the cabinets. If not, you'll have to use a mounting board as shown below. The mounting brackets are first secured to the bottom of the board. The board is then secured to the wall (above the window) using corner brackets. The corner brackets can alternatively be installed on the bottom of the board, so they don't show. If you're installing day-night blinds, you'll also have to re-install the two posts that keep the strings held tight.

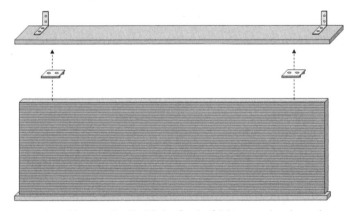

You can use a board for mounting the blinds after the fabric-covered enclosure is removed

Blinds and Shades

Shades and blinds are often interchangeable terms. In this book, blinds refer to day-night blinds and mini-blinds. Everything else is a shade. Don't ask why.

Pleated Day-Night Blinds

Day-night blinds, otherwise known as pleated shades, are installed by more RV manufacturers than any other type of window dressing. Designed to provide two basic levels of light blocking capacity, day-night blinds are both adored and despised – depending on who you talk to. When they do function properly, they offer an ingenious way to adjust the level of light and the degree of privacy. When they don't (function properly), they suffer the worst aspects of over-engineering.

For example, if the strings are too tight, the blinds can be hard to operate. If the strings are too loose, they fall down. In addition, the strings tend to break without any warning. When that happens, one side of the blind suddenly drops to the floor. To make matters worse, few people have the knowledge, the skill, or the patience to re-string them. We finally got rid of ours when they broke one too many times. I just didn't have the patience to deal with them anymore.

Fixing Day-Night Blinds

If the strings in your day-night blinds break, you can purchase a repair kit from www.dirtyblindman.com. This website sells and services day-night blinds and best of all – they have a kit that actually shows you how to re-string them. Also, there's a good document on Winnebago's website. Go to www.winnebagoind.com/resources/service/servicetips.php. Then select Service Tip 2006-09 (September 2006). This diagram shows the path of each line.

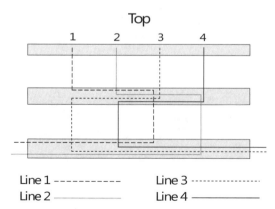

This diagram shows the path of the four lines that are inside each day-night blind

There are also a few steps that you can take to prevent the strings from breaking again. First, replace the original string with a stronger version. Some RVers use high-strength fishing line. Second, smooth out the holes that the strings go through with a small round file. This keeps the strings from fraying and breaking so often. You might ask why the manufacturers don't do this in the first place.

> **Note:** Adjust the tension of your shade by installing the cord retainers where you need them. Then adjust the tension as required by wrapping the cord around the cord retainers.

Mini-Blinds

The term "mini-blind" actually refers to a collection of louvered blinds that use revolving slats to control the amount of light that enters the room. Today, mini-blinds are available in a wide range of styles and materials from low-priced plastic to beautifully finished wood. In terms of choosing mini-blinds, here are a few things to keep in mind:

For Maximum Color, Don't use Mini-Blind

If you're trying to bring lots of color into your RV, especially during the daytime, don't use mini-blinds. Mini-blinds have solid slats that block light. Instead, go with a colorful fabric or honeycomb shade that is specifically designed to transmit diffused light.

Avoid Cheap Mini-Blinds

Inexpensive mini-blinds are sized for standard house windows. As a result, they're way too long for RV windows. While some can be shortened by removing slats, low-cost mini-blinds tend to disintegrate with use. This is particularly problematic for full-time RVers that use their blinds a lot. Even though they're inexpensive, cheap mini-blinds simply aren't worth the trouble.

Select the Style

At one time, mini-blinds were only available in either plastic or aluminum. Today, they come in a wide range of materials including wood, powder-coated aluminum, stainless-steel, fabric, and finished bamboo. They're also available in an endless array of finishes, widths, and colors. You may also want to install the clips that hold them in place (when they're lowered). Otherwise, they may swing and thrash about when you're on the road.

Fabric Shades

Fabric shades represent one of the most versatile window dressing options available for RVs because of the virtually unlimited selection of colors, patterns, and textures. In addition, by layering different fabrics, you can precisely control the desired level of light and privacy. For example, you might combine a colorful shade with a neutral colored sheer fabric. When you want privacy but a lot of light, you simply raise the colored shade to expose the sheer one.

For these and other reasons, fabric shades have a reputation for being highly suitable for small, awkwardly shaped areas – like an RV. If you order fabric shades from an established company, you'll also find a number of useful and stylish options ranging from elegant curtain rods and rings to decorative cleats and tassel sets. In addition, fabric shades can be ordered with top down/bottom up capabilities and continuous loop control that effectively eliminates dangling cords. Fabric shades come in many styles. These are some of the more popular designs.

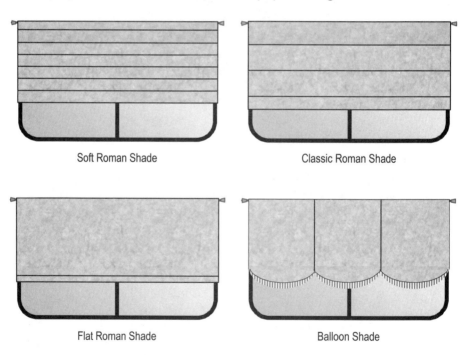

Soft Roman Shade   Classic Roman Shade

Flat Roman Shade   Balloon Shade

Honeycomb Shades

If you're looking for an upgrade to your day-night blinds, you should seriously consider honeycomb shades.

Honeycomb shades represent the ultimate window dressing for an RV

Honeycomb shades consist of horizontal cells (hence the name "honeycomb") that control the level of transmitted light and offer an extremely high level of privacy. They're easy to install, simple to use, and available in dozens of colors. What's more, their crisp design and colorful hues will deliver a stylish upgrade to any RV at a reasonable cost.

We installed them in our motorhome last year and would recommend them to anyone. They let in enough light to deliver stunning color yet they provide exceptional privacy – day or night. While they come in a wide variety of colors, honeycomb shades always use a neutral color for the side that faces the road. Consequently, your RV's exterior will always retain its uniform appearance – regardless of which color you select. If you've never purchased or installed honeycomb shades, here are a few tips:

Choose the Style

Honeycomb shades come in three basic styles. The most common is a single-cell version that provides a reasonable level of light-blocking capacity.

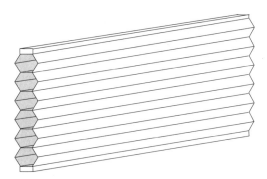

Single-Cell Honeycomb Shade

The next style is a multi-cell design that consists of two or three rows of cells. The thicker shade provides better insulating qualities and total night-time privacy. As a result, they're perfect for RVs.

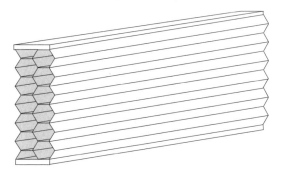

Twin-Cell Honeycomb Shade

The third style is a room-darkening model that utilizes a black coating on the inside if the cells. As a result, it blocks all available light. Room-darkening honeycomb shades are an excellent choice for bedrooms or rooms that simply get too much light. However, since they do not allow light to pass through, they aren't as colorful during the daytime.

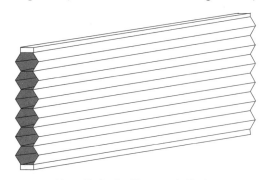

Room Darkening Honeycomb Shade

Using Honeycomb Shades with Atrium-Style Windows

If your RV has a grouped set of tall windows (sometimes known as atrium style windows), honeycomb shades would be ideal. First, they can be purchased cordless, which is preferable in grouped applications. Second, they offer highly effective room darkening capabilities – a must with large windows. And third, because of their design, they are extremely effective at keeping out unwanted heat or cold.

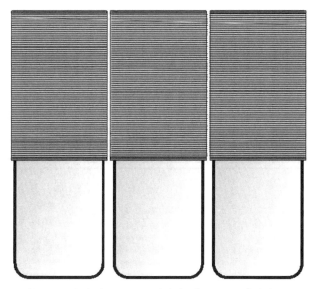

Honeycomb shades are a good choice for groups of windows

If you have two adjacent windows or one very wide window, consider purchasing a 2-in-1 model that comes with two shades on a single headrail. They're much easier to use than one large blind. Plus, with two shades on each window, you can fine-tune the desired level of light and privacy.

Selecting Options for Honeycomb Shades

Honeycomb shades typically come with a few options. They cost a little more, but if you can use the extra features – they're well worth it. Here are some examples:

- Most companies will let you specify which side you want the cord on (assuming you want a cord). Pick the side that's the most convenient for each window.

- If there are children (or mischievous cats) around, get the cordless version. With cordless models, the shades go up and down by simply lifting and lowering the bottom rail.

- If you want maximum control over light and privacy, look for top-down and bottom-up models (see photo below). They enable you to lower and raise the shade from the top or the bottom.

Top-down bottom-up honeycomb shades enable you to fine tune the level of light and privacy

Natural Woven Shades

Natural woven shades are usually made of bamboo, wood, or grasses. They typically lay flat when they're rolled down. When pulled up, they either form a roll or they stack evenly into flat folds like some of the roman style shades. Natural woven shades are very attractive, especially when used in a relaxed, casual setting that takes advantage of neutral colors, earth-tones, and natural materials.

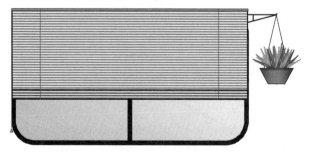

Natural woven bamboo shades help to create a more informal and relaxed looking RV

How to Clean Window Dressings

If you have fabric curtains, toss them into the wash with the rest of your laundry. Let them hang dry (unless they were pre-shrunk). Mini-blinds, day-night blinds, honeycomb blinds, and woven shades should be vacuumed every so often using a soft brush attachment. Mini-blinds should also be cleaned with a mild detergent and a damp sponge. Some fabric shades (i.e. roman shades) can be machine washed while others must be professionally cleaned. Refer to the manufacturer's directions.

Modifying your RV's Windows

The vast majority of RV window casings are constructed of black-colored extruded aluminum. The coating is bonded to the aluminum through a heat-based process known as powder coating. A few window manufacturers have white or tan colored windows but most RVs are still shipped with the black ones. The primary disadvantage of a black colored window is that it tends to create what is termed the "cage" effect. Technically speaking, darker colors absorb light whereas light colors reflect light. As a result, when a window frame is dark colored, it draws our attention to the window casing rather than the view outside. This is why it's called the "cage" effect.

White window casings help to make this RV more home-like (courtesy Monaco Coach Corporation)

That's why windows used in homes are almost always white. It also explains why RV manufacturers continue to use full-frame window cornices – even though they make no sense in a small environment. If they used white window frames, they wouldn't need to conceal them with fabric-covered boxes. You would also have a lot more light entering your RV.

Painting the Window Casings

If one of your objectives is to make your RV more cheerful and modern looking, you might want to consider painting your windows (no, not the glass). We've see the effect and it's undeniably dramatic. However, painting window casings in an RV can be a tedious task. The walls have to be protected as does the glass. In addition, there are lots of grooves, screw heads, and channels that can trap paint and cause drips. As a result, some people only paint the outer portion of the casing. It's not as clean looking but it's a reasonable compromise. Here are a few tricks that can help to make the task a little easier.

Painting the window casings in an RV will produce a brighter and more home-like interior

Always Use a Primer

Most RV window casings are coated in a smooth black powder finish. As a result, it can often take several coats to adequately cover the casings with paint. By using a primer that is specifically designed for coated metal surfaces, you'll reduce the number of coats required and the paint will adhere better. Use a good-quality 1¼-inch trim brush. It will produce a smoother coat and tackle the numerous grooves and details that exist in window casings. For latex or water-based paints, always use a brush with synthetic bristles.

Consider Using a Special Finish

If you want an unusual look for your RV's windows, check out some of the specialized paints that are now available. These include antiquing, marbleizing, simulated wood, bronzing, distressed metal, and more. However, avoid textured paints as they will be virtually impossible to keep clean. Windows attract a lot of dust and grime.

Remove any Window Stops or Spacers

RV windows, especially the sliding type, typically use rubber stops and spacers to control the way the window operates. Since these parts need to move freely for the window to perform properly, be sure to remove them before you start painting.

Use Masking Tape and Cardboard

There are two areas (besides the glass) that can make painting an RV window frame a challenge. The first is the surrounding wall. To avoid getting paint on the wall, paint carefully or use low-tack painter's tape (the blue stuff). However, make sure that the tape doesn't touch the window casing. The second problem area is the rubber gasket that lines the sliding window track. In some windows, the gasket can be removed. If not, insert pieces of cardboard between the gasket and the metal edging to protect the gasket from paint. The perimeter of the window glass should be covered with painter's tape as well. Last but not least, don't put a lot of paint on the brush. Instead, apply several thin coats. This will minimize dripping, running, and seepage.

Framing the Window Casings in Wood

If you want to enhance the appearance of your RV's windows without using paint, consider building a custom wood frame that fits over the existing metal casing. This strategy is often used by professional RV remodeling shops with considerable success.

The windows in this RV have been attractively embellished with wood trim

There are several ways to fashion a wood frame. One option is to construct the frame using wood trim and quarter-round molding as shown below. The associated dimensions are for a typical RV window. Since window casing shapes and sizes vary, construct a small section of frame to verify the fit before you build the wood frame.

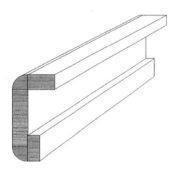

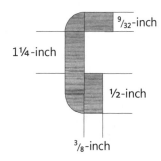

$^9/_{32}$-inch

1¼-inch

½-inch

³/₈-inch

Cross-cut dimensional view

Sectional view of wood window frame

The dimensions of pieces A and B (above right) are deliberately not specified. The reason is that these particular dimensions determine the depth of the frame – a matter of personal preference. You can use any depth you want as long as the ³/₈-inch horizontal difference between the two pieces is maintained. The corners are usually beveled at a 45° angle.

Another option is to create a much simpler frame that is made from rectangular pieces of wood. The pieces are attached to each other using carpenter's glue and screws (driven in from the back). The following illustration shows the frame pieces connected with butt joints. You could alternatively use beveled joints if you have a miter box and saw.

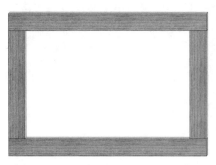

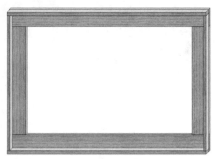

This wood window frame is easy to construct and a breeze to install (the front view is on the left)

After the frame is assembled, stain and lacquer the wood to match the surrounding woodwork. Finally, attach the frame to the wall with screws and anchors.

Conclusions and Recommendations

Windows are one of those topics that everyone has an opinion on and none are ever the same. Nevertheless, let's start by examining the principal advantages of each type of window dressing.

Table 7 – Comparison of Window Dressing Options

Window Dressing	Easy to install	Easy to clean	Lots of color during the day	Lots of color at night	Provides high level of privacy	Blocks out bright sunlight
Day-Night Blinds	✓				✓	
Fabric Curtains	✓	✓	✓	✓		
Honeycomb Shades	✓	✓	✓	✓	✓	
Darkening Honeycomb	✓	✓		✓	✓	✓
Mini-Blinds	✓				✓	✓
Fabric (Roman) Shades	✓		✓	✓	✓	
Natural Woven Shades	✓				✓	✓

Fortunately, once you move on from day-night blinds, you'll find a whole world of interesting possibilities. If you're looking for color and ease of use, consider installing honeycomb style shades. They even have room darkening versions that can block out 99% of the outside light. If you can sew, make some home-made fabric curtains or roman shades. The selection of fabrics, colors, and patterns is virtually unlimited. For unbeatable stylishness, look into installing wood cornices. They can be expensive, but they will instantly put your RV's windows into a whole new class.

Additional Resources

"The Encyclopedia of Window Fashions" by Charles T. Randall, Patricia M. Howard

"The Complete Book of Curtains and Drapes" by Caroline Wrey

"Curtain Design Directory" by Catherine Merrick, Rebecca Day, Clare Elwes, Day Rebecca, Hope Tony

"Windows with Style: Do-it-yourself Window Treatments" by The Editors of Creative Publishing international, The Home Decorating Institute

Chapter 11

RV Living Rooms

Because they are heavily used, highly visible, and centrally located, RV living rooms are remodeled and redecorated more than any other part of an RV. Accordingly, this chapter focuses on the interior aspects that shape most RV living rooms – specifically furniture, storage, lighting, and decorations.

Living Room Layouts

While most RV living rooms are fundamentally similar, the actual layout is usually dictated by the type, model, and size of the RV. For example, most travel trailers tend to have compact living rooms as a result of their highly-efficient design. However, as a result of slide-out technology, many travel trailers now have living room areas that can comfortably seat four or more people.

Travel trailers tend to have very space-efficient living rooms (Courtesy Monaco Coach Corp.)

Living rooms in fifth-wheels tend to be more open than those found in other types of RVs. With their boxy shape, tall ceilings, and prolific use of slide-outs, fifth-wheel layouts are starting to resemble those seen in efficiency apartments. As a result, fifth-wheels often provide the greatest level of flexibility for the creative remodeler.

Fifth-wheel trailers often have home-like living rooms (Courtesy Monaco Coach Corporation)

Most Class A motorhomes take advantage of the front seats (courtesy Monaco Coach Corp.)

Class A motorhome living rooms are similar to those found in travel trailers with one notable exception – the two front seats can often be turned around. Because these seats serve to expand the living room, Class A motorhome living rooms can usually accommodate a family of five or more. In addition, many Class A motorhomes have sofas that can be converted into a temporary bed.

Class C motorhome living rooms are pretty similar to those seen in travel trailers, except they're almost always in the front. However, by placing the dinette across from the sofa, most Class C motorhomes can seat a family of five or more. As with other RVs, the sofa and the dinette are often designed to function as an interim bed.

Class C motorhome living rooms generally consist of a single sofa (courtesy Monaco Coach Corp.)

Interestingly, truck campers, conversion vans, and pop-up trailers often accommodate more people than one would expect. In spite of their size, most have a small sofa and a dining area for relaxing and dining. When it's time to sleep, these areas often convert into beds.

Besides the type of RV, there's another factor that can influence the layout and configuration of the living room – the RV's length. In general, the longer the RV, the more furniture it has. Models that are less than 26 feet tend to have a single couch. RVs that are between 26 feet and 36 feet usually have an additional chair plus a small table. Models greater than 36 feet often have two sofas or one sofa plus a few chairs and a small table. In short, the larger the RV, the more furnishings it has.

Surprisingly, slide-outs, while making an RV roomier, don't tend to result in more seating room or furnishings. The reason has to do with the fact that slide-outs must be pulled in for travel. This inherently limits the actual use of the extra space they temporarily generate. That being said, who wouldn't appreciate a few more slides?

In spite of their limited space and attached furnishings, RV living rooms are the perfect place to unleash the creativity and imagination of the resourceful remodeler. Accordingly, this chapter includes some of the most popular and useful living room area remodeling ideas. Of course, they only represent a fraction of the modifications and improvements that can be made to an RV.

Changing the Layout

Needless to say, reconfiguring the furnishings in an RV isn't the same as rearranging the furniture in a house. In an RV, floor-space is severely limited, wall space is virtually nonexistent, and the furniture is usually attached to the floor. Yet in spite of these challenges, RVs aren't much different than any other living space. The furniture can still be detached, taken out, and exchanged with other pieces. In fact, many remodelers have totally stripped out the furnishings in their RVs and started from scratch.

At any rate, the real issue isn't about RVs. It's about your needs and your goals. If you like the furniture in your RV's living room but don't care for the fabric, consider reupholstering (described next). On the other hand, if the furniture is too big, too small, unattractive, or fatally flawed, it should either be removed or replaced. After all, there's no law about keeping your RV's interior the same as when you first purchased it.

The process of removing furniture in an RV primarily depends on the manufacturer and the object you're taking out. Likewise, when installing new pieces of furniture, you'll have to secure it so that it doesn't move around or present a hazard when you stop suddenly. Brackets, braces, and other similar hardware components can be used to hold the furniture in place. Also, be sure to use wall anchors to ensure a good grip.

  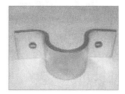

Brackets, braces, and clamps such as these are ideal for securing furniture to the floors and walls

Some Possible Living Room Layouts

The following illustrations show 12 potential layouts for a typical RV living room. The first six depict an RV with no slide-out rooms. The remaining six illustrations show an RV living room area with a single slide-out. The presence of dinettes, entrance-ways, kitchen cabinets, and built-in furniture will affect some of the possibilities shown here. However, the drawings can still be used for conceptualization purposes. The sofas with the rounded extensions are often referred to as j-lounges. The chairs shown with an extension are recliners.

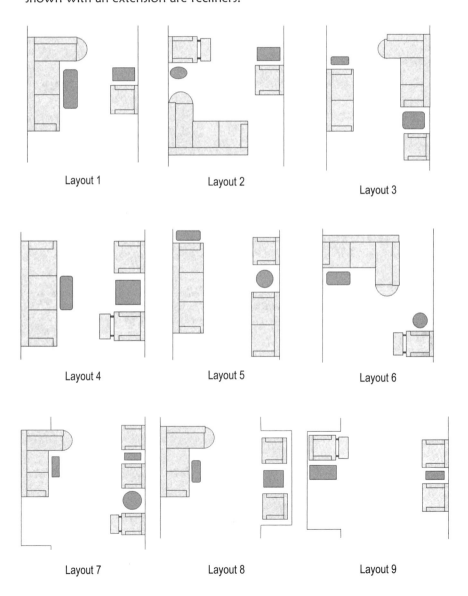

Layout 1   Layout 2   Layout 3

Layout 4   Layout 5   Layout 6

Layout 7   Layout 8   Layout 9

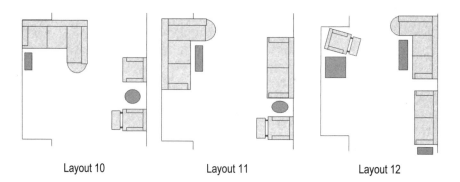

Layout 10   Layout 11   Layout 12

Reupholstering the Furniture

Furniture reupholstering is an effective way to dramatically improve your RV's appearance without altering its basic layout. However, reupholstering projects do tend to be disruptive since the furniture must inevitably be removed. As a result, you'll need to plan carefully and become familiar with upholstery fabrics and color selection criteria.

Also, unless you're experienced, we would strongly recommend that you hire a professional reupholsterer to tackle the job. If you're getting the front seats reupholstered in a motorhome, make sure that the shop is qualified to reupholster automotive seating as well as conventional furniture. Any good upholstery shop should have a photo gallery that highlights some of their work.

Choosing the Fabric

When selecting an upholstery fabric – there is usually a trade-off. For example, brightly colored fabrics such as polished cotton, linen, acetate, and rayon are not especially durable because their primary value relates to their ability to take on and retain color. To compensate, select a version (of these same fabrics) that's heavier or denser. On the other hand, if your primary objective is durability, consider canvas, cotton blends, micro-fibers, heavy cottons, or wool blends.

Normally – the higher the thread-count, the more tightly woven the fabric. Hence, fabrics with a high thread count tend to wear better and resist dirt and stains. Tightly woven fabrics also keep liquid spills on the surface, making cleaning up that much easier. However, comparing thread counts is only meaningful when you're evaluating similar fabric types. You might also want to consider using a fabric treatment like Scotch Guard®. The following table describes several commonly used upholstery fabrics:

Table 8 – Commonly Used Upholstery Fabrics

Material	Description
Brocade	Heavy material made of cotton, silk, wool, or a combination. Characterized by a raised floral design (known as a jacquard). Good for draperies and upholstery.
Cambric	Plain, tightly woven cotton or linen material with a sheen on one side. Used for pillows, curtain panels, and light-weight slipcovers.
Canvas	Rough woven cotton fabric available in varying thicknesses. Due to its durability and reasonable cost, canvas is ideal for draperies, slipcovers, and upholstery.
Chintz	Cotton material, often with a floral design. It's treated with a resin that gives it a glazed look. Used for curtains, pillows, and upholstery. Must be dry-cleaned.
Cotton Duck	Cream-colored cotton that's available in various weights. Ideal for curtains.
Crewel	Simple woven natural cotton material that is embellished with wool embroidery. Used for draperies and upholstery.
Damask	A popular fabric made of cotton, silk, wool, or a combination. Characterized by a raised satin design (a jacquard). Frequently used for upholstery and drapes.
Faux Leather	A leather-like material that is constructed of a rugged polymer (plastic). Some people insist that the faux leather is superior to the real thing.
Gingham	Plain-weave cotton material woven in a checked or blocked pattern. Popular for curtains, draperies, valances, bedspreads, and tablecloths.
Lace	Cotton or cotton-polyester blend with characteristic open-work designs. Frequently used for curtains or to embellish other fabrics.
Linen	Durable fabric made from processed flax. Ideal for simple, natural looking applications including tab-topped curtains, fabric blinds, and tablecloths.
Moiré	A watermark-like finish on a silk or acetate fabric. Some thicknesses suitable for upholstery and draperies. Must be dry-cleaned to preserve the finish.
Muslin	Coarse plain weave cotton in varying shades of white and tan. Frequently sheer. Often used for light slipcovers, curtains, and sheeting.
Organdy	Light cotton treated with acid for a crisp finish. Used for curtains and trimmings.
Satin	Satin is a silk, linen, or cotton weave with a shiny surface and a dull reverse. Often appears with a moiré finish. Used for draperies and light-use upholstery.
Silk	Soft glossy material made by silkworms. Used for formal draperies and swags.
Taffeta	Pliant silk and acetate weave with a shiny finish. Used in drapes and trimmings.
Tapestry	Heavy woven fabric that is made to look like hand-made tapestry. Frequently used for wall hangings, pillows, and upholstery.
Toile de Jouy	Eighteenth-century linen or cotton material typically printed with pastoral scenes. Used for curtains, pillows, and upholstery.
Velvet	Made of cotton, viscose rayon, or polyester. Velvet exhibits a smooth iridescent pile. It's manufactured in various piles. Heavier velvets offer more durability and thus are used for upholstery. Finer velvets, in contrast, are used for draperies.

Selecting a Color and a Pattern

When choosing an upholstery color, try to find one that you really like and then build the room around it. In other words, make the color of the fabric the foundation for the room. Natural colors and patterns tend to endure longer than trendy prints. Ironically, you're less apt to get tired of something that doesn't catch your eye the moment you walk into the room. Unless the patterns are subtle, don't use more than three patterns in the same area. Similarly, avoid large patterns since they can visually overpower your RV's interior.

Fortunately, there's an unlimited selection of available fabrics. You can even use unusual materials like leather, suede, designer fabrics, exotic silks, and elegant tapestries. To reupholster a typical 3-cushion sofa, you'll need anywhere from 10 to 14 yards of material. Most chairs require approximately 6 yards of upholstery fabric.

This leather covered sofa uses a neutral color and decorative pleats to create a modern look

Installing Slipcovers

As an alternative to reupholstering, you may want to consider using custom slipcovers. While they aren't as neat looking as the real thing, they're an excellent substitute. There are hundreds of available choices and best of all, they can be taken off and cleaned. Plus, if you get sick of a particular color or pattern, you can simply replace it. Check out the Web for companies that specialize in slipcovers. Then ask them to send you sample swatches so you can verify the color before ordering. The following picture proves that slipcovers aren't a bad way to go.

This good looking love seat is covered in a removable and washable slipcover

Musical Furniture

The actual process of having your furniture reupholstered is pretty straightforward. However, you'll have to first get the furniture out of your RV. Chairs are usually easier to remove than sofas – especially if the sofa is the type that can be converted into a bed. Some of the pieces may be fitted with seatbelts that will have to be unbolted from the floor. Detaching the furniture from the floor usually entails removing various screws and bolts. If you plan on removing the driver and passenger seats, you'll also have to detach the seatbelt warning system. Be sure to bag and label any loose pieces as you'll need them later on.

Getting the furniture out of an RV can be tricky. Couches (especially fold-out models) are notoriously tough to remove because of their weight and their awkward shape. You may have to remove the back of the couch in order to get it out the door. Some people take their door off its hinges while others have had to remove a window (to get the couch out). When you're ready to install the upholstered furniture, make sure that it's covered in plastic wrap. That way, you won't have to worry about getting it dirty while it's being re-installed.

Adding and Upgrading Furniture

When remodeling, you may wish to replace existing pieces of furniture or even add some new pieces to your RV. In any case, when purchasing furniture for an RV, you have two options. The first is to buy furniture that is specifically designed for recreational vehicles. The following is a partial list of companies that manufacture furniture for the RV market. Chapter 3 includes a list of RV salvage and overstock dealers. Some of them sell products made by these companies.

- Flexsteel (www.flexsteel.com)
- Bradd & Hall (www.braddandhall.com)
- Homestyle (www.home-style.com)
- Ekornes Collection (www.ekornes.com)
- Palliser (www.palliser.com)
- Lafer
- Villa (www.villainternational.com)
- Kustom Fit (www.kustomfit.com)

The second option is to purchase "regular" furniture from a conventional furniture or home furnishing store. Places like Target, IKEA, Kohl's, and even Wal-Mart often stock impressive selections of functional and stylish furniture at very reasonable prices.

Futons: Stylish, Adaptable, and Economical

If you need a sofa for your RV, check out some futons. These stylish pieces are becoming very popular with RVers because of their low cost, modern looks, and easy-to-use bed conversion features.

This attractive futon turns into a bed with very little effort (courtesy of futons.net)

Futons provide some other advantages as well. In particular, the mattresses have removable covers making them easy to clean. In addition, by switching out the cover, you can quickly transform the look of your sofa. As with any furniture in an RV, you'll need to secure the futon to prevent unwanted movement during sudden stops. Experienced RV remodelers use a wide array of products to secure their furnishings including pipe clamps, L-brackets, steel strapping, and hinges.

RV-specific furnishings, in general, offer a number of important advantages over furniture that was designed and manufactured for general use (i.e. for homes). RV furniture tends to be well made because it has to withstand the rigors of constant motion and vibration. That's why most RV furniture includes provisions for securing the piece to the floor or the walls of your RV. RV furnishings also tend to offer more flexibility than conventional furniture. For example, some pieces incorporate hidden storage provisions while others can be converted into a bed.

The principal downside to purchasing "RV furniture" is the relatively limited selection you'll find (when compared to traditional furnishing). Therefore, if you don't really need hidden storage provisions or a motorized sofa that turns into a bed, you might want to shop around. The following products should give you some idea of the furniture that is specifically made for RVs. To learn more about these products, please refer to their websites.

Chairs and Recliners

If you're looking for a little style or some added comfort, it's hard to compete with the value of a well designed chair. When shopping for a recliner, look for limited clearance models that can placed close to a wall. La-Z-Boy® usually stocks several low-clearance models. As you can see from the following examples, chairs and recliners are available in a wide array of designs, colors, materials, and configurations.

Billie® from Lafer, Bryson Recliner® from Lafer, and the Flexsteel 296 Swivel Rocker Recliner®

The Flexsteel 1300® storage chair comes with a cleverly designed foot stool

Sofas and J-Lounges

When it comes time to relax or catch a quick nap, you can't beat the comfort and versatility of a good sofa. Typically designed for two or three people, RV sofas and j-lounges tend to be well made and cleverly designed. If you get one that can be converted into a bed, you'll be able to handle overnight guests with ease. The following models are designed specifically for RVs.

The Flexsteel 4120® jacknife sofa can be secured to the floor or mounted in a box frame

Flexsteel 4132 Easy Bed Sofa® is converted into a bed by lifting up and pulling out the seat

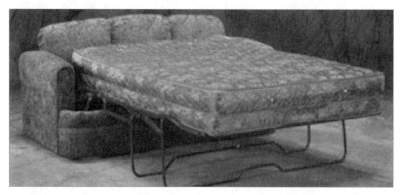

Flexsteel 4790 Sofa Sleeper® becomes a bed by removing the cushions and unfolding the mattress

Flexsteel 4403 J-Lounge® lays down into a bed and includes an optional drawer for storage

The Flexsteel Magic Bed® doesn't protrude into the room as far as a conventional sofa sleeper

Tables

Tables made for RVs tend to be better made and more adaptable than those found in regular home furnishing stores. Here are a few examples:

Bradd & Hall end table provides extra storage (22.5"H x 24"L x 14"W)

Bradd & Hall Hi-Lo® coffee table lifts up to 25" (from 17") for eating, games, or PC use

Bradd & Hall wall-mount table (24"W x 24"D x 27"H)

Removing Cupboards

For a variety of reasons, you may decide to remove the wall-mounted cupboards that are installed in many RVs. As a practical matter, most RV cabinets and cupboards are built in the same manner. A wood frame is first constructed and attached to the wall and/or ceiling with screws. The frame is then sheathed in wood or fiberboard to create the enclosure. The hinges, doors, and associated hardware are added last. To remove the cupboards, you essentially reverse the process by first removing the doors. You then remove the sheathing to expose the underlying frame. Finally, the wood frame is detached by removing a collection of screws.

> **Remodeler's Tip:** If there's a light fixture attached to the cupboard, either conceal the wiring or incorporate the fixture into your future plans.

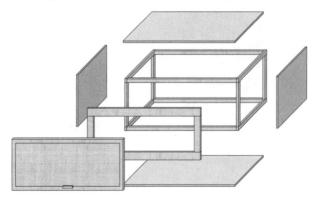

The primary components of a typical wall-mounted RV cupboard

Adding Storage in an RV Living Room

The storage requirements of a typical RV living room tend to be for smaller items such as books, magazines, coats, keys, remote control devices, CDs/DVDs, and other specialized items. Thus, from a remodeling perspective, it makes more sense to address the storage requirements of each item individually as opposed to creating a single storage repository for everything in the room. For example, remote control devices can be stored in a drawer or in a small wall-mounted box (see photo below) or basket. Alternatively, office supply stores sell a wide variety of metal and acrylic organizers that can be drilled out and mounted almost anywhere.

This home-made wood box, attached to the side of a cabinet, stores remote control devices

CDs and DVDs can be handled with a wall-mounted CD/DVD rack. Magazines can be stored in a magazine rack or a wall-mounted file holder (available from Staples or Office Depot). Books should be handled with bookshelves (please see next section).

To sum up, when it comes to adding storage to an RV living room, it's best to create specialized storage solutions that resolve identifiable problems. Living rooms are designed for people, not things. Thus, it rarely makes sense to take up comfortable living space with a bulky storage unit.

> **Remodeler's Tip:** Whenever you create additional storage capacity, make sure that the stored items are still accessible when the slide-outs are pulled in.

Installing Shelving

Even though almost everyone has a collection of books, few RVs come with much in the way of shelving. Consequently, no living room area remodeling project is complete without the creation of some badly needed bookshelves. Fortunately, it's a fairly straightforward process to add shelving to an RV. In general, most shelving systems tend to fall into one of the following three categories:

Shelving with Metal Brackets	Corner Shelving	Standards and Brackets
PROS: Inexpensive, easy to install. Available in several sizes and a few basic colors. Relatively strong and stable. Works with any type of shelving.	**PROS:** Inexpensive, easy to install, Wood supports can be cut to any size and thickness. Very strong and extremely stable.	**PROS:** Medium priced. Easy to install. Strong. Fully adjustable. **HINT:** Use the double-track type. They're sturdier, safer, and you can use screws to keep the shelves in place.
CONS: Must use a triangular shim for corners. Not adjustable. Not as strong as standards and brackets.	**CONS:** Limited usable shelf space. Not adjustable. Can only be used in corners. Wood supports must be painted or finished.	**CONS:** Not suitable for corners. Single track systems have shelf brackets that pose a safety risk (because they protrude beyond the shelf).

The first type uses inexpensive steel brackets that are available at any hardware store. The corner type uses pieces of wood to support the shelves. The third type (on the right) uses metal standards and (shelf) brackets. Not included here are plastic-coated wire shelves and pre-made shelving kits. As their quality varies significantly, these pre-made shelving products should be evaluated on a case-by-case basis.

Shelving can be made of wood (softwood or hardwood), plastic coated medium-density fiberboard (MDF), melamine-coated particleboard (MCP), or plywood. Most home supply stores carry a decent selection of pre-made shelving in a wide range of sizes and materials.

In terms of loading, hardwood is usually the strongest and MDF the weakest. Plywood is somewhere in between, depending upon the thickness. Shelving spans of less than three feet can generally handle most reasonable loads. However, for lengths greater than four feet, you may see some bowing. You can prevent this by using thicker shelving, reinforcement strips (see diagram on next page), or additional shelf brackets.

Reinforcement strips can add a considerable amount of strength to any shelf

RVer's Tip: Attach a thin strip of molding and a piece of non-slip drawer lining to the top each shelf. This will add some strength and prevent books and other objects from inadvertently sliding off.

Small strips of molding will help to prevent the books from sliding off the shelf

Drop-Leaf Window Shelves

It's nice to have a shelf beneath a window. You can keep plants there and other items that look good against the light of the window. Drop-leaf shelves are designed to fold down when they're not being used (i.e. while traveling). To use them, you simply lift up the shelf and swing out the two hinged supports.

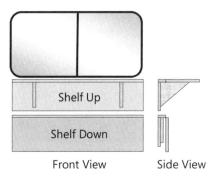

Drop-leaf window shelf shown in both raised and lowered position

Box Shelves

Box-style shelving is a stylish storage option that can be sized and configured to fit in virtually any available space. As a result, box shelves are often used in RVs. Moreover, because of their sturdiness; box shelves can be designed to hold anything from magazines to television sets. They can even be built with rounded sides to fit in trailers with curved or arched walls.

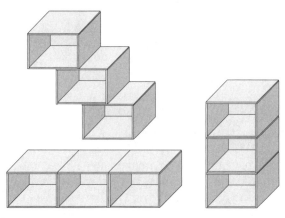

Box-style shelving is highly versatile because it can be sized and configured in a variety of ways

In terms of their construction, finished ⅜-inch plywood works very well. Quarter-inch plywood or particle-board can be used for the backing. The backing will also provide some added stability. Box-style shelving can be primed and painted, or stained and varnished. If you do use plywood, you'll need to cover the exposed front edges with veneer tape, wood molding, or wood trim. Screw the boxes together before mounting to ensure they're properly aligned. If you're using them to hold breakable objects, add a strip of wood to keep the objects from sliding out. Non-slip shelf lining is also advisable. The illustration on the right (the stack of three) is shown with wood trim installed. This not only helps to keep things in, it also results in a more polished looking appearance.

Crown Molding Shelves

Crown molding style shelves are another highly versatile storage option since they can be sized to fit in almost any space. These very attractive shelves not only look great – they're also easy to construct.

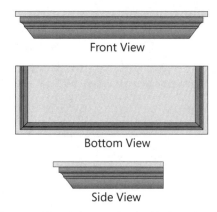

Front View

Bottom View

Side View

Crown molding shelves can be sized to fit any location

To build a crown molding shelf, attach crown molding to the underside of a board on three sides as shown in the previous illustration. You'll need a miter box and a saw to get the correct angle for the corners. In the example above, the shelf overlaps the crown molding a little. Alternatively, the shelf could be made to be flush with the outer edge of the molding. Crown molding style shelves are normally supported by a hidden strip of wood that runs the full length of the shelf. You can also find unfinished crown molding shelf kits at hobby marts and craft stores.

Crown molding shelves add a homey touch to any RV

Mounting Statues, Figurines, and Curios

Eye-catching figurines, decorative vases, candle sticks, knick-knacks, statues, and other similar items can make an RV feel warmer and more inviting. However, decorations like these must be secured firmly to a shelf or they'll inevitably fall and break. Fortunately, there's an effective way to secure any object to a surface without the use of permanent adhesives. It entails using a product known commonly as museum wax or museum putty. A small piece of the wax is first placed on the bottom of the object. Then, the object is pushed firmly against the shelf to hold it in place. To remove the object, you simply give it a gentle twist. There's even a clear version for holding glassware and crystal. It's available online and at craft stores. Try Quake Wax® from Conservation Materials, Ltd. At 800-733-5283. Supposedly, it can even hold objects during an earthquake. Someone should create a similar product for moving RVs. They could call it "Brake Wax".

Keeping Books In-Place

Storing books on a shelf in a house is a simple matter. But in a moving RV, it's a little more complicated. The first time we installed bookshelves in our RV, the books proceeded to rain down onto our dogs after a sharp right-hand turn. If you don't want to remove the books (or your dogs) every time you hit the road, you'll need to devise some way to keep the books secured. First, the books will need to be supported at each end. If the shelf is installed between fixed objects such as a set of cabinets, you're in luck. If not, you can create permanent book-ends out of pieces of wood. Alternatively, you can attach metal book-ends to the shelf by drilling holes and using screws.

Once you've devised a way to support the books at each end, you can then use a piece of wood (i.e. a dowel) to keep the books from falling forward. The dowel can be held in place with curtain rod brackets, screw-eyes, or anything else you can devise. We made u-shaped support brackets out of wood (shown below). The wood dowel basically functions like a small removable closet rod.

We used scrap pieces of wood to create support brackets for a piece of wood doweling

In the following photo, you can see that the wood dowel holds the books securely. The dowel is removed while camping and replaced when we're ready to hit the road. Note the support brackets at each end.

The space above the door was the perfect place to install an oak bookshelf

Adding More Surface Area

Tables and desks should be an integral part of every RV living room. Whether they are wall-mounted units or free-standing, they are the perfect accompaniment to an area where people congregate and relax. In addition to the usual end tables that can be found in stores, there are a few other ways to create additional surface area in an RV.

Wall-Mounted Desks

Space-saving workstations are becoming extremely popular in small homes and apartments. Wall-mounted desks can either be purchased at RV furniture and home furnishing stores or they can be fashioned from a round or oval-shaped table top.

Semi-circular, wall-mounted surfaces like these are perfect for RVs that have limited floor-space

The top should be mounted approximately 28 inches from the floor. It can be attached to the wall using metal or wood shelf brackets. If possible, consider using drop-leaf hardware so that it can be lowered when not in use. In any case, make sure that the supporting hardware is sturdy enough to support a reasonable amount of weight. Its rounded shape ensures that the desktop will be minimally intrusive (i.e. no injuries). However, make sure that the surface is deep enough to accommodate a laptop computer. After all, this little desk will quickly become very popular.

Creating a Dedicated Place to Work

Sometimes it seems that RV manufacturers haven't yet discovered that some people actually work while they're RVing. There are a few models that have a little desk in the bedroom but they're generally too small for serious work. Plus, a bedroom is no place for an office. If you try to use your dinette for working, you'll find yourself constantly wrestling with people that want to use the dinette for other activities (like eating).

You can purchase slide-out desk-tops that mount on the dash of a motorhome but they're too small for serious work. Plus, captain's chairs weren't designed for long-term computing. As a result, your lower back will pay the price. Similarly, there are rolling tables that can be wheeled up to any chair. But again, they aren't sturdy enough or large enough for serious computing and other similar tasks.

If your lifestyle includes extensive computer use – you'll need to create a dedicated workstation within your RV. The space will need to be suitable for a laptop computer, a small printer, and a rolling office chair. You'll also need to have an electrical outlet nearby and a place for your files. The standard design measurements for a work area are shown here.

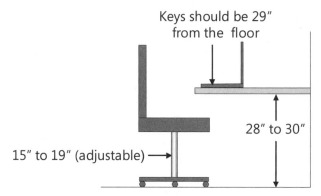

These figures should be maintained when designing a workstation for your RV

We solved our work-related needs by installing a wall-mounted, drop-leaf table from IKEA (www.IKEA-usa.com). The product is called the NORBO® and it cost around $30 plus shipping. Because it utilizes a drop-leaf design, it's only there when you actually need it (see photo).

This drop-leaf desk from IKEA provides a convenient place to work whenever it's required

Bradd & Hall (www.braddandhall.com) also has a nice wall-mounted table that folds up neatly against the wall. In terms of storing files, office supplies, and other work-related items, you may have to look at office supply stores and home furnishing outlets for a solution that works for you. We use a plastic file box and some wall-mounted magazine racks. It isn't perfect but it works.

Mini-Shelves

The theory behind mini-shelves is that a small table in the right location is a lot more useful than a large table in the wrong place. Mini-shelves basically operate like cup-holders in a car. They don't hold much but they do the trick.

This small wall-mounted mini-shelf is ideal for holding a single cup of coffee

Our mini-shelf was made from a piece of oak that was sanded, stained, and varnished. Be sure to smooth the edges and the corners to minimize potential injuries. The shelf is attached to the wall with two corner brackets, as shown here.

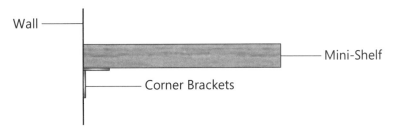

A small piece of wood and two corner brackets is all that it takes to create a mini-shelf

These little shelves are unobtrusive and more importantly, they provide exactly what is needed for that section of the room. Ours is installed on a small section of wall between a chair and a sofa.

Space Saving Furniture

RVs are the perfect application for space-saving furniture. One clever design is a set of coffee tables that fits inside one another. When stacked together, they only take up the space of the largest table. However, when the smaller tables are needed, you simply pull them out. Stackable tables are often found at home furnishing stores or on the Internet.

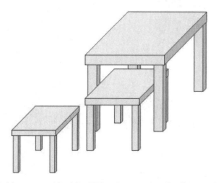

Stackable tables are perfect for RVs where space is always at a premium

Expanding the Size of your Table

If you've ever needed a larger table for card games, puzzles, or hobbies, you'll appreciate this clever design. It's essentially a large removable table-top that fits over a smaller table. When not in use, the removable top can be stored under a bed or in a closet.

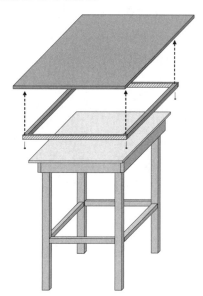

This table top can turn a small table into a larger one in a couple of seconds

The removable table-top can be constructed with a piece of ½-inch or ⅝-inch finished plywood along with four pieces of hardwood stock. The pieces of hardwood should be pre-drilled and attached to the plywood with carpenter's glue and screws. To ensure that the removable top fits tightly over the existing table, place the table (upside-down) on top of the piece of plywood. Then draw a line on the plywood using the small table top as a template. Remove the table and attach the four pieces of wood using the lines as a guide. Make sure that the table is sturdy enough to handle the bigger top.

A Multipurpose Foot Stool

Another useful piece of home-made furniture is a foot stool that doubles as a storage bin.

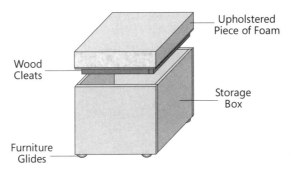

This simple foot-stool storage box will make a great addition to any RV

This versatile piece of furniture provides a seat, a place to rest your feet, and a bin to store your stuff. That's a lot of value for one object. The stool is nothing more than a simple wood box with a removable cover. The top consists of plywood and an upholstered piece of high-density foam. The cover has wood cleats attached underneath to keep it in place. The base can be painted, wall-papered, covered in fabric, or stained and varnished. You can even install furniture glides or wheels to make it easier to move. The foot stool should be approximately 18 inches high.

Improving the Lighting

Professional interior designers have long recognized that lighting can have a profound influence on the mood and appearance of a room. That's why manufacturers of high-end motorhomes put so much effort and expense into this particular area. For the do-it-yourselfer, lighting upgrade projects can bring sophistication, style, and illumination into virtually any section of an RV. Interior lighting is generally classified into three (sometimes overlapping) categories:

Task Lighting	Purely functional lighting that is designed to illuminate a specific area for a particular purpose. A good example is a light over a kitchen stove.
Accent Lighting	Lighting that normally draws attention to a specific area or a particular object. A ceiling-mounted lamp over a table is a good example of accent lighting.
Decorative Lighting	Lighting that is primarily designed to draw attention. Highly stylized wall lamps, chandeliers, and decorative floor lamps are typical examples.

The following guidelines and suggestions should help you to use lighting creatively and successfully in your RV's living room area:

- If you use your living room area for more than one purpose (who doesn't), don't hesitate to install different types of lighting. There's no reason to install matching fixtures.

- Start by installing task and accent lighting in areas where it's needed the most. For example, a wall-mounted lamp with a solid shade is ideal for providing light to a reading chair.

- Holiday (i.e. Christmas) lights are a great way to add mood lighting to various areas of your RV. For example, we've seen strings of lighted ornamental peppers used in very imaginative ways.

- Even though most RVs come with florescent ceiling fixtures, they should never be the principal source of light in a living room. Use florescent lighting in kitchens or bathrooms where high-intensity lighting is often desirable.

- Colorful translucent lampshades can introduce badly needed color into a room. Don't be afraid to pick vivid colors.

- Wall-mounted lights are ideal in areas where floor-space is limited. They can be used for both accent as well as decorative purposes.

- Check out some of the new battery-operated LED fixtures. The bulbs last forever and the lights can be installed practically anywhere.

- Don't use unfrosted bulbs or clear shades. Lighting in a living room should be soft and muted to create a warm and relaxing setting.

- Never place lighting at eye-level. Before you install a lamp, sit in the room and make sure that the fixture won't shine directly in anyone's eyes. Ceiling fan lights are notorious examples.

- Paint the white plastic light fixtures in your RV with a spray-can of brightly colored enamel that's specifically designed for plastic (i.e. Krylon Fusion®). You'll be surprised at the improvement.

This under-cabinet light fixture used to be white and boring. Now it's a beautiful red.

- Make use of dimmer switches. Lamps that illuminate a large area will benefit the most. Any good lighting store should be able to sell you a fixture with a 12-volt DC dimmer switch.

- Look into low-voltage track lighting. It can be installed and directed anywhere it's needed. For RVs, use small, delicate looking fixtures. The bulky fixtures used in homes will overwhelm an RV.

- Go slow. When you get a new lamp, use a cord with a simple switch to provide power at first. If it works out, you can then hard-wire the lamp for a cleaner installation.

Installing a New Lighting Fixture

When you look at most RVs, you'll notice that the majority of the lighting fixtures are attached to cabinets and cupboards. The reason is simple. In an RV, it's a lot easier to run wiring inside a cupboard than it is behind a wall. If you do want to install a wall-mounted fixture, you'll have to find a source of power in the same immediate area. In an RV, it's virtually impossible to run wiring through the walls for more than a couple of feet. If the nearest light fixture is further away, consider using surface wiring.

Surface wiring essentially runs along the outside of the walls or the ceiling. The wires are generally concealed behind plastic surface-mounted conduits. In an RV, there are two good things about surface wiring. The first is that it eliminates the need to run wiring through the walls. The second is that surface wiring enables you to take advantage of 120-volt AC lighting fixtures. For example, you can purchase a 120-volt AC lighting fixture, plug it into the nearest receptacle, and then conceal the cord behind a surface-mounted conduit that's specifically designed for that purpose.

Alternatively, you can install a 12-volt fixture and run surface wiring to the nearest 12-volt device. If the nearest device is a light fixture attached to a cabinet, here's what to do. First disconnect the power. Then remove the existing light fixture. Drill a small hole in the side of the cabinet. Insert a plastic or rubber grommet into the hole to protect the wiring from chafing. Run a section of wiring (of the right gauge) into the hole and connect it to the power source for the existing fixture (see illustration). Then re-attach the light fixture to the cabinet. Run the wire that comes out of the hole to the new wall-mounted fixture. Select a path that is the most inconspicuous. Finally, use surface conduit to conceal the wiring. The conduit should be of the same color as the wall.

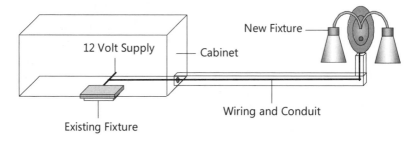

For many RV lighting projects, surface wiring is the way to go

When attaching the new light fixture, be sure to use expansion anchors. If there are any questions about the wiring in your RV, contact the dealer or get a copy of the manufacturer's wiring specifications and construction drawings.

Adding Back-Lit Crown Molding

Back-lit crown molding is a popular lighting solution that is frequently seen in high-end motorhomes. Essentially, a string of low-voltage lights is hidden behind a section of crown molding. It's often installed along the front edge of slide-out rooms, in bedrooms, and in other areas where subdued lighting is desirable.

You'll need a 12-volt DC power source and an expandable strip of cable-style lighting. An LED-based product called Flex-N-Lite® (www.innovativelight.com) works well and comes in several colors. To hold the lights in place, attach cable clips along the back of the crown molding (where it doesn't show) at even intervals. The gap between the top of the crown molding and the ceiling not only lets light escape, it also provides access if and when the lights require servicing or replacing. The width of the crown molding will ultimately control the amount of emitted light. Specifically – the wider the crown molding, the broader the emitted swath of light.

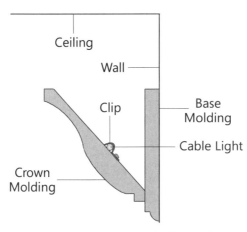

This cross-cut view shows how clips are used to hold the lights in place

The inside of the molding should be painted in high-gloss white to maximize the level of emitted light. Because of the pleasing effect back-lit crown molding can have on an RV – this is a project worth considering.

Improving the TV

One of the biggest complaints about RV interiors involves the location of the television set. In some RVs, the TV can only be seen from a few positions. In others, it's too far away. If your TV's configuration is problematic, consider some of these solutions:

- Install a pair of small, wall-mounted speakers and connect them to your TV with a simple switch. Then, everyone will be able to hear the television loud and clear.

- Consider using a smaller television. This way, you'll be able to place the TV where it's most appropriate (such as on a coffee table). For instance, you can put the television on a wheeled cart for viewing purposes. When you're traveling, simply put the television away.

  Techie's Tip: TVs are often connected to other electronic devices including video distribution units, DVD players, satellite receivers, cable connections, and inverters. Hence, make sure that you carefully label all cables, cords, and connections before moving the TV.

- If you have the space, purchase or build a small entertainment unit that's designed specifically for your television and DVD/VCR player. It can hold all of your CDs, VCRs, and DVDs and provide badly needed storage space for items like remote controls, magazines, computer accessories, and books. For added flexibility, you can install a TV turntable that will enable you to pull the TV out and swivel it around (like a motel room).

If you have the room, a small entertainment unit can be extremely useful in an RV

Accommodating the Kids

If you sometimes travel with children, they're going to need a place to read, play games, draw pictures, and store their toys. The dinette in an RV is generally suitable for these activities but in terms of storing their toys, you may want to purchase or construct a toy chest. The example shown here has drawers for storage and uses a foam cushion to make it comfortable for sitting on. There are also furniture glides on the bottom to make it easier to move. It can even be kept in the living room as an extension to a couch or as a foot stool.

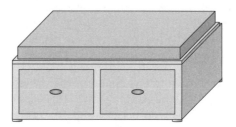

This easy to construct toy chest can also be used as a foot stool or a place to sit

Project: Upgrading to a Flat-Screen Television

In an RV, one of the most common TV upgrade projects entails switching from a large, bulky television set to a thinner, flat screen model. If one of your goals is to make it easier to see the TV from various locations, consider mounting the flat screen TV in a different place – one that is more strategically located. If you purchase an adjustable wall-mounted TV bracket (shown below), you can change the angle of the TV to accommodate a wider range of viewing scenarios. In addition, by installing the TV in a new location, you can make use of the newly created space that held the old TV.

In terms of using the old space (without the TV), you basically have two options. The first is to keep the existing TV cabinet the way it is. You could put in a shelf or two to make the space more useful. The second option is to remove the old TV cabinet altogether. You could then install a book shelf or a small cupboard in its place. In any case, one of the biggest hassles in moving the TV set is re-routing the various cables and wires. Be sure to tackle this job first to make sure that the project is feasible. Most people end up purchasing longer coaxial cables and an extension cord. This makes it easier to hide the cables.

If you plan to install the new TV in the same location as the old one, consider using a TV turntable (shown below). Often used in entertainment units, turntables enable the TV to be pulled out and rotated for optimum viewing.

When you're done viewing, you simply push the TV back into the cabinet. With this device, you could even install a door on the cabinet to conceal the TV when it's not being used. Some people have even used a painting to conceal the TV set. Similar to the ones used to conceal a wall safe, the painting is basically fitted with hinges and a magnetic latch.

Heating Things Up

If you're looking for a more efficient way to heat your RV, think about installing a propane-driven catalytic heater. They can either be wall-mounted or free-standing. They're extremely efficient and best of all, they don't require any electricity. This makes them particularly suitable for dry camping and boondocking.

Catalytic heaters are ideal for dry-camping because they don't use any electricity

Warning: Like many heating devices, catalytic heaters produce carbon monoxide, an odorless gas that is extremely toxic at elevated levels. Consequently, when installing a catalytic heater, carefully read over the product literature. Install a carbon monoxide detector and always leave a window partially open when the unit is operating.

For a cozier atmosphere, consider installing a ventless fireplace. These 12-volt wall-mounted units come with blowers, remote controls, and realistic looking flames (sort of). Alternatively, you may want to install a flush-mounted space heater. These 120-volt AC units put out lots of heat and often take up less than two square feet of wall space.

Taking Advantage of Area Rugs

One of the best kept secrets in the interior decorating profession is the creative use of area rugs.

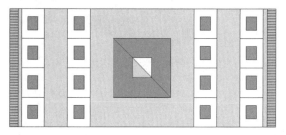

An area rug represents a practical and highly decorative addition to any section of an RV

Available in an infinite variety of sizes, types, and colors, "scatter" rugs can work wonders in virtually every region of an RV. Besides adding style and color, rugs help to deaden sound, protect your floors, and prevent slipping. And unlike wall-to-wall carpeting, area rugs can be replaced, moved around, and taken out for a routine cleaning.

When shopping for small rugs, pick bold colors and attention-grabbing patterns to add some excitement to a room. If you're trying to make your RV look longer, install a carpet runner from the front to the back. In this case, choose a color and a pattern that complements the existing décor. This will help to create a greater sense of length.

Make sure that any rug you buy is rubber backed to prevent slipping. Otherwise, you'll have to find some way to secure the rug to the floor (i.e. tacks), effectively eliminating one of its best qualities (portability). These are some of the more common types of rugs:

- **Oriental** – Authentic oriental rugs are made of highly durable hand-knotted wool or silk. Machine-made reproductions are a good alternative.

- **Braided** – These oval or round shaped rugs are made from a single, continuous braid of cotton or wool. Look for thin (i.e. flatter) versions as they're easier to maintain.

- **Dhurrie** – These flat-woven rugs are made of wool or cotton. They are often decorated with tribal motifs.

- **Kilim** – Kilim rugs are flat-woven and usually made of wool. They are often characterized by their lengthwise slits that mark the point where two colors intersect.

- **Aubusson** – These are tapestry-style rugs that are extremely tough as a result of their tight, flat-woven design.

> **Full-Timer's Tip:** Place a doormat just inside the entrance of your RV. It should be heavy, highly textured, and have a rubberized backing to prevent slippage. This simple addition will help to preserve the floors in your RV. Be sure to shake the mat out every so often.

Installing Wall-mounted Accessories

No remodeling project is complete without wall-mounted accessories and decorations such as mirrors, coat hooks, key racks, pictures, and clocks. A small wall-mounted coat rack will become invaluable for storing hats, umbrellas, keys, and other essential items. Make sure that it's mounted near the door for convenience. Mirrors are particularly useful because they increase the level of light while creating the illusion of more space.

This rack, located by the door, is perfect for holding keys, pet leashes, scarves, and hats

When putting up artwork or framed pictures, try mounting them in groups of two or three, stacked vertically. This arrangement tends to make a wall look bigger (see next section). Avoid over-sized clocks, heavy coat racks, and other bulky accessories that could potentially overwhelm your RV's interior. In a small area (like an RV), the idea is to use decorating tricks to make a room look larger than it actually is. Over-sized accessories tend to achieve the opposite effect.

Hanging Pictures in an RV

Adding pictures to a room is one of the most effective ways to add interest, style, and color. However, when hanging pictures in an RV, there are a few unique issues to keep in mind. The most important one involves finding a way to keep the pictures attached securely to the wall as you drive down the road. Fortunately, with the help of special mounting hardware, it's a pretty straightforward process. Mounting brackets, like the one shown here, are typically attached (in pairs) to the back of the picture frame. They then slide over the heads of screws that are partially inserted into the wall. Your pictures will remain secure, no matter what.

Special mounting brackets, like this one, will keep your pictures on the wall – where they belong

Conventional strategies like double-sided tape are not recommended because the tape dries up over time. Likewise, mounting wax, (used for securing objects to a shelf) is also unsuitable for the same reason. The following techniques are used by professional decorators when working with small spaces:

- When hanging groups of pictures, lay them on the floor and move them around until you see an arrangement you like. Then attach them to the wall.

- Since RVs are short on wall-space, use thin, brightly colored frames that deliver some excitement without overpowering the room.

- Don't hang pictures too high. In an RV, a picture should appear balanced when it's configured properly.

- Use existing features to visually anchor the artwork. For example, hang the pictures between two windows, next to a door, or above a piece of built-in furniture.

- Two or three pictures tend to look better stacked vertically than mounted next to each other. If the pictures are different sizes, mount the smaller picture below the larger one. If you plan on grouping a set of pictures, mix frame types (like oval frames with rectangular ones).

Remembering the Pets

Considering that more than 60% of all RVers travel with their pets – it makes sense to factor them into your remodeling projects. This home-made drop-leaf bowl stand has swing-out supports and a hinged top. When it's not being used, the supports swing in and the top drops out of the way. The bowls fit snugly inside holes that are made with a saber saw.

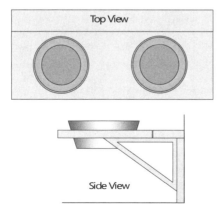

Drop-down dog food and water bowl stand (top view and side view shown)

Conclusions and Recommendations

Living rooms are the center piece of every RV. They are the first place you see when you enter and the last place you look at when you leave. In addition, RVers spend more time in their living rooms than any other location. Consequently, if you're going to limit your RV remodeling efforts, focus on the living room.

Beyond that, it's hard to give bottom-line advice about living rooms. If you do a good job on your floors and your windows, you're already half-way there. The rest is primarily a function of the upholstery fabrics and decorations you use. That being said, there are two essential things to keep in mind. Remodel to accommodate your lifestyle and decorate to satisfy your tastes. After that, it's mostly a matter of opinion.

Additional Resources

Some Online Furniture Dealers:

- www.braddandhall.com
- www.countrysidervinteriors.com
- www.glastop.com
- www.campingworld.com
- www.pplmotorhomes.com
- www.rvfurniturecenter.com
- www.rv-interiors.com
- www.swego.com
- www.rvtoystore.com
- www.IKEA-usa.com

"Upholstery: A Beginner's Guide" by David James

"Complete Step-by-Step Upholstery" by David Sowle and Ruth Dye

"Organizing Plain and Simple: A Ready Reference Guide with Hundreds of Solutions to Your Everyday Clutter Challenges" by Donna Smallin

"Home Organizing Idea Book" by Joanne Kellar Bouknight

"New Built-Ins Idea Book" (Idea Books) by Sandor Nagyszalanczy

"Taunton's Home Storage Idea Book" (Idea Books) by Joanne Kellar Bouknight

"Design Ideas for Home Storage" (Design Ideas Series) by Elaine Martin Petrowski

"Built-In Furniture: A Gallery of Design Ideas" (Idea Book) by Jim Tolpin

"Trim Carpentry and Built-ins" by Clayton DeKorne

"Decorating with Architectural Details" by Philip Schmidt

"Decorating With Interior Trim" by Lisa Stockwell Kessler, Scott Fitzgerrell

Chapter 12

RV Kitchens

If you enjoy cooking and preparing large meals, you'll know what I mean when I say that most RV kitchens have a long way to go. Counter space is meager. Lighting is barely adequate. Pantries are skimpy. Refrigerators are too small. The pint-sized sinks rarely have sprayers. Dishwashers are scarce, and there aren't enough drawers. In fact, from a remodeling perspective, RV kitchens are the veritable land of opportunity. Put another way – there's no place to go but up. This chapter covers virtually every aspect of an RV kitchen except the floors, wall, and windows (covered separately in Chapters 7 through 10). We'll start with the cabinets.

Upgrading your Cabinets

One of the best ways to give your kitchen a face-lift is to improve the appearance of your cabinets. Accordingly, this section describes four manageable projects that can make a big difference:

1. Upgrading the Handles
2. Painting or Refinishing
3. Refurbishing
4. Adding Crown Molding

Upgrading the Handles

The cabinet handles (or pulls as they're often called) that come with most RVs are usually pretty dull. After all, cabinet handles are one of the areas where manufacturers can cut corners. Who's going to notice such small details? You would be surprised.

Fortunately, it's easy to find replacement handles. At places like The Home Depot or Lowe's, you can find dozens of cabinet handles. If you don't see anything you like, move on to the Internet. There are cabinetry hardware websites that literally stock thousands of unique handles and knobs. In fact, the range of available designs is nothing short of amazing. You can get handles that look like bugs, birds, dogs, plants, and even Elvis Presley (seriously). At the high end, you can find handles and pulls made of every material imaginable including marble, granite, exotic hardwood, pewter, silver, and blown glass. We replaced our unexciting "faux brass" handles with polished red marble handles and were delightfully surprised at the impact it had on our cabinets (see photos).

The original kitchen cabinets handles were replaced with polished red marble handles

When replacing cabinet handles, always use the same type. In our case, we had to replace the handles on 24 cabinets and drawers. Before you purchase a single handle or pull, be sure that the size you order matches the ones on your cabinets exactly. Handles and pulls are always measured from post to post as shown below. Since custom handles are normally made to order, there are no refunds. Therefore, if you order the wrong size, you may find yourself in the drilling and filling business after attempting to install a 3-inch handle into holes that are 2½ inches apart.

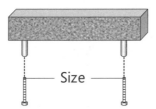

Cabinet handle sizes are equal to the distance between the centers of each mounting bolt

When professional cabinet makers install handles and knobs, they always use a drilling jig. A drilling jig is a simple device that ensures that the holes are always drilled at the correct location. Fortunately, you can make your own drilling jig with a small piece of hardwood and some scrap lumber. In essence, a small piece of ⅜-inch hardwood is sandwiched between four pieces of scrap wood (please see illustration on next page). The actual dimensions of the drilling jig are based on the type and size of cabinet handles you're installing.

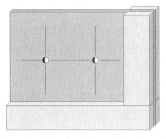

A drilling jig enables you to install cabinet handles and knobs quickly, easily, and accurately

To use a drilling jig, simply hold the jig against the corner of the cabinet door and start drilling. If you're installing knobs (instead of handles or pulls) make a jig with one hole instead of two.

Painting or Refinishing Cabinets

While new cabinet handles can make a big difference, it's hard to compete with the impact that painted cabinets can have on any kitchen. Because wood cabinets have been installed in so many RVs, they rarely generate much in the way of excitement. That's one of the reasons why many high-end RVs now come with attractively painted or lacquered cabinets. Painted cabinets have the capacity to create a sense of elegance and spaciousness that is very difficult to achieve with wood – unless the wood is a very unusual variety. Fortunately, painting kitchen cabinets is a fairly straightforward task.

The kitchen in this RV appears bright and cheery largely as a result of the all-white cabinets

> **Designer's Tip:** Before you can paint your cabinets, you'll need to first determine if the cabinets are the type that can be painted. If your cabinets are coated with a plastic laminate, they won't accept paint. To make a determination, brush on a small amount of paint in some inconspicuous spot. When it's dry – try to scrape it off with your fingernail. If the paint flakes right off, it probably means that your cabinets are covered in a plastic coating. To paint them, you would first have to remove the plastic coating with sandpaper – a task that is both tedious and time-consuming.

If they can be painted, you'll have to first remove all the drawers, doors, and hardware. Be sure to mark each door and drawer so they can be put back in their original location. For the doors, use a sharp object to make a mark where the hinge goes. That way, it won't show later on. For the drawers, place the identifying mark on the bottom.

You'll first need to clean the cabinets thoroughly with a strong detergent to remove any grease and grime. Then give them a light sanding with 200-grit sandpaper. Start with a coat of primer. To apply the primer as well as the paint, use a roller that's specifically designed for smooth surfaces. Finish up with a brush to cover any areas the roller couldn't access. For latex or water-based paints, always use a brush with synthetic bristles and a roller that's specifically designed for water-based paints.

Cabinet Finishing Options

When choosing a color, select a light tone to make your kitchen feel and look bigger. Use a semi-gloss or high-gloss finish for easier cleaning. For added durability, give the cabinets a final coat of varnish or polyurethane. Since cabinet interiors take a beating, consider leaving the insides unpainted. When finishing kitchen cabinets, you can use any combination of paint and/or lacquer you want. Keep in mind, wood cabinets hide dirt better than painted ones. That's why some people paint the cabinets but leave the doors natural. The following illustrations will give you some idea of the possibilities.

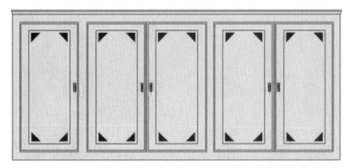

Paint and stencils can give your cabinets an appealing country look

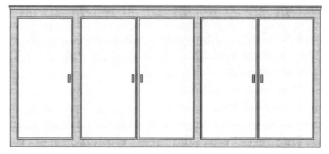

Painting just the doors creates a very clean, attention-grabbing look

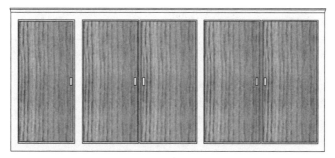

Painting the cabinets but leaving the doors unpainted is both practical and attractive

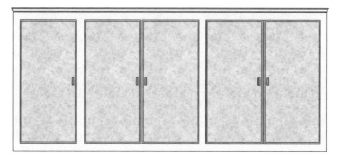

The doors are painted using a special marbleized technique. The rest is covered with a solid color

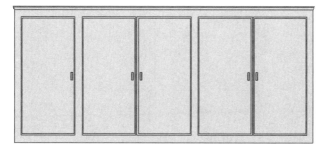

Painting the entire cabinet a single light color will make your kitchen seem bigger and brighter

Refurbishing the Cabinets

Instead of painting your cabinets, you might want to consider restoring them to their original condition. Start by lightly sanding the entire surface with 200-grit sandpaper. Then, using a good brush, apply several coats of high-gloss polyurethane, sanding lightly with 200-grit sandpaper between each coat. Try to perform the job in a dust-free environment.

On the other hand, some people re-face their cabinets instead of resurfacing. This essentially involves replacing the doors and the hardware but leaving the rest in-place. The cost, including installation, can run as high as $300 per cabinet. The cabinet doors shown below represent some of the more popular styles. If you're looking for more light, consider the frame and mirror door or the Mullion panel with mirrors instead of glass. However, these styles require greater maintenance as a result of fingerprints and smudging. If you're trying to modernize your kitchen, look for colorful flat slab cabinet doors. They're typically made of plastic coated medium-density fiberboard (MDF) or melamine-coated particleboard (MCP). As a result, they're normally available in bright, high-gloss colors. These are some of the more common cabinet types.

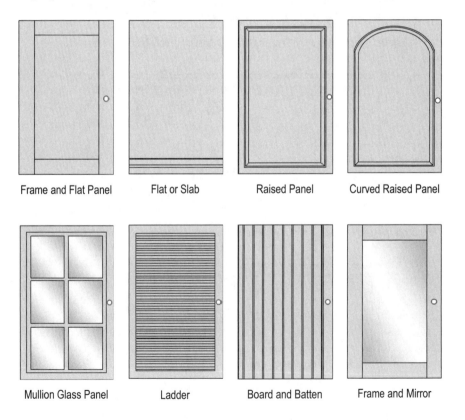

| Frame and Flat Panel | Flat or Slab | Raised Panel | Curved Raised Panel |

| Mullion Glass Panel | Ladder | Board and Batten | Frame and Mirror |

Adding Crown Molding to your Cabinets

If you're looking for an easy way to add some style to your kitchen cabinets, embellish them with crown molding. Besides making your cabinets look more elegant, crown molding helps to create a built-in appearance by concealing the gap between the cabinet and the ceiling.

For this project, you'll need 3 types of molding along with a miter box and a miter saw. Start by measuring, cutting, and marking each pieces of molding. Then stain and varnish the pieces to match your cabinets. When you're ready to install the molding, begin by attaching the plain molding and the base molding to the top of your cabinets (see illustration). Then, using finish nails, attach the crown molding to the two pieces of molding. Sink the nails with a punch; fill them with wood putty; and sand smooth.

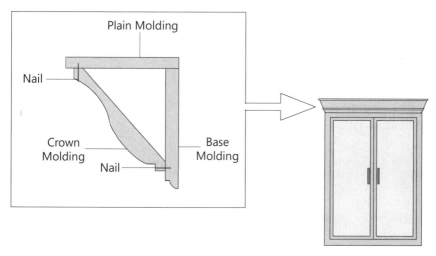

Crown molding will add an element of elegance and sturdiness to any kitchen cabinet

Upgrading your Kitchen Countertop

The vast majority of RVs are shipped with plastic laminated kitchen countertops (i.e. Formica®). While laminated surfaces are both durable and vibrant, they do have their limitations. In particular, as they age, they tend to suffer from fine surface scratches, stains, and cracked edges (just like us).

Fortunately, there are several alternative materials that are considerably more durable than traditional plastic laminates. These include solid surface polymers (i.e. Corian®, Avonite®, and Surell®), ceramic tile, engineered stone, stainless steel, and hardwood butcher block. The following table summarizes the pros and cons of each countertop material. The prices shown in the table may vary considerably so always confirm the actual cost in your area.

Table 9 – Comparison of Countertop Materials

Material	Advantages	Disadvantages	Cost (installed)
Laminate	Durable; low cost; easy to maintain; lots of colors and designs; can mimic wood, stone and tile; lightweight.	Prone to fine scratches; cannot be refinished; visible seams. High-gloss laminates tend to show smudges.	$10 to $30 ft^2
Solid Surface	Durable; wide range of colors and designs; Small nicks and scratches can be repaired.	Expensive; heavy; not heat resistant; prone to fine scratches; costly to refinish. Dark colors show flaws.	$35 to $80 ft^2
Ceramic Tile	Inexpensive. Easy to install. Durable; heat, stain, and water resistant; wide range of colors, textures, and patterns.	Tile is prone to cracking and chipping. Moisture and dirt can stain grout; difficult to repair if cracked; heavy; must be sealed every so often.	$10 to $30 ft^2
Quartz (engineered stone)	Available in lots of colors; no sealing required.	Expensive; heavy; needs to be sealed occasionally; Prone to chipping and fine scratching.	$45 to $90 ft^2
Granite	Extremely durable; heat resistant.	Expensive; heavy; must be occasionally sealed.	$40 to $100 ft^2
Stainless Steel	Easy to clean; durable; water and heat resistant; modern looking; lightweight.	Shows fingerprints and smudges; prone to denting and scratching; expensive.	$120 to $140 ft^2
Marble	Attractive; very durable; stain and heat resistant.	Expensive; heavy; needs to be sealed occasionally; Prone to chipping and fine scratching.	$40 to $100 ft^2
Limestone	Attractive; extremely durable; heat resistant.	Expensive; heavy; must be sealed occasionally. Stains, even when sealed. Chips and scratches easily.	$60 to $100 ft^2
Concrete	Hard wearing; long lasting; easy to clean; colorful and versatile; can be dyed and textured.	Prone to staining and fine cracks; chips easily; heavy; requires regular sealing.	$80 to $120 ft^2
Butcher Block (wood)	Inexpensive; lightweight; perfect for cutting; water resistant; lasts forever; provides a warm, natural look; easy to clean; can be refinished.	Some woods dent easily; some finishes wear unevenly; requires on-going maintenance; If sealed, you cannot cut on the surface.	$40 to $65 ft^2

Bear in mind that solid surface and engineered stone countertop are almost always installed by the manufacturer. This clearly adds to the cost but many people feel that it's worth it. Conversations with several RVers suggest that there's a fairly wide range of prices being paid for some of these materials. This means that you can probably save significant amounts of money by shopping around. In addition, if your remodeling plans entail replacing your kitchen cabinets, you may be able to find a competitively priced package deal that includes a sink and a pre-built countertop.

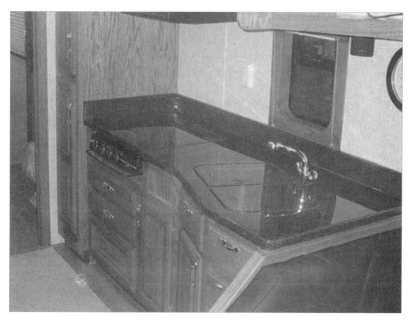

This RV's kitchen counter is made of highly polished granite – an attractive and durable material

Refinishing Solid-Surface Countertops

Solid surface countertops (like DuPont Corian®) are gaining in popularity, largely because of their durability, color selection, and sturdy-looking appearance. However, solid surface countertops are not impervious to stains and scratches. Fortunately, they can be cleaned up and refinished with a little effort.

Professional Cleaner's Tip: When cleaning a countertop, always start with the mildest cleaners. Avoid the use of abrasive cleaners unless you are actually refinishing the surface. If you are dealing with hardened food, first soak the area with warm water and soap. Then use an old toothbrush to remove any remaining material. To remove calcium and hard water stains, spray the area with white vinegar. After a few minutes, wipe the area with a cloth rinsed in cold water. Finally, towel dry the area to remove any water stains.

The actual process of refinishing a solid surface countertop depends on the countertop's original finish. Most solid surface countertops fall into one of three surface finish classifications: high-gloss; semi-gloss; and satin (or matte). The method for refinishing each type is described below.

- **High-Gloss Surface Finishes:** For deep cleaning, apply some soft scrub to the surface with a cloth or a sponge until it's clean. To refinish the surface, you'll need a high-speed rotary finisher with sanding and polishing capabilities. Start with 400-grit sandpaper, wiping frequently with a damp cloth. Then move up to finer sandpaper (such as 600-grit). After cleaning the surface with a damp cloth, apply a white polishing compound with a low-speed polisher fitted with a polishing pad. When you're done, clean the surface thoroughly and finish with a commercial wax that is specifically used for countertops. Janitorial supply stores carry these products.

- **Semi-Gloss Surface Finishes:** For deep cleaning, apply a non-abrasive cleaner to the surface with a white colored Scotch-Brite® pad. The white ones are much softer than the green colored pads. To remove surface scratches, sand the surface with 400-grit sandpaper, wiping frequently with a damp cloth. Then finish off with a non-abrasive cleaner on a white Scotch-Brite® pad.

- **Satin (matte) Surface Finishes:** For deep cleaning, apply soft scrub to the surface with a white colored Scotch-Brite® pad. To remove surface scratches, sand the surface with 220-grit sandpaper, wiping frequently with a damp cloth. Then finish off with a non-abrasive cleaner on a white Scotch-Brite® pad.

Tiling your Kitchen Counter Backsplash

If you're looking for good looks and trouble-free maintenance, consider installing a tiled backsplash behind your sink or stove. It's a great project for do-it-yourselfers, even if you've never installed tile before. In terms of the cost, expect to spend around $10/ft² for tumbled marble tile and around $50 for tools and other supplies.

The full-tile backsplash in this kitchen includes a decorative centerpiece for added color

There are two types of tiled backsplashes – single or full-tile. A single tile backsplash consists of a single row of tiles that runs along the back of your countertop. The row is usually topped off with a decorative cap or a piece of molding. In contrast, a full-tile backsplash is completely tiled all the way up to your cabinets.

While there are numerous sources of information on how to tile a backsplash, the first step always entails test-fitting the design on a flat surface. However, be sure to protect the underlying surface from scratches. Decorative components such as border pieces and accent tiles are normally cut and fit at this time. Once the pattern is completed, use a trowel to apply mastic over the entire surface to be tiled (except around electrical outlets). Then, starting at the bottom, begin to apply the tiles. When you encounter an outlet, trace the edges of the outlet box on the surrounding tiles. After cutting them to fit, apply some mastic and finish the job. The following illustration shows the various ways that tile backsplashes are installed and finished off.

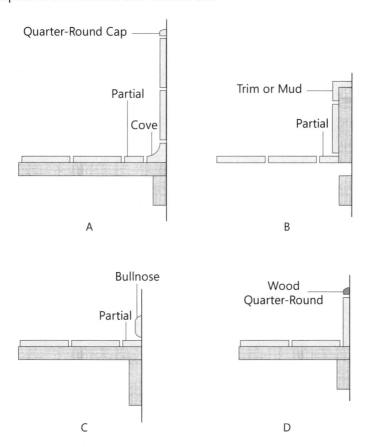

Most tile backsplash projects conform to one of these techniques (grout not shown)

The Finishing Touches

Stone tile should always be sealed before grouting to prevent the grout from sticking to the tiles. After the grout firms up, remove the excess with a sponge and a dry cloth. When the grout has cured for 48 hours, apply a final coat of sealer to the entire surface.

> **RV Remodeler's Tip:** Leave a ⅛-inch gap between the bottom tiles and the counter top (and between the uppermost tiles and the cabinets). Then fill the gap with silicone caulking instead of grout. This will minimize the likelihood of cracked tiles when things shift around, as they often do inside an RV.

How to Clean Ceramic Tile

Over time, the grout in between the tiles will eventually become stained with mildew. Dip a toothbrush into household bleach and scrub the area until it's clean (wear safety goggles and old clothes). With colored grout, use a commercial cleaner that's designed for colored grout. For really stubborn stains, try a commercial acid-based grout cleaner. Make sure you have plenty of fresh air since these product give off noxious fumes.

Damaged grout can be removed with a special grout saw with a durable tungsten carbide blade. When the old grout has been cut out, use a vacuum cleaner to remove any loose particles. Mix up a batch of matching grout and apply it with your fingers. If you're replacing the grout for a large area, use a grout float. Be sure to match the depth of the new grout with the existing grout. Use a damp sponge to clean the area. When the grout has dried completely, apply a coat of grout sealer. Use a cloth to remove any sealer that gets on the tiles.

Tiling your Kitchen Countertop

Tiling a countertop is another great way to add character and color to your RV's kitchen. The process is similar to installing a tile backsplash except that you're dealing with a flat surface. You'll need to remove your sink and faucet before starting. In addition, you'll have to decide how you want to finish off the edge of your countertop.

As with the backsplash, stone tile should always be sealed before grouting to prevent the grout from sticking to the tile. When the grout firms up – clean off any excess with a damp sponge and a dry cloth. After the grout has cured for two days, apply a coat of sealer to the entire countertop. The following diagrams show the more commonly used edging options.

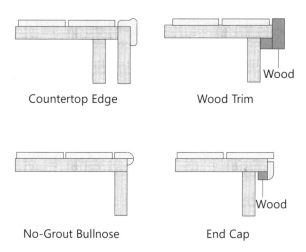

Countertop Edge   Wood Trim

No-Grout Bullnose   End Cap

These proven tile edging techniques have been used by professionals for years

Adding More Kitchen Cabinets

The diagram below shows the standard dimensions for most RV kitchen cabinets. These specifications are for RVs that have a ceiling height of 77 inches. When working in RVs with taller ceilings, simply increase the (18-inch) vertical distance between the upper and lower cabinets.

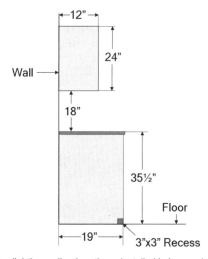

RV kitchen cabinets are slightly smaller than those installed in homes (side-view shown here)

RV kitchen cabinet assemblies are typically smaller than those found in regular homes. However, you may be able to find discontinued models or partially damaged residential cabinets that can be modified to fit in your RV. Since these cabinets are heavily discounted, they're often worth the trouble. At any rate, when comparing cabinets, there are four types.

Table 10 – Summary of Kitchen Cabinet Types

Cabinet Type	Advantages	Disadvantages
Custom Cabinets	Designed from scratch to fit any situation. Unlimited choice of designs, materials, and hardware. Exotic woods and high-quality workmanship such as dovetail joints and hardwood sub-frames.	Very expensive. Entails professional design and installation services. Custom-cabinets must be ordered several months in advance.
Semi-custom Cabinets	High quality materials and workmanship. Hundreds of available designs and options.	More costly than stock cabinets. Must be ordered a few months in advance.
Stock Cabinets	Good quality. Low cost (especially on sale). Can often be purchased and delivered on same day.	Lower quality materials and workmanship. Not as durable or attractive as custom cabinets. Fewer choices and options than custom cabinets.
Ready-to-Assemble (RTA) Cabinets	Low cost. No waiting (cash and carry).	Low-grade composite materials (i.e. MDF). Must be assembled. Not as durable or attractive as higher-priced cabinets. Limited choices and options. Heavy.

RV kitchen layouts tend to adhere to configurations that have been used for decades. However, with the arrival of slide-outs and longer vehicle lengths, there are now a few remodeling options that didn't exist in the past. The following illustration shows how a single cabinet can be added to a row of cabinets to create a traditional L-shaped work area.

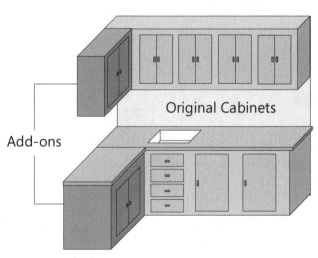

The addition of an extra set of cabinets can provide more storage and badly needed counter space

Creating More Workspace

If there is a universal flaw in most RV kitchens – it would have to be the ubiquitous shortage of usable counter-space. The fact that RV dealers consistently place stove and sink covers on all of their display models only serves to underscore this fact. Some dealers even put a vase of flowers on the kitchen counter in the hope that you'll somehow forget that you have to prepare meals there.

At any rate, if you intend on doing some real cooking or plan on living in your RV full-time, you'll need to find some way to get a little extra workspace. The easiest and quickest option is to contact your RV dealer to see if there's a ready-to-install countertop extension for your particular model. If not, many dealers sell the hardware that will enable you to construct your own countertop extension. Normally, this includes a piano style hinge and a locking leaf support device. You will have to supply your own counter top. Plastic coated medium-density fiberboard (MDF), melamine-coated particleboard (MCP), or plywood will work just fine.

This home-made countertop extension gave us an additional 4 square feet of usable workspace

The photo above shows the countertop extension we made for our kitchen. The extension is very sturdy and represents one of the best additions to an RV that we've ever seen. We purchased a table-top (made of MDF) from a discount furniture store and cut it down to a more manageable size. You could also use a piece of finished ⅝-inch plywood.

It was attached to the end of our kitchen counter with a piano hinge and locking leaf support hardware (obtainable from most RV parts departments). It's supported by a removable plank that is cut at a 45°

angle at each end. The 24-inch long by 3-inch wide plank is held in place by two beveled blocks of wood, each cut at a 45° angle. The wood blocks are roughly 3 inches wide and 5 inches long.

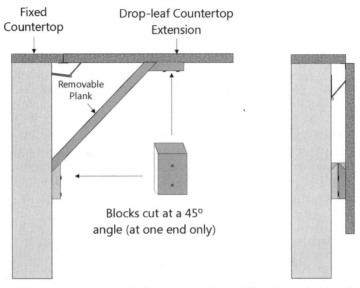

Drop-leaf countertop extension details: operational (to the left) and in the stored position

To prevent the plank from accidentally slipping out, we installed wood stops next to each block (see above illustration on right). To keep the extension pinned against the side of the cabinet when we're traveling, we installed a hook and eye.

Cabinet Extensions

A simple cabinet extension is an easy way to add counter space as well as more storage capacity.

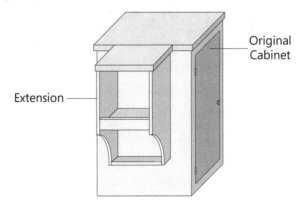

A cabinet extension can provide badly needed counter space along with some extra storage

The base of the extension normally consists of a small wall-mounted shelf or cupboard. The top can be made of anything solid. If you have some extra material that matches your existing countertops, you'll be able to create a more seamless looking installation. If not, use a piece of unfinished butcher block.

Flip-up Countertops

Another commonly used method for adding more counter space is to install a concealed flip-up countertop. The device attaches to the underside of your kitchen counter – inside one of the cabinets. To use it, you simply open the cabinet door and pull the countertop out until it locks in place. One minor drawback to this innovative device is the fact that the extension isn't flush with the existing countertop.

This flip-up countertop provides more counter space (courtesy www.starmarkcabinetry.com)

Pull-Out Tables

Another highly effective solution for obtaining more counter space is a pull-out table. These units are designed to fit inside most kitchen cabinets and can be stowed away when not in use. They provide a significant amount of workspace as well as a place to sit. Kitchen remodeling stores sell these units along with other cleverly designed storage solutions.

Detachable Table Tops

Another way to add some extra counter space is to take advantage of a specialized piece of table-top hardware. Available in some home supply stores, this two-piece bracket enables you to attach or remove a table top from a vertical surface in a matter of seconds.

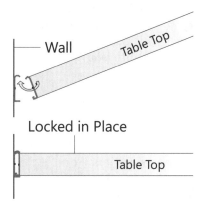

This simple device makes it easy to install a removable countertop extension

The device can be cut to any size with a hack saw. You'll need to use long screws to ensure that the bracket holds tight. To install the table, you simply push the top into the wall-mounted bracket and lower it into place. Keep in mind – this design does not eliminate the need for a support. As a result, most people install a swing-out leg fashioned from a board and a hinge.

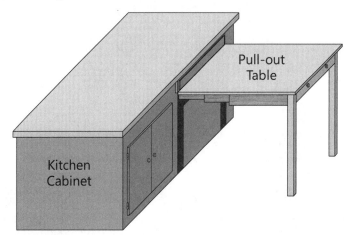

Pull-out tables provide additional counter space as well as a place to have a meal

Cutting Board Inserts

If you're looking for an easy way to create a little more counter space, try this clever adaptation of a kitchen drawer. First, trim a cutting board to match the outside dimensions of your kitchen cabinet's top drawer. Attach four strips of wood to the underside of the cutting board to form a frame. Whenever you need a little more counter space, simply open the drawer and drop the cutting board in. Since it's removable, you can wash it off in the sink.

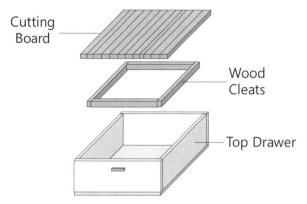

Cutting Board

Wood Cleats

Top Drawer

It's easy to turn any top drawer into a pull-out cutting board

You can also find a good selection of space-saving devices at kitchen remodeling shops and home furnishing stores.

This pull-out cutting board and wastebasket combo are available at www.starmarkcabinetry.com

Mobile Workspaces

If you're looking for the ultimate in portability and versatility, consider purchasing a rolling kitchen cart. While kitchen carts vary in quality and size, most have multiple shelves, locking wheels, and a top surface that's made of laminate, plastic, butcher block, or stainless steel. They can be found in discount stores, home furnishing super-centers, and kitchen supply outlets.

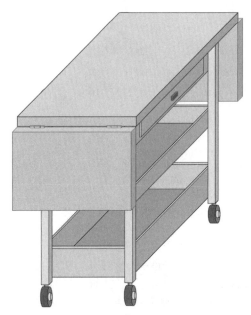

Rolling kitchen carts provide a portable work space along with some extra storage capacity

For RVs, look for smaller models that offer adequate surface area, a decent size drawer, shelves with tall sides, drop-leaf capabilities, and a top surface that's both durable and easy to maintain. You'll also need a place to keep the cart when it's not in use – a major problem for some RVers.

Creating More Storage

If too little counter-space is the number one weakness in RV kitchens, insufficient storage capacity is a close second. Because of their compact size, most RV kitchens simply don't have enough places to keep things. Non-perishable foods, pots and pans, baking accessories, and small appliances are the worst offenders. Consequently, creating more kitchen storage capacity is a goal worth focusing on.

Eliminating Wasted Space

The first step in creating additional storage in any environment is to maximize the space you already have. In RV kitchens, nearly all of the available storage space is provided by the cupboards. However, because of the way they're designed, kitchen cupboards are extremely inefficient. In fact, studies have shown that most people utilize less than 40% of the available space in the average kitchen. Therefore, the first step towards creating more storage capacity is to find ways to organize the space you already have. This is where things like shelving, organizers, bins, rotating platters, dividers, and creative thinking come into play.

> **Decorator's Tip:** The trick to maximizing cupboard space is to use an organizational strategy that is specifically designed for the contents of your kitchen. So don't run out and buy an assortment of organizers until you know exactly what you're going to use them for.

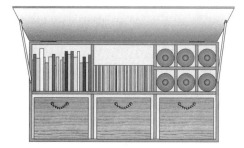

Dividers, shelving, and boxes are essential for making the most of any available space

Tiered Cabinet Organizers

Storing canned goods and bottled foods has always been a challenge because it's hard to find a specific item when you need it. Tiered organizers solve this problem by putting each item on display. Because of their stepped design, they're also good at storing tall items.

Tiered cabinet organizers represent an inexpensive solution for storing canned goods and bottles

The one downside to tiered organizers is their tendency to dump their contents when you hit a bad bump or slam on the breaks. Fortunately, you can solve this problem with bungee cords. Install screw eyes at the end of each step. Then stretch the bungee cords horizontally across the middle of each step to hold the contents in place. The organizer will also need to be securely attached to the cabinet floor.

Storage Turntables

Storage turn-tables or "lazy susans" provide quick and easy access to small items that frequently get buried inside deep cabinets and tall cupboards. They range from inexpensive plastic trays to solidly built multi-tiered models that are permanently installed inside a cabinet. Look for ones with a tall lip to keep the items in place. Then insert pieces of non-slip shelf liner to prevent things from sliding around.

Storage turntables can be permanently installed or simply inserted into any cabinet

Saddle Shelves

Saddle shelves are especially useful in RVs where both storage space and surface area is at a premium.

Saddle shelves are sturdy, versatile, and easy to make

Placed on a table or a counter, they instantly deliver more surface space without taking up any room (since you can still place things underneath). In a cupboard, they enable you to stay more organized while packing more things in. We keep our printer on one and store paper and office supplies underneath. You can sometimes find them at office supply stores. Better yet, make your own out of ⅜-inch plywood or MDF. The home-made shelves tend to be better because they're sturdier plus they can be accurately sized to meet your specific storage requirements.

Storing Utensils

A sturdy canister can be a real asset in a small kitchen. By storing commonly used utensils in this fashion, you can save valuable drawer or wall space for other important kitchen items. Clay crocks are an excellent choice because they're heavy and washable. Glue a round piece of anti-slip shelf liner on the bottom to keep the holder from sliding around.

Kitchen utensils kept in a simple canister will free up your drawers and walls for other items

> **RVer's Safety Tip:** During emergency braking and accidents, canisters and other items on the countertop will become deadly projectiles. Consequently, be sure to put them away before you hit the road.

With the help of two screw-in hooks – you can store a rolling pin under any shelf

Utilizing your Cabinet Doors

Once you've organized and optimized your cupboards by any means possible, take a close look at the cabinet doors. If there's enough clearance, install a few door-mounted organizers like the ones shown in the following illustration. The cabinet beneath the kitchen sink is an ideal candidate because of the lack of shelving. We installed a plastic-coated wire rack to hold dishwashing soap, glass cleaner, and other commonly used maintenance items. The rack was supposedly designed for items like plastic wrap, wax paper, and aluminum foil but it can be used for anything you want.

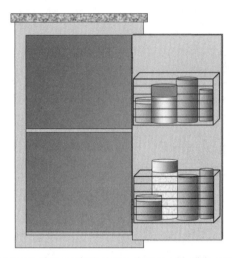

Cabinet doors are often overlooked as a place to add a little extra shelving

Storing Spices and Herbs

Given that space is at such a premium in an RV, storing small items such as spices and herbs can be a real challenge. The trick with spices and herbs is to take advantage of their small size. In other words, make use of areas that are too small for anything else. For example, a narrow rack that fits on the inside of a cabinet door is ideal. To provide adequate clearance, you may have to cut the shelves back by a few inches.

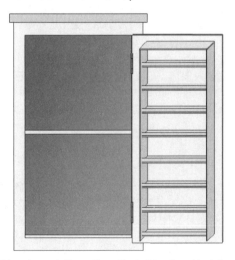

This spice rack fits neatly on the inside of a cabinet door

Alternatively, some experienced cooks store spices in small tins and keep them in a drawer. The tins are labeled on the top so they can be easily identified. Short (4-oz.) jelly jars are ideal.

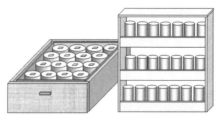

Spices and herbs, stored in jars, can either be kept in a drawer or in a wall-mounted shelf

Pull-Out Storage Solutions

Pull-out storage solutions are part of a growing collection of cleverly-designed space-efficient products that are essentially hidden inside a cabinet until you need them. The one thing they all have in common is the creative use of full-extension drawer slides – the technology that enables anything to be easily pushed in and pulled out. One of the most useful applications is a pull-out waste basket and maintenance shelf. This clever device enables you to keep your waste basket out of the way until you need it. In addition, it provides a convenient place to store cleaning and maintenance supplies.

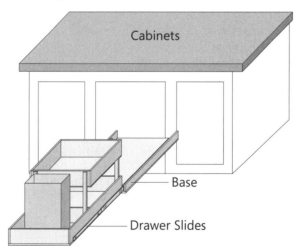

This slide-out unit holds a waste basket along with your cleaning supplies

You can purchase pull-out storage solutions at home furnishing stores or construct your own from easily obtainable parts. You'll need a set of 100-lb. full-extension drawer slides (see Additional Resources at end of chapter for sources), some ⅝-inch plywood, and a few pieces of wood. The base that keeps the unit in place is made from plywood. The two sides are used for mounting the drawer slides. The base is screwed to the inside floor of the cabinet. The unit is basically a two-tiered set of drawers. The bottom drawer is longer than the top, effectively leaving room for the waste basket. The two drawers should have sides that are tall enough to keep the cleaning supplies in place. The illustration doesn't show the cabinet door that conceals the unit when it's pushed in. Other pull-out storage solutions include covered bins like the ones shown in the following photo.

These pull-out storage baskets are perfect for odd-shaped items (starmarkcabinetry.com)

Pull-Out Produce Bins

As a result of limited storage provisions, keeping fresh produce like onions and potatoes can be a real challenge in an RV. That's why pull-out produce bins are so handy. The bins can be made of any "breathable" material. Wicker or wire baskets are ideal. The wood tray (on left) should be varnished to protect it from moisture and make it easier to clean. The full-extension drawer slides should be able to handle at least 50 pounds (see Additional Resources at end of chapter for sources).

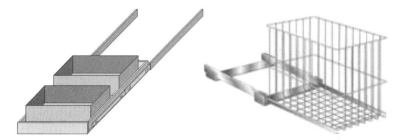

Slide-out trays and baskets are a convenient and efficient way to store produce

Pull-Out Pantries

The storage of non-perishable foods (i.e. flour, sugar, and canned goods) has always been a big problem for RVers. The reason is that conventional kitchen cabinets and cupboards are not particularly suited for these types of items. That's why pantries were invented.

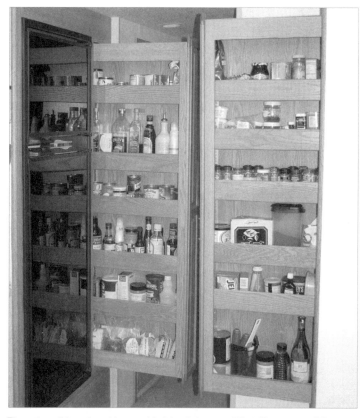

These two slide-out pantries provide lots of storage while taking up very little space

Well-designed RV pantries are a pleasure to use. They make it easy to find things. They're conveniently located. They have adjustable and removable shelves (for cleaning), and they slip away inside a wall or a cabinet.

While they aren't always easy to construct, pull-out pantries can be built using sliding cabinet hardware that's specifically designed for this purpose. The ones shown in the photo above are designed to take advantage of narrow (11 inches) spaces, usually located next to refrigerators and walls. Alternatively, you can purchase smaller, ready-to-install sliding racks that deliver a surprising amount of storage within a relatively confined space. The next photo shows an example of a pre-built pantry.

Small slide-out pantries can be installed in narrow spaces (starmarkcabinetry.com)

If you're looking for a way to convert an under-counter abyss into an efficient storage system, consider building your own pull-out pantry. You'll need an 8-foot section of 1¼-inch by ⅛-inch aluminum angle (for easy drilling), three shelves, and a set of heavy-duty full-extension drawer slides (see Additional Resources for sources). The aluminum angle is first cut into four 2-foot sections and drilled out to accommodate the flat-head screws that are used to secure it to the boxes. Construct the bottom drawer with high sides to provide adequate support for tall items.

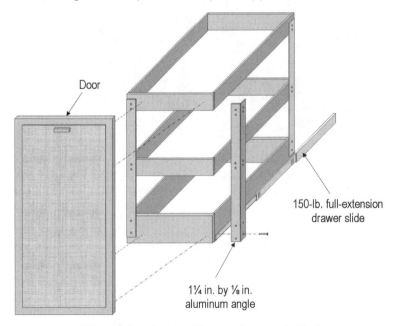

Door

150-lb. full-extension
drawer slide

1¼ in. by ⅛ in.
aluminum angle

This pull-out pantry can hold an amazing amount of food

Toe-Kick Drawers

Toe-kick drawers are named after the wood trim (the toe-kick panel) that runs along the bottom of kitchen cabinets. They're designed to take advantage of the wasted space that exists underneath most cabinets. Since toe-kick drawers are extremely shallow, the drawers are perfect for things like pie plates, cookie sheets, pot holders, utensils, and dish towels.

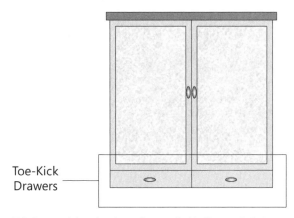

Toe-Kick Drawers

Toe-kick drawers take advantage of space that isn't normally being used

> **Note:** Because RVs are inherently short on space, some manufacturers conceal utility lines and electrical devices underneath the cabinets. If this is the case, you might not be able to install a toe-kick drawer.

Assuming you have the room, first remove the toe-kick panel that covers the bottom of the cabinet. Then measure the space to establish the actual dimensions of the drawer. The toe-kick drawer slides in and out of a wood cradle base via a set of drawer slides (see Additional Resources for sources). The cradle base is simply a piece of ½-inch plywood with two sides. The cradle base with the drawer is then secured to the floor. Make sure there's adequate clearance between the drawer and the base. The following illustration shows the basic construction details.

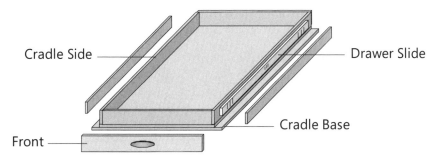

Cradle Side — Drawer Slide

Cradle Base

Front

Toe-kick drawers are mounted on a wood cradle to simplify the installation

Using the Walls for Storage

If your kitchen area has any free wall-space, consider using it for storage. One of the most overlooked areas in a kitchen is the wall behind the stove. This is a perfect place to install a magnetic knife rack, measuring cup holders, utensil racks, and other storage solutions. The photo below also shows a Plexiglas™ guard attached to the wall next to the range top.

The wall space behind the stove is ideal for storing knives, measuring cups, and utensils

Measuring Cup Racks

A simple wall-mounted measuring cup rack can be fabricated from a single piece of wood. The measuring cups are first laid out on a sheet of paper and outlined to create a template. The template is then used to determine where to cut the notches (to hold the cups) in a piece of wood. The wood is notched by sawing half way through and chiseling out the unwanted portion. The illustration shows how the cup holder appears from both sides. The two holes (at each end) are for attaching the cup rack to the wall.

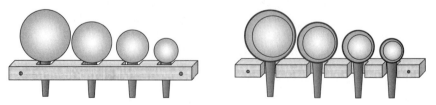

This simple measuring cup holder keeps the cups in place – even when you're on the road

Plate Cupboards

Storing plates in an RV is always a challenge because of potential breakage and the fact that storage space is always in short supply. A wall-mounted plate cupboard can address both of these issues. The dividers should hold the plates tightly but without any binding. A horizontal strip of wood at the base of each shelf normally keeps the plates in place. Small drawers can be added at the bottom to store things like tableware and napkins.

This wall-mounted plate cupboard is designed to keep your plates safe

Drop-Leaf Shelves

Drop-leaf shelves started appearing in Airstreams® during the 1940s. In spite of their "age"– they're still an efficient and stylish way to store things in an RV. You can build your own with a single piece of wood, two hinges, some light-duty chain, and a little hardware. The hinges are first attached to the bottom of the shelf and then secured to the wall. Screw eyes are screwed into the shelf and into the wall (see illustration). Two sections of chain (with a crimped s-hook at each end) are used to hold up the shelf. When you're ready to break camp, you simply disconnect the chains and let the shelf hang down. Attach a few stick-on felt disks to the bottom of the shelf to keep it from thumping against the wall.

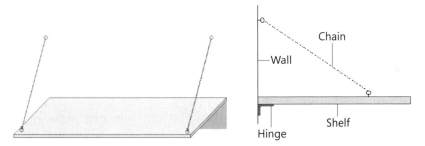

These simple drop-down shelves have been used in RVs since the 1940s (side-view on right)

Organizing your Drawers

If you want to keep the contents in your kitchen drawers organized, you'll need to use drawer dividers. You can purchase inexpensive plastic ones but homemade dividers are a lot better. First, they can be custom designed to fit the exact dimensions and contents of each drawer. This means there's no wasted space. Second, you can build the divider high enough to ensure that the contents don't accidentally overflow into other sections. Use ¼-inch wood planking, #4 screws, and white glue. You'll need to drill holes to prevent splitting. The bottom can be made of ¼-inch particleboard. Secure it with glue and small finish nails.

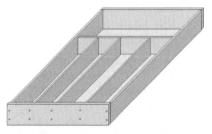

A custom made drawer divider will keep everything in its place

Specialized Storage from a Drawer

If you want to store dishes in a drawer, use wooden pegs to keep them in place. You can find the pegs in craft stores. First, arrange the dishes in the drawer and use a pencil to mark where the pegs should go. You'll need enough pegs to keep the dishes in place but it shouldn't be hard to get the dishes in and out. After drilling the holes, put a little wood glue on each peg. To protect the dishes, insert pieces of shelf liner between each one.

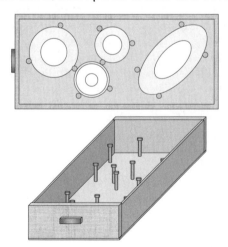

Wood pegs, installed in a drawer, will keep plates and bowls in their place

In an RV, pots and pans can be a real problem because they take up so much room. In addition, the lids prevent the pots from being stacked together. One clever solution is to use a deep drawer with tilted dividers. The lids are inserted between the tilted dividers and the pans are placed in the open section (on the right).

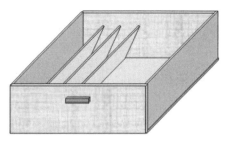

This drawer is specifically designed for holding small sauce pans and their lids

Upgrading your Kitchen Sink

The vast majority of kitchen sinks installed in RVs are made of molded plastic. They look okay when they're new, but over time, they invariably become scratched and discolored. You can brighten them up with a bleach-based cleaner, but they quickly become stained again as a result of the fine surface scratches. The only way out of this high-maintenance treadmill is to replace the sink with a more durable model.

Self-rimming stainless steel sinks represent an excellent upgrade choice

Most sinks are made of porcelain, stainless steel, polyresin, or fiberglass. Porcelain is an attractive, low maintenance option but it's much heavier than stainless steel and fiberglass. Porcelain sinks are also a little harder to install. Polyresin and fiberglass sinks resembles porcelain but they're more prone to fine scratches. Stainless steel sinks are inexpensive, lightweight, and durable. They're also the easiest to install because they're self-rimming (they have a lip that overlaps the hole in your countertop).

Before you begin looking for a replacement sink, contact the dealer. They might sell a replacement sink that drops in without any cutting or retrofitting. If not, you may have to expand the opening in your countertop to accommodate a new model. Under-sink access in an RV is often very limited, so re-attaching the water lines and drains can be especially frustrating. The good news is that the replacement sink will dramatically improve both the appearance and the maintainability of your kitchen. Here are some tips regarding the installation.

The Installation Process

First install the faucet and basket strainer. It's a lot easier while the sink is fully accessible. Use plumber's putty to form a watertight seal but don't over-tighten anything. If you're installing a stainless steel sink, apply a rope of plumber's putty to the bottom of the sink's rim. Don't use silicone caulking. The mounting clips that come with most stainless steel sinks are designed to fit ¾-inch countertops. You can find longer mounting clips at a plumber's supply store. Be sure to use locking washers, especially in an RV. Use a rag to wipe off any excess putty.

When connecting the drain lines, you may have to shorten the tailpiece so that it fits into the existing trap adapter. If the sink drain lacks cleanout provisions, use this opportunity to install one. When you drop a piece of jewelry down the sink drain, you'll be able to retrieve it without taking everything apart. When you're done with the installation, turn on the water (both hot and cold) and check for leaks above and below the faucet. Then fill the sink and look for any leaks in the drain assembly.

Installing a Modern Faucet

Since few RVs come with dishwashers, most RVers wash their dishes by hand. In spite of this fact, very few RV kitchen faucets include a sprayer. As a result, it takes more water (and time) to rinse dishes and clean up. Since many RVers need to conserve water and minimize the generation of wastewater, the lack of a sprayer is a real problem. Fortunately, there are a couple of ways to add a sprayer to an RV. The first is to purchase a kitchen faucet set that comes with a separate sprayer unit. However, try to find a faucet set with a sprayer unit that's stored in the faucet's base. If the faucet set has a sprayer hose that extends out from the bottom of the base, you'll have to drill a new hole in your countertop to accommodate the sprayer.

The second and better option is to install a new faucet set that has a sprayer built into the spout. You won't have to drill a new hole in your countertop. Plus, you'll be able to enjoy the benefits of a faucet that can spray water.

Look for a faucet with a single handle control and a spray head that's built into the spout

Installing a new kitchen faucet in an RV can be difficult because everything is so tight. As a result, you may want to pay someone to perform the installation. If you plan to do it yourself, make sure that you have a basin wrench to loosen (and tighten) the nut that holds the faucet in place. In addition, you may need to purchase special fittings to connect the hot and cold water lines. It's one of those projects where it's vital to have a good hardware store nearby. Use plumber's putty to create a good seal between the faucet and the sink. Lastly, don't tighten the nut (that holds the faucet down) too much because you could damage the faucet.

Installing an Under-sink Water Filter

If your RV doesn't have an under-sink water filter, you should seriously consider installing one. They offer an economical and highly effective way to remove sediment, odors, and unpleasant tastes. The most economical filters take a standard 9¾-inch filter cartridge (like the ones shown here).

Make sure that your under-sink water filter uses standard 9¾-inch cartridges

In terms of which type of filter cartridges to use, start with a sediment removing filter that also contains activated charcoal. They're often referred to as "taste and odor" cartridges. If you have room, consider installing a dual-cartridge filter. You can insert a sediment filter in the first chamber and an activated charcoal filter in the second chamber. Stay away from overpriced RV "water treatment systems" that come with screw-on metal filters. The replacement cartridges are not only expensive – they also reduce your water flow down to a trickle over time.

When installing an under-sink unit, filter the cold water only. In addition, be sure to tie in the water line that feeds the icemaker. It will produce better tasting ice cubes. If you're RVing in an area that has a questionable water supply, drink bottled water. If you travel with pets, give them bottled water as well. Under-sink filters are not designed to purify chemically or biologically contaminated water. For that, you would need to consider installing a reverse-osmosis (RO) based system. RO systems produce purified water gradually, which means you would have to utilize your RV's water tank for storage.

Upgrading your Kitchen Lighting

In a kitchen, the primary goal is to illuminate your work surfaces without generating shadows. That's one of the reasons why under-counter lights and track lighting are so popular. Ease-of-maintenance is another requirement for kitchen lighting. Fixtures should either be recessed or encased in an easy-to-clean housing. Light fixtures that have a tendency to collect bugs and other debris should not be installed in areas where food is routinely prepared.

If you're looking for a quick and easy way to add some additional lighting to your RV's kitchen, consider installing some puck lights. These small hockey-puck shaped halogen lights are available in packs of two or more. Since most are less than 5-inch in diameter, they can be mounted precisely where you need them. The wiring is similar to that used in Christmas tree lights. Each light essentially snaps into the next. The last light in the string is connected to a low-voltage transformer which is plugged into a nearby receptacle. They're inexpensive, very bright, easy to maintain, and simple to install.

Puck lights can be installed exactly where you need them

For a more advanced solution, consider installing a strip lighting system. They typically use 3, 6, or 10 watt bulbs that are mounted on a track. As a result, they provide a continuous line of high-intensity lighting with no shadows. Check out the Clikstrip Low Voltage Lighting System® (704-482-2811 or www.ardeelighting.com). While you're at it, consider installing some GFCI outlets in your kitchen (if they aren't already installed). GFCI receptacles are easy to install and they can prevent deadly shocks. For this reason, GFCI receptacles are now mandatory in all new kitchens and bathrooms.

> **Full-Timer's Tip:** If you're looking for a simple way to improve the lighting in your kitchen, replace the florescent bulbs that are currently in your ceiling fixtures with special "Kitchen and Bath" bulbs. Unlike regular florescent bulbs, these bulbs produce a softer, more pinkish light with considerably less glare. We never liked the florescent lights in our RV because they made the area feel like a drab corporate office. Now that we've replaced them with "Kitchen and Bath" bulbs, we use them all the time.

Installing a Dishwasher

If you spend a lot of time living in your RV, you might want to install a dishwasher. They're relatively inexpensive, they don't consume as much room as you might think, and they use less water than doing dishes by hand. Last but not least, dishwashers provide a place to store dirty dishes, which in turn, keeps the sink free for other uses.

There are five types of dishwashers that can be installed in an RV.

1. Compact Built-ins
2. Compact Portables (like compact built-ins except they have wheels)
3. Drawer Types (fit inside a cabinet)
4. Countertop Models
5. In-Sink Models

The most convenient models are built-in compacts and drawer types. The table below shows the dimensions and estimated prices of seven different models. All dishwashers require access to 120-volt AC power, a hot water supply, and a drain (with a trap) to your RV's gray water waste tank. If you can obtain a plumbing diagram for your RV, you should be able to determine the best way to tap into your RV's plumbing and wastewater systems.

Table 11 – Sampling of Dishwashers

Manufacturer	Type	Price	Height (in.)	Width (in.)	Depth (in.)
Frigidaire FDS252RBS	Portable	$447	36	19	27
GE GSM1860JSS	Built-in	$498	32½	18	23
Danby DDW1802W	Built-in	$329	32	17½	22½
KitchenAid KUDD01SSPA	Drawer	$833	16¼	23½	22½
Fisher & Paykel DS603SS	Drawer	$839	16¼	23½	22½
Danby DDW496W	Countertop	$189	17¼	22½	18¾
KitchenAid KIDS42EP	In-sink	$1,879	21	41	22

Where to Install the Dishwasher

One of the best places to install a built-in compact or drawer-style dishwasher is right below the cooktop (where a gas range usually goes). If you have a stove with an oven, you would have to exchange it for a drop-in cooktop. Then again, if you have a microwave/convection oven, this might not be much of a sacrifice.

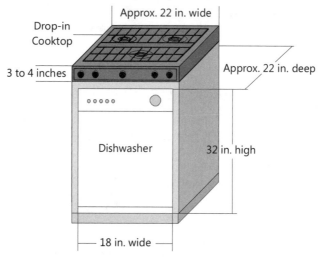

A good place for a dishwasher is under the cooktop (where the gas oven normally goes)

If you are going to install a drop-in cooktop to make room for a built-in dishwasher, you'll have to go with cooktops from either Atwood or Suburban. The reason is that these two cooktops are less than 3 inches high – enabling you to stay within the "regulation" counter height of 36 inches. You'll also have to find a built-in dishwasher that's less than 33 inches tall. Table 10 includes two built-in models that fit the bill – the GE GSM1860JSS® and the Danby DDW1802W®.

Drawer style dishwashers are starting to appear in some RVs (courtesy Monaco Coach Corp.)

If you decide to install a drawer-style dishwasher, you can use any cooktop since drawer-style dishwashers are less than 17 inches high. However, drawer-style dishwashers are a few inches wider than most cooktops. As a result, you would have to make the necessary adjustments.

Upgrading your Refrigerator

There are two principal reasons to upgrade a refrigerator. The first is to get more space. After all, most RV refrigerators have less than one third of the capacity of a typical home model. The second reason is to obtain features that weren't included in the refrigerator that came with your RV. These typically include icemakers, water dispensers, and more recently, automated defrosting capabilities (now available from Dometic).

Fortunately, some RV manufacturers skillfully build in the capacity to accommodate larger models. If you plan to replace your existing refrigerator with a larger model, contact your local RV dealer. They'll be able to tell you what specific models fit in your RV (without major modifications). Bear in mind, there is always a sacrifice. In our case, installing a larger refrigerator would mean losing a pantry. In effect, we would be sacrificing one type of food storage for another.

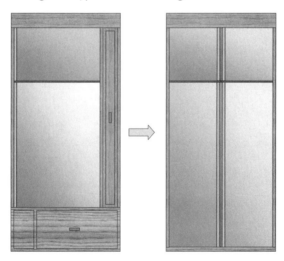

Upgrading to a larger refrigerator means the loss of potentially valuable storage space

If you plan on installing a new LP-gas/electric refrigerator in another part of your kitchen, you could be in for some major modifications. For starters, you'll need to install a refrigerator roof vent as well as an exterior access panel. You'll also need dedicated 12-volt DC and 120-volt AC power sources along with a connection to your LP-gas supply. If the unit has an ice maker, you'll also need to tap into a filtered, cold water line. It's easy to see why people rarely relocate their refrigerator.

Customizing your Refrigerator

If you want to give your kitchen a custom-made appearance, cover your refrigerator with decorative panels that match the cabinets. In fact, some refrigerators have front panels that are interchangeable. They're usually accessed by removing the plastic edging that borders the front of each door. There will usually be one panel for the door and another for the freezer. Contact the manufacturer or a dealer for details. Alternatively, you can fabricate your own decorative panels from wood veneer, artwork, posters, paint, fabric, contact paper, wallpaper, or cork sheeting. Use your imagination.

The refrigerator in this RV matches the surrounding woodwork (courtesy Monaco Coach Corp.)

Installing a Separate Freezer or Icemaker

There's nothing like having lots of freezer space. You can buy meat, chicken, and fish on sale and freeze it for later. You can keep plenty of frozen entrees and leftovers on hand as well as baked goods and ice cream. However, as a practical matter, you'll rarely get much freezer space from an RV refrigerator. Fortunately, there are some things you can do. Places like Compact Appliance (www.compactappliance.com) specialize in small appliances – many of which are suitable for RVs. They sell 1.4 to 8 cubic-feet stand-alone freezers along with a wide array of stand-alone icemakers. The main drawback to these specialized appliances is finding a place to put them. However, if you do have the space, they represent a terrific addition to any RV.

Installing a Microwave-Convection Oven

We didn't really understand combination microwave-convection ovens when they first came out. In fact, we thought they were just another appliance gimmick that was doomed to fail. Not anymore. While the microwave function is nothing new, the convection oven is a great addition to any kitchen. It bakes perfect bread, flawless cookies, and beautiful casseroles. To boot, since it's located above the kitchen counter, it's easier to access and keep clean.

Installing a combination microwave-convection oven is as easy as installing a microwave oven. In fact, many RVers that install microwave-convection ovens report that they removed their propane-fueled ovens. As a result, they were able to acquire some extra storage space.

Microwave-convection ovens are perfect for RVs where space is always at a premium

Using Space-Saver Appliances

There are a number of small appliances that incorporate space-saving features. Because they're usually installed on the underside of your cupboards, these appliances help to free up valuable counter space. The list includes coffee makers, toaster ovens, CD players, clock radios, TVs, electric can openers, space heaters, and more. Keep in mind, most of these appliances can be located anywhere in an RV – not just the kitchen.

Hanging Produce Baskets

For fresh fruit and other produce, consider installing a three-tiered hanging basket. These metal baskets can be found in most discount stores. They can be hung from the ceiling using a hook or supported by a plant hanger mounted on the wall. They should be installed out of the way but in a convenient location. Ours is attached to the wood trim that surrounds our living room slide-out. These baskets also keep the produce in-view – which helps to ensure that it's quickly consumed.

Hanging baskets keep fresh produce in view, but out of the way

Freeing up Space under the Cupboards

One of the most space-hungry devices in an RV kitchen is the paper towel holder. Because of their design, they are almost always installed on the underside of the kitchen cupboards. Consequently, they tend to crowd the area above the counter. Fortunately, there's a readily available alternative – commercial paper towel dispensers.

Commercial paper towel dispensers are perfect for RVs

These slender units are specifically designed to fit in small rooms. Unlike a regular paper towel roll holder, these models can be mounted on walls, cabinets, and doors. What's more, you can grab a towel with one hand – a real blessing in some situations. Commercial paper towel dispensers are available at janitorial supply stores and on the Internet.

Installing a Central Vacuum System

In an RV, central-vacuum systems offer a number of advantages over conventional vacuum cleaners. There's no cumbersome appliance to drag out and put away. There's no power cord to plug in. In fact, the only thing you have to deal with is a hose and a vacuum head.

Central vacuums offer convenience and quieter vacuuming (courtesy Monaco Coach Corporation)

Central vacuums typically come with assorted attachments for cleaning floors, carpets, walls, blinds, upholstery, and ceilings. Most models have an automatic shut off in case the collection bag is full or the unit starts to overheat. Central vacuums are normally quieter than regular vacuum cleaners because the base unit (that contains the noisy motor) is usually tucked away in a closet, a cabinet, or inside a cargo bin.

Installing a central vacuum system is fairly straightforward but it does require some planning. For starters, you'll need to decide where you want to install the base unit. Since it contains the motor, the fuse, and the dirt collection bag, it will have to be kept within reach. While each model is different, most central vacuums require roughly 10 ft³ of space, a 120-volt AC power source, and a circuit that can safely handle 8 amps. The area that contains the base unit must also be vented to allow the exhaust air from the vacuum to escape.

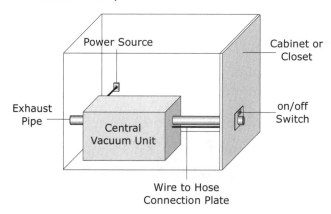

A central vacuum system can be installed in a closet, a cabinet, or in a basement storage area

The next step is to find a suitable place for the hose connection plate. This is where the hose is attached when you're ready to vacuum. The connection plate must be installed in a location that is central enough to ensure that a 20 or 30 foot hose can reach every part of your RV. The best way to find this location is to have one person hold one end of the hose while another person tries to reach everywhere in the RV.

To install the hose connection plate, you'll need to first cut a hole in the cabinet or closet that contains the base unit. There's also an on/off switch on the hose connection plate that must be wired to the base unit. The conduit that goes from the base unit to the hose connection plate usually consists of 1½-inch PVC pipe. If the pipe has to be routed through walls or floors, use a 1¾-inch door-knob saw to make the holes. For turns and bends, you'll have to use the appropriate fittings. The exhaust pipe that attaches to the base unit is made of flexible tubing to simplify the installation. After that, it's simply a matter of deciding where to store the hose and all the attachments.

Adding the Touches of Home

It's easy (as well as tempting) to focus on the functional aspects of remodeling a kitchen. After all, who doesn't need a little more storage room or some extra counter-space? Yet, the things that really make an RV more inviting and comfortable tend to be trivial items like decorative dish towels, colorful soap trays, and attractive curtains. Use your kitchen remodeling project as an excuse to attend to the little things as well. Here are a few small decorating ideas that can make a big difference:

- The next time you're at a yard sale or a flea market, pick up a colorful salt and pepper shaker or a stylish napkin holder.

- Place a bonsai tree on the dinette table or countertop next to a window. These miniature trees will add an element of style to any RV. If you follow the directions for care (including spraying the leaves with water every few days), they'll flourish.

- Install a mini-shelf in some out-of-the-way location. Place a decorative vase on the shelf and fill it with some fresh flowers. Silk flowers will last longer. Use glue (or museum wax) to keep the vase in position. The arrangement will add some color and style to your kitchen.

- Grow some culinary herbs in a colorful pot. They'll be useful as well as pleasing to the eye. You can hang the pot it in one of your windows and keep it in the sink while you're traveling.

- Replace your dishtowels with a more colorful set. These small accents can make a big difference.

- Refrigerator and freezer doors can also be turned into something useful as well as attractive. Use a silicone-based (i.e. removable) adhesive to attach a cork board to the front of your refrigerator door. It will be invaluable for holding recipes, phone numbers, reminders, and photographs. If you're looking for a little more color, wrap the cork board in fabric. The material should cover the board tightly and be glued on the back side.

- Replace your conservative looking wall clock with something more interesting and colorful.

- Put up a colorful calendar on your refrigerator. Each month, you'll have a new image to brighten things up.

- Add some colorful café style curtains to the window near your sink (keep the mini-blinds in place). Your kitchen will look brighter, homier, and more cheerful.

- Put a colorful floormat in front of your kitchen sink. It will provide a measure of safety while sprucing things up. Be sure to get one with rubber backing to keep it in place.

Conclusions and Recommendations

While living rooms have been described as the centerpiece of an RV, kitchens are clearly the control room. Not only do they keep us fed, they also provide an element of security and comfort that make us feel at home – no matter where we are.

From a practical perspective, good compact kitchens are conceptually the same, whether they're on a boat, in a small apartment, or in an RV. The key to creating a good RV kitchen, in essence, entails making incremental improvements until it eventually becomes the proverbial "model of efficiency". This efficiency is achieved with a number of key attributes that include a well-designed pantry, sufficient counter space, a good double sink, highly organized storage, conveniently located utensils, and the creative use of every square inch.

That being said, any kitchen can manage toast, eggs, and coffee. The real test of a good RV kitchen is its capacity to put out tasty, home-cooked meals for hungry campers – day in and day out.

Additional Resources

Some online sources for drawer slides:

- www.thehardwarehut.com/
- www.udb.cc/
- www.thehardwarehouse.com/
- www.ovisonline.com/store/
- www.mcfeelys.com/
- www.ahturf.com/catalog/

"Building Kitchen Cabinets" by Udo Schmidt

"New Kitchen Idea Book" (Idea Books) by Joanne Keller Bouknight

"Remodeling a Kitchen: Taunton's Build Like a Pro: Expert Advice from Start to Finish"

"Complete Tile" by Steve Cory

"Ideas for Great Tile" by Sunset Books

"Tiling 1-2-3 (Home Depot 1-2-3)" by Catherine Staub

"Ceramic Tile: Selecting, Installing, Maintaining" Creative Homeowner

"Tile Your World: John Bridge's New Tile Setting Book" by John P. Bridge

Chapter 13

RV Dining Areas

RV dining areas are more than a place to have a meal. They're also where families and friends play cards, have a drink, tell stories, surf the Internet, and more. Thus, the measure of a well-designed RV dining area goes much further than its ability to handle place settings, serving bowls, and coffee.

From a design perspective, RV dining areas fall into two basic categories. The first is the ever-present dining booth. Many include under-seat storage provisions and the ability to transform into an extra bed for the occasional guest. The second is a set of table and chairs that is little different from those seen in a typical home. These two configurations, along with others, are discussed in some detail in this chapter.

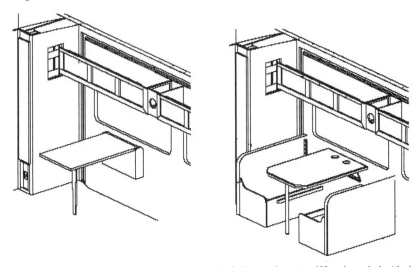

When it comes to RV dining areas, there are two basic layouts (courtesy Winnebago Industries)

Giving your Dinette a Facelift

One of the easiest ways to renovate a dinette is to reupholster the cushions. Because of their relatively simple shape, many do-it-yourselfers have been able to perform this task themselves. For a description of suitable fabric types, please refer to Table 7 in Chapter 11. In addition, we've included a standard template (see next page) that's designed to work with most rectangular cushions. When measuring the size of your cushions, add a little extra to compensate for shrinkage. After cutting the fabric, stitch up the corners to create a cloth "box" with four flaps. Then use glue and/or staples to secure the flaps to the bottom of the cushion.

Conversely, many RVers take their dinette cushions to a professional upholsterer. They can assist you with the selection of an appropriate fabric. Plus, they can use sophisticated reupholstering techniques to create a very elegant and polished looking dinette. After all, it's hard to compete with the skills and the experience of a professional.

> **Decorator's Tip:** You might want to consider getting each side of your dinette's cushions reupholstered with a different material. This will enable you to change your dinette's appearance by simply reversing the cushions. If you have family members that like to swim, get one side upholstered in a waterproof material such as plastic-coated rayon or nylon. When they come in from the lake or the pool, simply flip the cushions over.

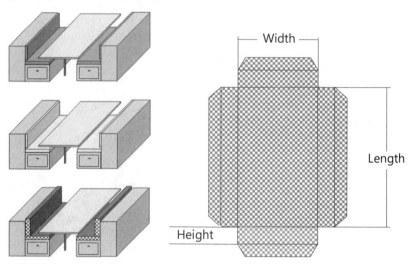

Width

Length

Height

You can dramatically change the way your dinette looks by reupholstering the cushions

In addition to upgrading the cushions, many remodelers focus on the table as a means of giving their dinette a face-lift. Your options are extensive since you could theoretically use many of the same materials that are used to create kitchen counters. However, the material costs and labor requirements would have to be accurately established first. Most people utilize the same hardware that's used with their current dinette table. In any event, it would be hard to compete with a dinette table made of finished cherry, polished granite, or imported marble.

This attractive dinette fits in with the RVs highly stylized décor (courtesy Newell Coach Corp.)

Commercially Available Dining Furniture

Several companies make dinette furniture (please see Chapter 11). The following examples will give you some idea of what's currently available.

This elegant looking Flexsteel 124® dinette offers easy access and extra storage

The Bradd & Hall CWSBS3 ® dinette chair includes under-seat storage

The Big Horn® Dinette Table has an expandable top (30"H x 26"W x 38"D → 47"D)

This Bradd & Hall dinette table expands from 27" x 36" to 27" x 48")

Designed for toy haulers, these Flexsteel wall mount dinette seats quickly convert into an extra bed

Switching Out the Dinette

Removing a dinette and replacing it with a table and set of chairs is a commonly performed RV remodeling project. Many people feel that RV dinettes are often too small, too confined, and not flexible enough to handle large groups of people. Therefore, if your plans entail replacing your dinette with a table and set of chairs, make sure that the new layout successfully eliminates the major shortcomings of the original setup. It would be a shame to go through all the trouble only to find out that you still didn't like sitting at the table.

On that note, minimum design standards do exist for domestic dining areas (see below). Bear in mind, these design standards are for homes, not RVs. As a result, when you build and install a dining area for your RV, simply try to maintain as much wiggle room as possible.

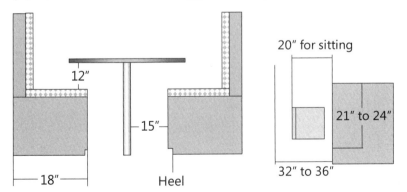

Minimum design specifications for dining and sitting (the heel space is 3" high x 2" inches deep)

Since dining areas aren't simply used for meals, you'll need to factor in other potential applications into your final layout. To help, we've included a number of dining area designs that are currently being used in RVs. Each one can be constructed using a combination of off-the-shelf furnishings and commercially available building materials. In addition, each design can be installed perpendicular or parallel to a wall.

> **Designer's Tip:** Whenever possible, use a tabletop with a drop-leaf extension. This way, you'll be able to accommodate larger groups of people. Likewise, if your plan entails installing a table and chairs, try to find chairs that can either be stacked or folded. This will simplify the process of packing up when it's time to go.

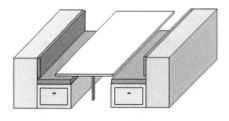

1. Standard dinette with under-seat storage

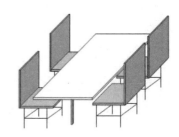

2. Typical table and chairs

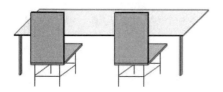

3. Counter-style with front legs

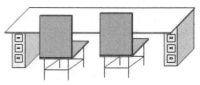

4. Counter-style with storage units

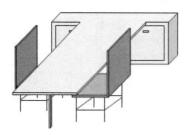

5. Table attached to a full-length storage unit

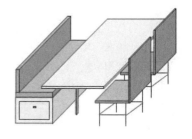

6. Combo dinette with bench and chairs

Removing a Dinette

RV dinettes are typically secured with an assorted collection of screws, staples, bolts, and brackets. So get your hands on a rechargeable screwdriver, and socket set. Be sure to save any loose parts as they'll come in handy when constructing and installing other furnishings.

Full-Timer's Tip: Before you remove your dinette, make sure that you can sacrifice the unit's bed-conversion feature. Likewise, if you currently rely on the dinette's under-seat storage provisions, you'll need to find an alternative location for the existing contents. Fortunately, many dining area set-ups now offer integrated storage.

Take Care of the Floor and the Walls

When you remove your existing dinette, you may want to refurbish or replace the original flooring (under the dinette). If so, deal with it now because it's a lot easier without any obstructions. For information on flooring options, please refer to Chapter 7. When you remove the dinette, you'll inevitably leave a number of screw holes, scratches, and scrapes. Patch them up and finish the walls with paint, paper, or wainscoting before you begin the new dining area project. For information on RV walls, please refer to Chapter 8.

Getting Creative with Storage

Some dinette designs can actually create more storage than you already have. The supporting units shown in figures 4 and 5 (previous page) could consist of bookshelves, bed-side stands, file cabinets, small bureaus, bathroom vanities, or end tables. Use what's best for your specific needs.

Decorator's Tip: If your dining area design incorporates a piece of furniture with doors or drawers, be sure that you can access and open them easily when the unit is completed and the table top is in place.

Enjoying the Best of Both Worlds

This dinette is usually installed with the two chairs facing the outside wall. With this design, people will have their choice of seating type (table or booth). This flexible design also provides some beneficial under-seat storage (under the bench seat).

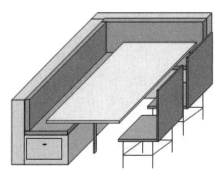

This flexible design offers plenty of seating, lots of breathing room, and some under-seat storage

Taking Advantage of Ready-to-Use Components

While table tops can be constructed from a wide range of materials, it's a lot easier to purchase off-the-shelf products from home furnishing stores like IKEA (www.ikea-usa.com). They look good, they're inexpensive (under $100), and they can be installed with a variety of commercially available table legs. IKEA sells chrome-plated table legs that are adjustable from 27 to 42 inches. The table tops are sold finished or unfinished. They also have some tops with rounded ends which are very desirable in tight quarters (see bottom photo).

When we first removed our dinette, we tried a design that offered more room and some shelving

We finally ended up with a simple wood table, a few chairs, some wainscoting, and a black cat

Secure Everything

If you install a table and set of chairs, you'll need to find a way to keep them secure while traveling. If you simply stack the chairs together or lay them on their side, they will still pose a deadly threat during a serious collision. Consequently, you'll need to use brackets, braces, clamps, or even bungee cords to keep things in their place. In most cases, you should be able to install the brackets in places that aren't that noticeable. Chairs are more challenging because they can't be permanently attached.

Brackets, braces, and clamps are ideal for securing furniture to the floors and walls

Traditional Dining Area Decorating Techniques

There are many ways to make an RV dining area look better. Here are some of the techniques used by professional decorators:

- Get a brightly colored tablecloth or an unusual set of placemats.

- Leave a few throw pillows on the dinette cushion. They'll add color and provide support.

- Place a vase of flowers on the table. Silk ones make sense in an RV.

- Install a small table lamp with a colorful shade at the end of the table. It will add light, color, and warmth. Alternatively, mount a wall-mounted fixture in the corner.

- To add a little life to your RV, hang a small house plant in the window. You can put the plant in a cupboard when you're traveling.

- Put a small, colorful tray in the middle of the dinette table. Then fill it with a decorative salt and pepper dispenser, a sugar bowl, a napkin holder, and so on.

- Place a bowl of fruit (imitation fruit works fine) on the table. It will provide a sense of comfort and hominess.

- Keep appliance like coffee makers and toasters off the table. They take up valuable space and they'll make the area appear cluttered.

- Put a narrow piece of brightly-colored cloth on the table and let it drape over by a foot or so. Use a bowl to hold it in place.

This dining area table looks more appealing with a piece of cloth and a bowl of fruit

Conclusions and Recommendations

The dining arrangement that you ultimately choose should fit your lifestyle. If the dinette's sleeping feature is essential, you have no choice but to go with a fixed booth design. If the extra bed is seldom used or you have an alternative solution, it's hard to beat the flexibility, comfort, and modern look of a well designed table and set of chairs. If you've owned your RV for a while, you'll already know what's best for you. If you haven't, don't do anything until you've established familiar and predictable routines. Then the decision will be obvious.

Additional Resources

"Debbie Travis' Painted House Living & Dining Rooms: 60 Stylish Projects to Transform Your Home" by Debbie Travis

"Dining Rooms & Kitchens (Design Ideas for Small Spaces)" by Norman Smith

"The House & Garden Book of Kitchens & Dining Rooms" by Leonie Highton

"Dining Rooms (Interior Design Library)" by Alison Aves

"Dining Room Makeovers" by Salli Brand

Chapter 14

RV Bathrooms

Lots of homeowners remodel their bathrooms. After all, it's not hard to tear down a wall, throw in a new tub, and upgrade all the plumbing fixtures. But in an RV, it's a whole different story. RV bathrooms are small, there are no walls to tear down, the plumbing is largely hidden, and "throwing in a new tub" is easier said than done.

Yet, we've seen remodeling projects that have produced dramatic improvements to both the appearance and the functionality of several RV bathrooms. How is this accomplished? The same way most RV remodeling projects are pulled off – by using selective upgrades and tasteful decorations to enhance an area without altering the basic structure or floor plan.

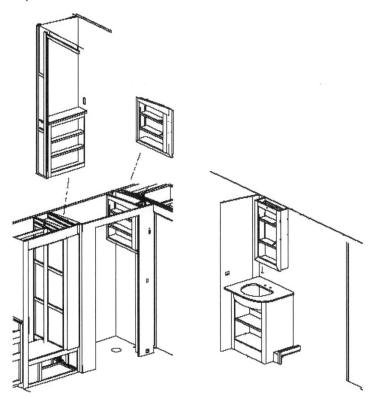

RV bathrooms tend to be highly functional but difficult to remodel (courtesy Winnebago Industries)

Replacing the Bathroom Sink

Most RV bathroom sinks are made of injection molded plastic or reinforced resin. They look just like porcelain when they're new but over time, they become covered in fine surface scratches that hold dirt and promote staining. As a result, you inevitably use an abrasive cleaner to get them clean again – which of course, only makes matters worse.

Fortunately, it's neither difficult nor expensive to replace your sink with a porcelain or stainless steel model. Porcelain sinks are easy to clean and they rarely become stained. They're also available in a wide array of colors and shapes. Our new bathroom sink is shaped like a scalloped sea shell, as shown here.

We replaced the plastic sink in our RV with a stylish porcelain model that's easy to maintain

Stainless steel sinks are usually round or oval shaped. They're easy to install, low maintenance, light weight, and very stylish looking.

A stainless-steel sink will add an element of style to any RV bathroom

When purchasing a new sink, make sure that it will fit in your existing vanity. Check the depth as well as the diameter. If the shape of your new sink is different from the old one, you'll have to use a saber saw to cut a larger hole in the top of your vanity. All sinks come with a paper template for this purpose. Choose a sink that includes holes for the faucet. Otherwise, you'll have to install the faucet behind the sink. This is a bad design because water will invariably collect outside the basin making the vanity much harder to keep clean and dry.

When installing the new sink, place a bead of plumber's putty around the bottom edge of the basin. Don't use silicone caulking. Then carefully lower the sink into the hole. Use a knife and a damp cloth to remove any excess putty. Most stainless steel sinks come with mounting clips that are installed from underneath. When you're re-connecting the drain line, you may have to shorten the tailpiece so that it fits into the existing trap adapter. After you've re-installed the faucet and drain assembly, turn on the faucet (both hot and cold) and check for leaks above and below. Then fill the sink with water and look for any leaks in the drain assembly.

> **Contractor's Tip:** The plastic sinks that are installed in many RVs are considerably thinner than porcelain models. Thus, your existing drain assembly might not be re-usable. Before you begin the installation, check to see if you'll need a new drain assembly. If you're upgrading to stainless steel, you can probably re-use the existing drain assembly.

Upgrading the Bathroom Vanity

One of the easiest ways to improve the appearance of your bathroom is to replace the vanity with something more stylish. Fortunately, reasonably priced vanities are available at home-supply stores like The Home Depot and Lowe's. Here are a few tips to help you select and install a new bathroom vanity:

- Most vanities come bundled with a sink and a faucet assembly at very competitive prices. Look for the sales.

- Pick a vanity with a countertop that is durable and attractive. To simplify maintenance, look for a seamless backsplash.

- When possible, choose a design that's somewhat consistent with your bathroom's existing décor. For example, try not to mix dark and light woods. Otherwise, your vanity will appear out of place.

- Measure carefully to ensure that the new vanity will fit. In most cases, there will be a little cutting and trimming required. In addition, make sure that there's enough clearance for the vanity doors to open all the way.

- Try to match the fixtures. For instance, if your shower fixtures are brass, try to find a vanity and sink combo with a brass faucet.

- If possible, choose a sink color that matches the color of your toilet and tub/shower enclosure. If your vanity is in a different room (than the toilet or shower), this requirement isn't as important.

- Secure the vanity to the wall using corner brackets. The brackets can be installed from the inside, so they don't show.

- Make sure that when you're done, there are no open pathways to the outside. In some RVs, the drain pipe from the vanity goes directly to the holding tank without any barriers. Consequently, pets can escape and insects and rodents can pay a visit. Use pieces of wood and spray insulating foam to seal any openings.

Adding a Tile Backsplash

If you're looking for a sure-fire way to add some style to your bathroom, consider installing a single-tile backsplash. A single-tile backsplash is simply a single row of ceramic tile attached to the wall behind the vanity. In addition to providing some protection from moisture, tile backsplashes are a good way to add some color and texture to a bathroom. Be sure to select colorful tiles that have a high-gloss finish.

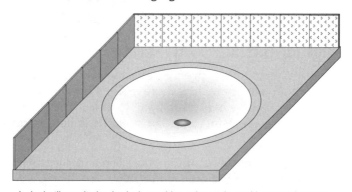

A single-tile vanity backsplash provides color, style, and lower maintenance

Fortunately, installing a single-tile backsplash is an easy task. Start by applying some blue painter's tape to protect the wall and the countertop. This will enable you to apply thin-set mortar (or solvent-based mastic) without having to be too careful.

> **Contractor's Tip:** Use a thin strip of wood to create a ⅛-inch gap between the row of tiles and the top of the vanity. After the tiles have been installed, fill the gap with silicone caulking instead of grout. This will minimize the likelihood of cracked tiles as things shift over time.

Starting at one end of the countertop, install the first tile. The end tile will typically be a bullnose tile (a tile that's rounded along the side and top). Then lay the other tiles, making sure to twist each one slightly to ensure a good bond. When the mortar has dried, fill the gaps with grout. After a few days, brush on a grout sealer to keep moisture out. As an alternative, you might want to install a double row of tiles. The tiles should extend beyond the vanity until you reach either a corner or an obstruction, as shown below.

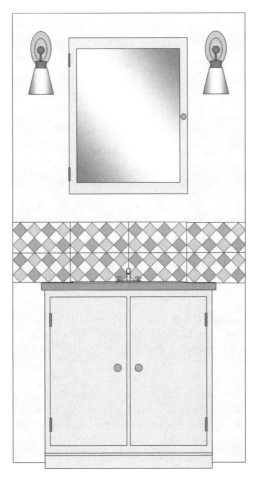

A double row of tile installed along the wall can really jazz things up

Installing a New Toilet

If your toilet is unattractive, uncomfortable, operates poorly, or is difficult to keep clean, consider an upgrade. Replacement toilets aren't difficult to install and there are dozens of models to choose from. Here are a few things to keep in mind:

- RV toilets are constantly being improved and re-engineered to make them more like the ones in homes. However, this progress comes at a price. Some high-end models use electric pumps while others rely on sophisticated hydraulic systems. As a result, they cost more and have considerably more moving parts. If you can live without the frills, you may want to stick with a basic ceramic model that operates with good old-fashioned water pressure.

Purchase a basic porcelain toilet and simply upgrade the seat (courtesy Winnebago Industries)

- Always go with porcelain (ceramic). They stay cleaner and they're easier to maintain. Try to select a color that matches your sink.

- For flushing and filling, most models are equipped with either foot pedals or a hand lever. Pick the one that best suits your physical capabilities. If bending over is difficult, get one with foot pedals. If you sometimes have trouble using your legs, consider installing one with hand-operated controls.

- Consider installing a grab handle near the toilet to make it easier to get up and down. Experiment with different locations before permanently attaching the grab handle.

- Toilets come in various heights. The tallest toilets are more than 17 inches high whereas the shortest models are less than 13 inches from the floor. If you're dealing with a disability, go with a taller model. Regardless, select a height that is the most comfortable. Which is the basis of rule one. Always sit on a new toilet before it's installed.

- Get a model that comes with a hand sprayer. They're invaluable for general maintenance.

- Most manufacturers sell inexpensive, well-made porcelain toilets. However, they keep the cost down by fitting them with low-grade plastic seats. Purchase the toilet but replace the seat. If your bathroom has wood cabinets, consider installing a solid oak seat. Otherwise, look for a well-made seat with stainless steel, brass, or chrome-plated hardware.

- Get a diagram of your RV's plumbing system. It will help you to understand how your bathroom plumbing is configured.

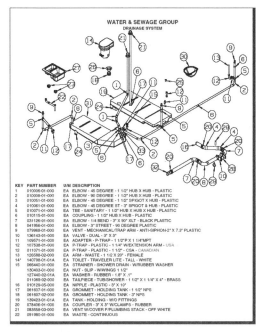

Plumbing system diagrams are useful for many types of projects (courtesy Winnebago Industries)

Improving the Shower

There's an entire industry that specializes in RV tub and shower related products. Accordingly, you can now find one-piece molded tubs, whirlpools, shower seats, ready-to-install shower enclosures, fiberglass panels, sliding glass doors, tub molding kits, and more. In short, no matter what you have now – it can probably be upgraded to something better.

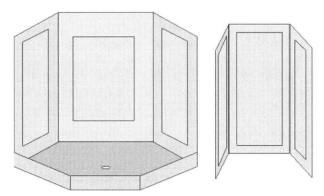

Tub and shower enclosures are available in a wide range of materials, colors, sizes, and styles

In terms of available materials, shower and tub enclosures are currently available in fiberglass reinforced gelcoat, molded acrylic, plastic laminate, and synthetic marble. Shower bases are usually made of fiberglass, terrazzo, cast polymer, and solid-surface materials. For most applications, fiberglass reinforced gelcoat is a good choice. It's inexpensive, lightweight, and can be found in a wide range of sizes, colors, and configurations. Acrylic is more durable and scratch resistant than fiberglass but it's very heavy and costs twice as much as fiberglass. Besides, acrylic shower enclosures (unlike fiberglass units) usually come with a ceiling attached.

This RV bathtub doubles as a whirlpool bath (courtesy Monaco Coach Corporation)

When choosing a molded unit, look for panels with integrated soap dishes, ledges, and grab bars. Shower stalls should be at least thirty inches in diameter at the base. Thirty-six inches is even better (as shown below).

The actual process of upgrading a shower or tub depends on the job and the product. There are bathroom remodeling books that include step-by-step illustrations for replacing or adding a new tub or shower unit. In addition, some manufacturers include good instructions. With some patience, helpful instructions, and the right tools, most resourceful do-it-yourselfers should be able to handle this type of project. There are also several RV remodeling companies that can perform the work.

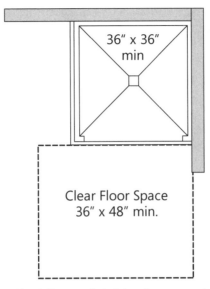

You should have at least 12 square feet of clear floor space outside the shower

Installing a Better Showerhead

One of the best and easiest bathroom upgrades entails replacing your existing showerhead with a more advanced model. The benefits often include improved flow, water massaging options, and hand-help spraying capabilities. Another popular upgrade project entails the installation of a rain-style showerhead. Capable of producing a wide spray that feels like soft rain, these showerheads have a large flat head with lots of tiny holes (see diagram). Switching out a showerhead is a straightforward process. However, be sure to use Teflon® plumbing tape on the threads and don't over-tighten the fittings.

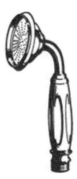

A rain-style showerhead delivers a soft, delicate stream of water (courtesy Winnebago Industries)

Upgrading the Shower Door

One of the most popular (and beneficial) remodeling projects entails replacing a flexible shower door with one made of tempered glass. Hinged shower doors are generally available in widths from 21 inches to 37 inches. Heights vary up to 68 inches. In tight situations, consider installing sliding glass doors. Two-panel tempered glass door systems are commonly available in 36-inch and 48-inch (total) widths.

The installation process is generally the same, regardless of the model. A bottom track is first secured with screws and silicone caulking. Then side channels are installed in the same manner. The doors are subsequently test-fitted with the top track held in place. Finally, the top track is permanently installed and everything is tightened firmly. Most units have a knob at the top that keeps the doors secured during travel.

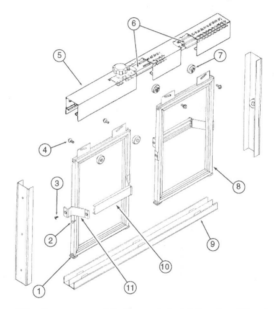

Tempered-glass sliding doors are surprisingly easy to install (courtesy Winnebago Industries)

Adding a Shower Closet Rod

By installing a removable closet rod in your shower stall, you'll have one more place to store clothes while you're traveling. Closet rods and mounting brackets are readily available from most home supply stores. The rod will have to be finished with varnish or polyurethane to protect it from moisture. Also, use stainless steel screws that won't rust. If you slide a piece of corrugated flexible plastic tubing over the closet rod, it will prevent the hangers from sliding back and forth. Corrugated tubing can be found at industrial plumbing supply dealers.

A piece of corrugated flexible plastic tubing over the rod will keep the clothes from sliding around

Making your Bathroom Safer

One of the best improvements that you can make to any bathroom entails the installation of a few, well-placed grab handles. Made of either textured plastic or corrugated metal, grab handles are designed to help people safely navigate the shower or toilet. They're also something to grab should you begin to slip. Consequently, when installing grab handles, always use anchors to ensure that the handle is securely attached.

Grab handles should be installed in every tub or shower enclosure

Creating More Storage Space

Surprisingly, it's not that hard to create a little extra storage space in an RV bathroom. They're out of the way and they often have plenty of overlooked wall space. Here are some successful ideas that have been used by other creative RVers.

Installing a Vanity Extension

If you have some room next to your bathroom vanity, construct a narrow shelf to store things like hand-towels, cleaning supplies, and toiletries. You can add a door or use wood molding and non-slip shelf lining to keep the items in place. If you need some extra counter space, add a top.

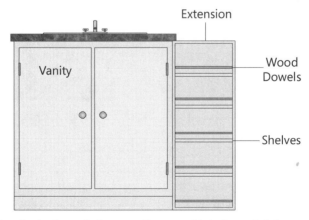

An extension to your bathroom vanity can provide badly-needed storage space

Adding a Medicine Cabinet Extension

Most medicine cabinets installed in RVs are somewhere between 15 and 24 inches wide. As a result, there is usually a small section of wasted wall-space next to the cabinet. With a small medicine cabinet extension, you can create more storage capacity without changing the basic layout of the bathroom.

The extension itself is essentially a narrow wooden shelf that is the same height and depth as the existing cabinet. The width of the extension is determined by the available wall space. Small wood dowels or wood strips in front of each shelf keep the objects in place. The extension is attached to the medicine cabinet (and the adjacent wall) with screws.

A simple medicine cabinet extension can give you a 50% increase in storage capacity

Taking Advantage of the Vanity Door

One of the best ways to create a little extra storage is to take advantage of your bathroom vanity's door. As with kitchen cabinets, the inside of the door is frequently overlooked. While you may have to cut the shelving back a little, you should have enough room for a small wastebasket, a clothes hamper, or some utility shelves. For the clothes hamper or wastebasket, drill two holes and hang them on cup hooks. That way, they can be removed for emptying and cleaning.

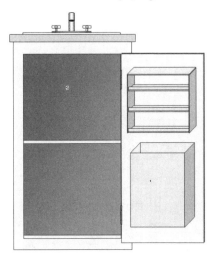

Vanity doors are often overlooked when searching for ways to create more storage capacity

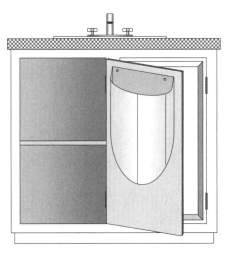

A small canvas bag attached to the inside of the door makes a great clothes hamper

Adding Storage to the Toilet Room

Some RVs have a separate room, just for the toilet. As it turns out, this particular layout provides remodelers with some real advantages in terms of adding storage to an RV. For example, you can create more space for toiletries and personal items by simply installing a wall-mounted medicine cabinet above the toilet. By adding a simple towel rack (see next page), you can increase the cabinet's usefulness.

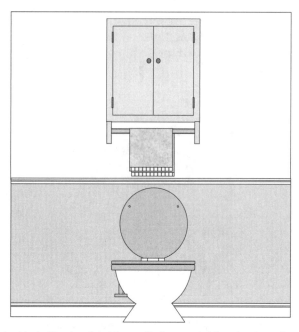

A wall-mounted cabinet with a towel rack is an effective way to take advantage of a small bathroom

Likewise, at discount stores and home furnishing outlets – look for narrow storage units that are specifically designed to fit behind toilets.

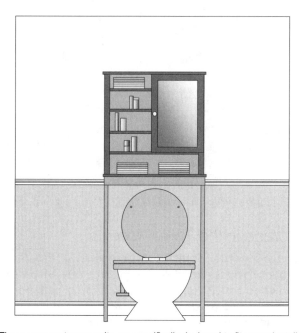

These narrow storage units are specifically designed to fit around a toilet

When we were looking for a quick and easy way to store some extra towels, we installed an inexpensive, wall-mounted shelf high up on the toilet-room wall. It isn't fancy but it does the job.

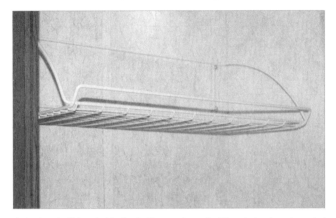

A coated-wire shelf, located in the bathroom, is perfect for storing towels and sheets

As full-time RVers, we have an expanding collection of small, assorted items that are difficult to store and even harder to find. To resolve this growing problem, we bought a small storage box that is comprised of multiple rows of small plastic drawers. Available at places like The Home Depot and Wal-Mart, these storage boxes are typically used for small parts like screws, nails, and washers. We attached the storage unit to the wall that faces the toilet, as shown below.

This storage box with drawers holds all the little things that we accumulate (note the bungee cords)

We then drilled small holes at the top and bottom of each column to secure light-duty bungee cords. When we set up camp, we take the bungee cords off. There aren't enough words to describe how useful this inexpensive storage device has become.

Bathroom Shelving

For storing odds and ends that don't fit in your medicine cabinet, consider building or purchasing a simple wall-mounted shelf like the ones shown below. Although these shelves are easy to build, you can usually find them at craft shops and unpainted furniture stores. They're reasonably priced, surprisingly useful, and look terrific with a coat of paint or some stain and varnish.

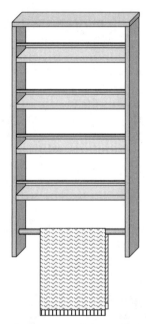

This simple wall-mounted shelf takes up very little room – yet it can hold a lot of toiletries

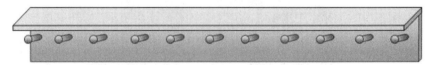

If you only have room for one shelf – this is the type to install

If you're looking for a convenient way to store commonly used items such as a razor, toothbrushes, or soap – consider building a small, wall-mounted shelf like the one shown here. This particular example has two holes and a small box attached to the middle.

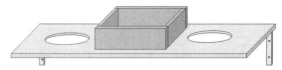

This small shelf is designed to hold two cups plus other miscellaneous items

One hole is for a plastic tumbler that can be used to store things like toothbrushes, a comb, scissors, and other tall items. The other hole is for a drinking glass. The 2½-inch diameter holes can be made with a door-knob saw or a saber saw. The small box in the center is used for storing other miscellaneous items. The shelf can be mounted on the wall using small corner brackets. The best part about a shelf like this is that it can be installed anywhere.

Another option is to install a narrow chair-rail shelf along one of the walls (see illustration on next page). The shelf is actually a 3-inch board supported with a strip of chair-rail molding (underneath) for a little added elegance. Chair-rail shelves are perfect for holding soaps, lotions, tooth brushes, and other small items. Sand the edges of the shelf before painting or finishing.

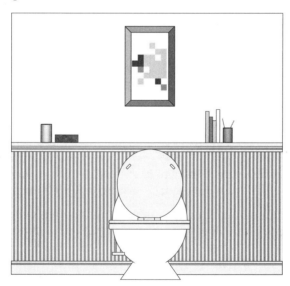

A chair-rail shelf offers a convenient place to put miscellaneous items

Since bathrooms walls are often overlooked, consider installing a set of bookshelves. Books are heavy so be sure to use plastic anchors when attaching the shelf brackets to the wall. The bookshelves shown in the following photo are supported with fully adjustable, double-track standards and brackets. The interior walls are hollow so winged anchors were used to attach the vertical standards.

The bathroom is a great place to catch up on your reading – especially with some shelving

Painting the Bathroom Cabinets and Trimwork

The RV industry's long-standing use of unpainted wood cabinets makes a lot of sense in a kitchen. After all, unpainted wood is easy to clean, it hides dirt, and it's attractive. However in a small bathroom, wood has a tendency to make the room seem smaller – especially with darker woods.

If you want to make your bathroom seem much bigger and brighter – paint the cabinets a light color. You'll be astonished at the results. Use good quality paint with a high-gloss finish and be sure to paint the trimwork as well as the vanity and cabinets. Choose a color that doesn't clash with the sink and toilet. This might also be a good time to do something with the walls (please see Chapter 8 for details). When you're done, purchase a toilet seat that complements the new color scheme.

Jazzing Up the Hardware

As expected, little details can make a big difference in a small bathroom. If your toilet paper dispenser, towel hooks, cabinet handles, and towel racks are ordinary looking, give your bathroom a make-over by replacing them with something more stylish. Remember, in a small area – it's important to maintain a consistent design. As a result, try to use fixtures that adhere to a similar style or era such as modern, art deco, Victorian, and so on.

Stylish toilet paper holders and towel bars can have a big impact (courtesy Winnebago Industries)

Upgrading the Bathroom Lighting

In the interior decorating industry, lighting upgrades represent one of the proven tools of the trade. The reason is simple. Improved lighting is the easiest way to enhance the overall look and feel of a room without altering the layout or changing the furnishings.

Most RV bathrooms come with no-frills, run of the mill lighting fixtures. Luckily, it's easy to remedy this shortcoming. For instance, wall-mounted sconce-style lamps will make any bathroom feel warmer and more welcoming. If you currently have a florescent light fixture on the ceiling, replace it with a glitter-dome style ceiling lamp. It will instantly make the room seem brighter as well as more elegant.

The general idea is to install a variety of fixtures so you can adjust the lighting to the specific situation. For evening use, look for a small wall-mounted fixture that puts out just enough light to make the bathroom seem warm and inviting. For putting on makeup or shaving, install a stylish vanity-style fixture that illuminates the area above the sink. When you need to clean the area or find a lost contact lens, flip on the ceiling lamp. For daytime use, skylights and roof vents are the ideal solution.

Reducing Glare

Many RVs come with make-up style lights mounted above the medicine cabinet. This type of fixture often comes with three round bulbs mounted on a narrow base. The problem with this particular design is that it tends to emit excessive amounts of glare – right at eye level.

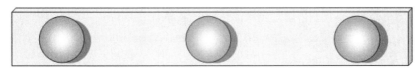

Many RV vanities come with cosmetic-counter style lights that give off too much glare

Besides installing smaller bulbs, there are two ways to alleviate this problem. The first is to create a shield to reduce some of the glare. Use a lightweight, non-combustible material that can be painted, varnished, or covered in fabric. One good choice might be stiffener, a flexible material that's available at most fabric stores. It's easy to cut and can be purchased with a peel-off style adhesive on one side. To attach the fabric, you simply peel off the protective layer and press the fabric into place (overlapping the edges). The inside should be painted white to reflect as much light as possible. Use brackets to attach the shield to the wall.

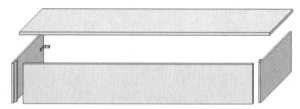

A simple shield like this can help to cut the harsh glare of your vanity's overhead lights

The second option is to replace the light fixture with one that emits less glare. The new fixture can be installed above the medicine cabinet or on each side. Side lighting should be installed approximately 65 inches from the floor and 36 to 40 inches apart to minimize shadows. Use frosted bulbs and opaque lamp shades to minimize glare and direct the light where it's needed.

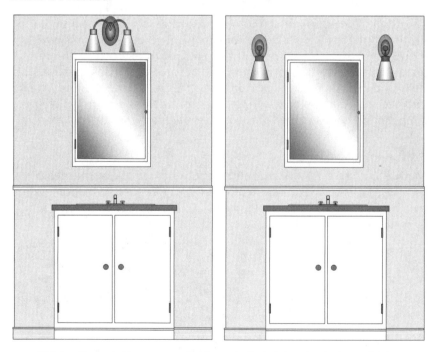

Stylish wall-mounted lamps are perfect for producing soft, low-glare bathroom lighting

Improving the Ventilation

RV bathrooms tend to generate lots of unwanted moisture. As a result, they should always be well ventilated. Here are some options:

- If it doesn't have one, add a small window to your RV's bathroom. The added light and fresh air will make your bathroom seem bigger and brighter. For details, please refer to Chapter 10.

- Upgrade your roof vent. The newer models have automated rain protection, reversible fans, thermostats, and variable speed controls.

- Install an exhaust fan in one of your windows. A small table-top fan can move a considerable volume of air.

Adding and Upgrading Doors

One commonly overlooked but effective way to enhance the appearance of an RV is to upgrade the interior doors. Doors can help to reduce noise, bring in more light (French doors), hide clutter, and deliver more privacy. Here are a few possibilities:

- Use ¼-inch thick wood strapping to convert a plain wood door into a raised panel style door. You can also attach wainscoting-patterned particleboard to provide some visual texture.

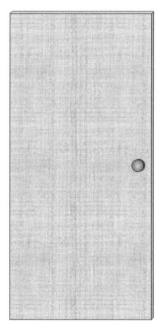 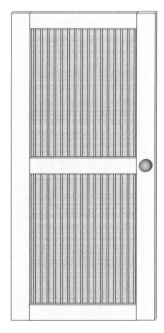

Contractor's Tip: To attach items to a hollow door (i.e. a mirror or a towel rack), use small winged plastic anchors.

- Replace your existing door with a French door. The small glass panes will increase the level of light while adding an eye-catching degree of elegance. For privacy, install a sheer curtain with a rod at both the top and bottom of the door.

French-style doors add light and elegance to this RV bedroom (courtesy Monaco Coach Corp.)

- Add some privacy with a set of sliding doors. They're easy to install and they can accommodate openings of any size. In short, you first install a track along the ceiling. The sliding doors are then hung on the track and secured (at the bottom) with special hardware.

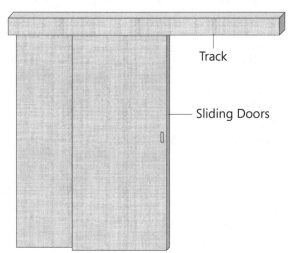

Track

Sliding Doors

Sliding doors can be used to close off any opening – regardless of its size

- Replace your existing hollow door with a solid wood door (see photo below). The improvement in quality will have a positive influence on the entire RV. It will also help to deaden sound.

A solid wood door provides a measure of elegance and quality to this RV bathroom

- Attach a full-length mirror to a door. It will add more light and be useful for checking your appearance. Use winged plastic anchors when attaching the mounting clips.

Adding a Fold-away Ironing Board

There are now wall-mounted ironing boards that fold out of the way when they're not being used. If you're handy, you can probably construct your own out of wood.

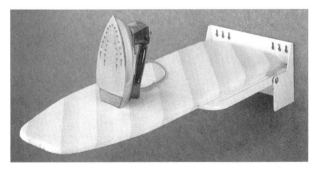

This wall-mounted fold-down ironing board is available from www.rockler.com

Other Bathroom Decorating Ideas

As with any decorating and remodeling venture, it's the little things that make the biggest difference. With a bathroom, the trick is to use small, carefully selected items to make the area look more elegant and comfortable. Here are a few ideas from the experts:

- Instead of putting up a single framed piece of art, install a set of four small prints. They'll create a more stylish effect while adding some extra color. The frames don't have to be the same color, type, or shape.

- Put a small, colorful area rug in the bathroom. The color and pattern aren't that important as long as the rug is attractive and interesting. Make sure that it has a rubber backing to prevent slippage.

- Jazz up your bathroom by mounting a small, framed mirror. It'll also help to generate more light.

- Attach a decorative basket to the wall or on the side of the vanity. The basket will make an attractive storage bin for a hair dryer, a sponge, or some hand towels.

Grouped sets of pictures tend to make a wall appear larger than it actually is

- Use double-sided adhesive or museum wax to attach a colorful glass tumbler to the top of your vanity. It will make an attractive tooth brush holder.

- Attach a decorative ceramic bowl to your vanity (with double-sided adhesive). It'll be perfect for soap, sponges, cotton balls, and other similar items.

- Place candles, perfumed soaps, potpourris, and scented oils on your vanity. They'll add a nice touch while providing a pleasing scent.

- With a small hook attached to a suction cup, hang a small plant from the skylight in your shower. Make sure that it likes a lot of light and moisture. Some people use this approach to grow herbs or keep their cats supplied with fresh catnip.

- Line a wicker basket with a plastic bag for trash. It'll be a stylish alternative to the usual plastic waste basket.

- Install a wall-mounted swing-away (magnified) mirror near the medicine cabinet. Perfect for close-up work, it'll become a real hit.

- Place a small vase of silk flowers on the vanity. Use double-sided tape or museum wax to keep the vase in-place. The flowers will add some elegance and color.

- Place an artificial hanging ivy plant on top of your medicine cabinet. The leaves hanging down will add a nice touch.

Conclusions and Recommendations

RV bathrooms, like kitchens, are largely measured in functional terms. Either they do a good job at what they do, or they don't. Therefore, in terms of remodeling, always put functionality first. For example, if there isn't enough room in the bathroom to sit comfortably on the toilet, find a way to fix this shortcoming before you do anything else. Likewise, if your shower door lets water out and cold air in – consider upgrading to a sliding glass door.

Only after your bathroom is properly configured should you look into upgrading the fixtures and changing the décor. Tile flooring, ceramic toilets, and porcelain sinks are the gold standard of a home-style bathroom – so begin there. Stainless steel sinks are another popular choice. After that, focus on storage. Medicine cabinets are usually too small and vanities are notoriously cluttered. Then start looking at the décor. Stick with proven design strategies such as decorative borders, stenciling, tiled backsplashes, wallpaper, wainscoting, improved lighting, and framed artwork. Finally, add little decorative items to make the bathroom area feel more inviting and relaxing. Over time, you'll have a bathroom that is both beautiful as well as functional.

Additional Resources

"New Bathroom Idea Book" (Idea Books) by Andrew Wormer

"Renovating a Bathroom" (For Pros by Pros Series) by Fine Homebuilding

"Bathroom Makeovers" (Do It Yourself) by Fine Homebuilding Editors

Chapter 15

RV Bedrooms

Recreational vehicle bedrooms are rarely the focus of major remodeling efforts. In fact, few RVers do little more than upgrade their mattress, change the blinds, and replace the bedspread. Yet, with their built-in wardrobes, accessible wall-space, and relatively large dimensions, RV bedrooms are rich in potential and ripe for possibilities. Hence, the principal objective of this chapter is to demonstrate ideas in order to promote some of these possibilities.

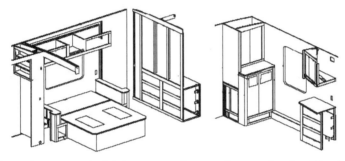

RV bedrooms have more potential storage space than any other room (courtesy Winnebago Ind.)

Creating a Dual-Zone RV

One of the more recent concepts in floor plan design strategies is the idea of the "dual-zone" RV. Put simply, a dual-zone RV has two separate places where people can sit and relax. In a dual-zone RV, the kids can watch a video in the living room while the folks relax in the back with a cold beer and some TV.

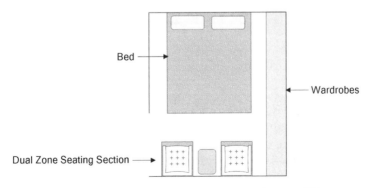

This bedroom illustrates the basic idea behind a dual-zone RV

As a practical matter, creating a dual-zone RV essentially involves adding a down-sized sitting area in the bedroom. Assuming that you have the space to begin with – you'll probably have to remove or rearrange some of the furnishings. You'll need to create enough room for a couple of chairs and a table for snacks, beverages, and reading material. Below are two examples. Note that the illustrations include the use of a recliner. Fortunately, companies like La-Z-Boy® manufacture space-saving recliners that require very little clearance between the chair and the wall.

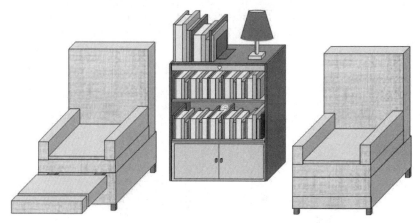

This first arrangement is designed to create a small library-like setting

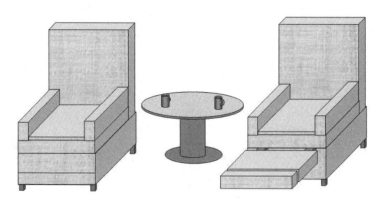

This second setup is perfect for relaxing with a drink and some good company

Optimizing the Space under the Bed

Some RVs enable you to store things underneath the bed. Typically, the mattress sits on a hinged sheet of plywood that can be tilted up to access the area underneath. However, because the space resembles a giant drawer, stored items have a tendency to shift around until the entire area becomes a disorganized and tangled mess.

The solution is conceptually the same as it is for drawers. In short, wood planks are used to divide the area into smaller sections. The boards are held in place with pieces of wood that essentially create a track (see diagram on next page). With this design, you can remove boards to accommodate larger objects or add boards to create more sections. You may want to add a cabinet handle to each board (as shown) to make it easier to get hold of. The dividers also provide extra support for the bed. Once you've inserted the dividers, you can then use boxes, bins, or bags to keep the contents better organized. If possible, use the dividers to accommodate your actual storage requirements. For example, if you plan on keeping some folding chairs under the bed, size one of the divided sections to hold the chairs securely.

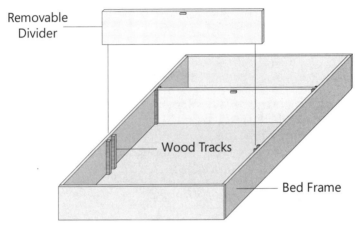

Removable Divider

Wood Tracks

Bed Frame

The space under the bed is divided into smaller sections to keep the contents organized

Adding More Beds

RV industry market data indicates that growing families are now purchasing RVs in record numbers. Yet, when it comes to something as crucial as sleeping arrangements for children (and friends) – most RVs are woefully inadequate. In truth, many pop-up trailers have better sleeping arrangements for large families than expensive motorhomes.

Consequently, if your plans entail RVing with a group of people – you may have to design your own sleeping solutions. However, since RV floor space is always at a premium, you should try to take advantage of the types of furnishings you already have. Chapter 11 (living rooms) describes a number of pieces that can be converted into a bed, such as a futon or a convertible sofa. In contrast, the designs shown in this section are generally limited to the bedroom. For example, the following bunk-bed is designed to fit in small areas. The storage area at the bottom could easily be drawers.

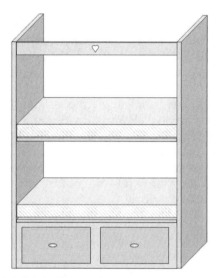

This built-in bunk bed is designed to handle two people

This second bunk bed takes advantage of the often unused space that exists above most beds. This unique design also provides some additional storage in the form of the loft's supporting shelf. Note that this shelf even has some cubbyholes (at the bottom) for storing small items like shoes.

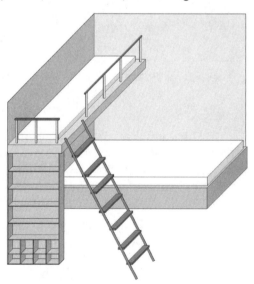

This loft-style design takes advantage of the unused space above many beds

This next unit is basically a window seat that was converted into a single bed by adding a small foam pad. The window seat is framed in cabinets and drawers for storage while the drapes provide privacy.

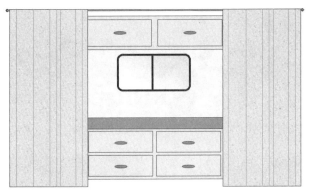

This built-in unit is actually a window seat with a mattress (and drapes for privacy)

When designing and installing beds in an RV – be sure to build in some redundant support so that the entire unit isn't dependent on a few bolts, one board, or a couple of brackets. Take advantage of toggle bolts and over-sized supports. When using nuts and bolts, always use lock washers.

These bunk beds were added to the bedroom of a thirty-four foot motorhome

Hide-Away Beds

Several companies now sell beds that can flip up into the wall or hide away inside a piece of furniture. Originally known as "Murphy" beds, these ingeniously designed devices have been used in hotels and efficiency apartments for years. In an RV, it means that the bedroom can be used as a daytime office or a conference room while the bed is conveniently tucked away. Not bad.

This desk turns into a bed, making it perfect for RVs with limited floor space (murphybeds.com)

As can be seen from these beauties, Murphy beds come in many styles (murphybedusa.com)

If you look for "Murphy beds" on the Internet or in the yellow pages, you'll find numerous companies that specialize in hide-a-way beds. The cheapest units are basically mechanized steel frames that attach to a wall. You simply add a mattress and you're ready to go. On the other end of the spectrum are beautifully designed wall units with built-in shelves and hand-painted doors (see above photo). Their small footprint makes them the perfect solution for many RVs.

The Flexsteel wall mount bed is ideal for toy haulers

Upgrading your Mattress

While some RVers might argue that mattress upgrades are outside the realm of remodeling, the issue is raised enough to include it here. In terms of getting a good night sleep – these are your current options:

- Add a foam mattress topper. These supplemental foam covers will significantly improve any mattress. Some take advantage of memory-foam type materials while others use an egg-crate foam design. Memory-foam based toppers tend to add stability while egg-crate foam toppers tend to deliver more softness. In any case, try it out before you buy, if you can (and keep the receipt). Queen-size mattress toppers cost between $20 and $250, depending on the thickness and the amount of memory-foam used in the construction.

- Purchase a better spring-style mattress. The mattresses that come with most RVs are of low quality. If you install a high-quality spring-style mattress, you'll immediately notice a big difference. A queen-size mattress costs between $150 and $950, depending on the manufacturer, the model, and the quality. Low-priced spring mattresses deteriorate very quickly. These are the standard mattress sizes. Actual sizes may vary.

  - Bunk/Twin: 35" x 75"
  - Extra Long Twin: 38" x 80"
  - Double or Full: 53" x 75"
  - Short Queen: 60" x 75"
  - Queen: 60" x 80"
  - Extra Long Queen: 60" x 90"
  - King: 76" x 80"
  - California King: 72" x 84"

- Install a bigger bed (if you have the floor-space). It's hard to sleep soundly when the bed you're sleeping on is too small. The box on the next page shows a method for increasing the size of any bed.

- Purchase a high-tech mattress such as the Sleep Number® System. These innovative mattresses utilize modern technology to provide adjustable and individualized levels of firmness. If your preferences are significantly different than your partner's – this might do the trick. A queen-size Sleep Number® mattress costs between $1400 and $1800, depending on the model and the dealer.

- Install a high-tech memory foam mattress like a Tempur-Pedic®. Built from ultra-modern foam composites, these beds represent the top of the line in reliability and comfort. They're heavier than most spring mattresses but they're extraordinarily comfortable and remarkably stable. In fact, they're the only type of mattress that enables one person to move around without affecting the other. A queen-size Tempur-Pedic® mattress costs between $750 and $1200, depending on the dealer.

Project: Making your Bed Bigger

If your bed isn't large enough, you can build a simple drop-leaf extension that will give you the extra length (or width) you need. Once the extension is installed, you can either fill in the extra length with a piece of foam (as shown below) or purchase a larger mattress.

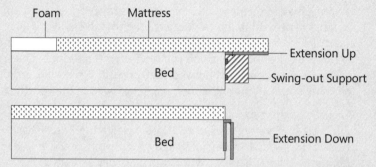

This drop-leaf extension (side view) enables you to expand your bed in any direction

To start, you'll have to cut and attach a fixed support as shown below. The support should be wide enough to attach some hinges. This piece can be made of ¾-inch plywood or a strip of hardwood. The support is attached to the edge of the bed frame using L-brackets (from underneath). The drop-leaf extension is then sized to give you the total length (or width) you need. The drop-leaf extension is attached to the fixed support with hinges. You'll need at least two hinges to provide enough strength. To keep the drop-leaf extension up, you'll need to cut two pieces of wood to serve as swing-out supports. These supports are attached to the bed frame with hinges (2 for each swing-out support).

Remodeler's Tip: To prevent injuries, be sure to round off the outer corners of the drop leaf extension.

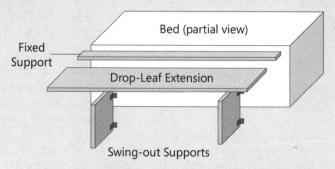

You'll need at least 4 pieces of plywood and 6 hinges for this project

Improving RV Closets and Wardrobes

In an RV, closets and wardrobes represent the single largest source of storage space. In fact, these storage provisions are so significant – many home decorating professionals make a good living helping people organize and optimize their closets. Unfortunately, RV wardrobes and closets have a long way to go before they could be described as organized or optimized storage solutions. In fact, it seems that once a wardrobe has been built, most RV manufacturers install a closet rod and call it good. Consequently, the majority of RVers are left with a cavernous space that is capable of little more than storing clothes on a hanger. Accordingly, this section focuses on proven strategies for upgrading and enhancing RV closets and wardrobes.

Shelving is the Key

The first step towards improving any closet or wardrobe entails adding some shelving. One of your best options is to use adjustable shelf standards and brackets. The double track versions are exceptionally sturdy and they're fully adjustable.

The shelving can be made of wood planks (softwood or hardwood), plastic coated medium-density fiberboard (MDF), melamine-coated particleboard (MCP), or plywood. Most home supply and hardware stores carry a good selection of pre-made shelving in a wide range of sizes and materials. Shelving spans of less than three feet can usually handle most reasonable loads. However, for lengths greater than four feet, you may see some bowing. You can minimize this problem by using thicker shelving, adding reinforcement strips, or using additional shelf brackets.

If you don't need adjustable shelving, consider using wire closet organizers. There's no painting, they're easy to install, and wire closet organizers are cheaper than other options.

Compared to wood shelving– wire closet organizers are easy to install and relatively inexpensive

This first illustration represents a typical RV wardrobe. Note the single closet rod and set of drawers. To highlight their interior features, all of the examples in this section are shown without doors. In actuality, most RV closets and wardrobes have hinged or sliding doors.

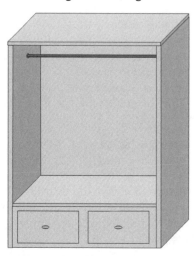

If everything you stored could be hung on a hanger, this RV wardrobe might actually be useful

The next illustration shows how a little shelving can quickly increase the usable storage capacity of any wardrobe. Note that this enhanced version retains some of the closet space for hanging clothes.

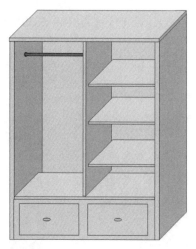

A single column of shelves instantly increases the usable storage capacity of the basic wardrobe

If you already have a place to keep clothes on hangers, you can further optimize the storage capacity of this hypothetical wardrobe by filling the entire interior with shelves and drawers as shown here.

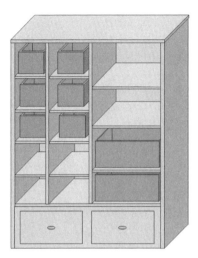

The storage space in this wardrobe was maximized with shelving, dividers, bins, and drawers

Note the use of boxes and bins. Snug-fitting storage containers are one of the best ways to effectively use all of the available storage space. The containers also help to keep the contents from sliding around when your RV is in motion.

Modifying Wardrobes for Specialized Uses

Wardrobes and closets can also be modified in other ways. The example shown below has been converted into a computer workstation. It offers shelving for books and files, cubby holes for mail and small supplies, and a pull-out support for a keyboard. With the doors closed, this workstation would be entirely concealed.

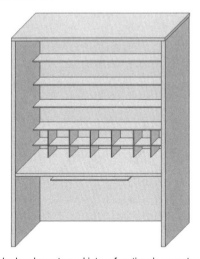

This wardrobe has been turned into a functional computer workstation

Another option is to convert your closet or wardrobe into a full set of drawers. This unique design offers highly organized storage for small items of clothing, jewelry, art supplies, maps, and the like.

This design is ideal for storing things that must be segregated as well as organized

This last example shows a wardrobe that has been converted into a large bookshelf. The open shelves would be ideal for clothing, linens, towels, blankets, coats, and other similar items. Bins would also make sense here.

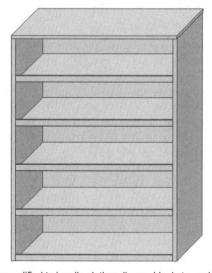

This wardrobe was modified to handle clothes, linens, blankets, and other similar items

Before you modify any wardrobe, make sure that you have a clear idea of what you want to store and how you want it arranged. The following picture shows a wardrobe that's been successfully optimized.

Well organized closets take advantage of every cubic-inch of available space (easyclosets.com)

When adding a closet rod to a wardrobe, use the following table to determine the installation height:

Table 12 – Closet Rod Installation Clearances for Various Types of Clothing

Men's Clothing		Women's Clothing	
Pants, folded	32 inches	Bathrobe	52 inches
Pants, unfolded	48 inches	Blouse	36 inches
Shirts	38 inches	Dress	58 inches
Suits	40 inches	Evening Gown	69 inches
Ties, folded	32 inches	Skirt	35 inches
Topcoat	56 inches	Suit	37 inches
Winter Coat	55 inches	Winter Coat	52 inches

Decorator's Tip: A cedar-lined closet is now a do-it-yourself project thanks to cedar closet kits. Companies like Giles & Kendall's CedarSafe® and Mountain Home Cedar make kits from Eastern red cedar. You can choose from solid cedar planks or pressed board cedar panels. Most kits cover about 20 square feet. A cedar closet lining kit from Mountain Home costs around $140.

Using Storage Containers

When stocking wardrobes, closets, or shelving, always try to store things in boxes or bins. Make sure that the boxes are sized to fill all of the available space. Without bins and boxes, you would be forced to keep everything in carefully arranged piles. This might be an acceptable strategy in a house, but in an RV, these piles would be the first thing to go when you hit the brakes. If possible, use clear plastic boxes since they make it much easier to locate specific items.

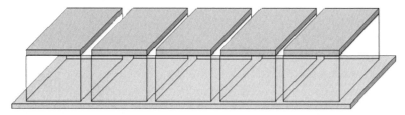

By using clear boxes, you'll be better organized and you'll be able to locate things easier

Building a Window Seat

If you have a free wall in your bedroom that has a window, consider installing a window seat. It'll give you a place to sit along with some additional storage capacity.

The following example is very easy to construct. The hinged seat is a piece of ¾-inch plywood topped with a piece of fabric-covered foam. The box itself is constructed of ⅝-inch plywood. The front of the window seat is embellished with recessed panels that are made from wood molding cut at 45° angles. The window seat can be secured to the wall using brackets or scrap pieces of wood that are attached from the inside.

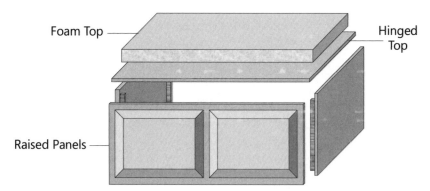

Foam Top
Hinged Top
Raised Panels

This window seat provides a place to sit in addition to more storage capacity for your stuff

Designing Custom Storage Units

One of the most beneficial RV remodeling projects entails designing and installing custom storage units. These units are typically installed in bedrooms since they're the only place that has enough room. In most cases, you'll still have to remove some existing cabinets or shelving. The illustrated storage units shown in this section were intentionally deigned to accommodate the presence of a single window. If you don't have to deal with a window, you'll have even more options.

The first example is a small workshop – complete with a bench vise and overhead storage for supplies and scrap lumber. Note that the window has been retained for ventilation and light. This same concept could just as easily been used for a small office.

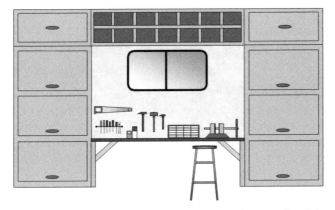

This custom storage unit has been (partially) converted into a small workshop

This second example shows a custom storage unit that's also being used to hold a kayak. With the right mounting hardware, these units can be adapted for storing a small boat, golf clubs, and other recreational items.

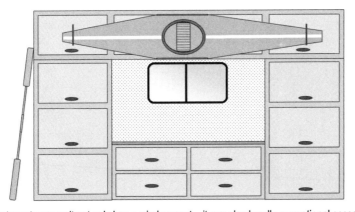

This custom storage unit not only has a window seat – it can also handle recreational accessories

The last example represents a custom storage unit that incorporates a window seat and multiple cubby holes. Its simplicity obscures the fact that it provides an extraordinary amount of storage.

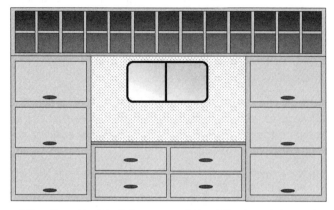

This unit provides lots of storage capacity in addition to a window-seat

Surrounding your Bed in Storage

You can never have too much storage space – especially in a bedroom. The following design is sometimes seen in Class A motorhome bedrooms. The advantage is that it provides a substantial amount of storage capacity without using much floor space. Plus, it can still be used if there's a window above the head of the bed. Note the shoe caddy that's attached to the foot of the bed. This device, made of canvas, holds five pairs of shoes. You can find them at Camping World.

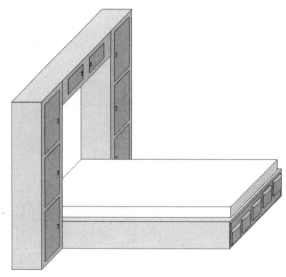

This design offers considerable storage capacity without taking up a lot of valuable floor space

Adding a Headboard

In some RVs, there's a free wall behind the head of the bed. If this is the case, you can create valuable storage space by adding a headboard with a built-in shelf. The headboard is attached to the wall with anchors and screws. If there's a window, construct the bed board around the window opening. Be sure to round off any sharp corners to prevent the possibility of an injury.

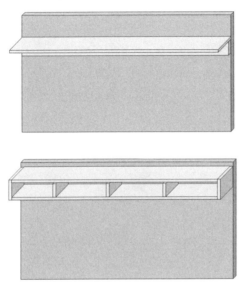

Headboards provide useful storage where it's often needed the most

Improving Air Flow

If you find that your bedroom gets a little stuffy at night, consider installing a ceiling fan. In a bedroom, ceiling fans are generally preferred over a roof vent because they don't generate unwanted light. However, if you do want the features of a roof vent – consider purchasing a spring-loaded shade to block the morning light. RV ceiling fans typically have 36 to 42-inch blades and require approximately 5 to 6 inches of headroom. Fortunately, headroom isn't usually an issue over a bed since you can't walk there anyways (unless you have a hide-away bed). Look for a 12-volt model with a reversible fan. This will enable you to pull in as well as push out air. There are also models that can be remotely controlled – an especially nice feature in a bedroom.

Putting Up some Pegs

Install a strip of Shaker-style pegs approximately two-thirds of the way up the wall. In addition to being stylish, these pegs will quickly become indispensable for hanging clothes, towels, and other similar items. Peg boards are normally installed by counter-sinking screws. The holes in the board are then filled with small hardwood plugs.

After you install one of these in your bedroom, you'll wonder how you lived without it

Traditional Bedroom Decorating Ideas

You can greatly enhance the overall appearance of your bedroom by applying some time-honored decorating tricks. Here are a few ideas:

- Upgrade the lighting fixtures with more stylish and colorful models.

- Replace the day-night blinds with something more fashionable and colorful such as room-darkening honeycomb blinds (see Chapter 10). Then add some sheer curtains to soften the look.

- Paint the walls in a beautiful, warm color. Then, add a decorative border along the middle of the wall for some real elegance.

- Place cedar-filled sachets in your closets and drawers.

- Mount some Trompe l'oeil artwork on the wall. It will give the room a whole new look.

Conclusions and Recommendations

Bedrooms are basically private affairs. Tucked away from public view, they operate under different rules than the rest of an RV. That's the good news. The bad news is that RV bedrooms have a tendency to become the proverbial junk drawer for the entire RV. Can't find a place for that pile of magazines? Stick them in the closet. Don't know what to do with that monopoly set? Throw it under the bed. You get the idea.

The real problem isn't the fact that things end up in the bedroom. After all, the stuff has to go somewhere. The problem is that most RV bedrooms aren't designed to deal with complex storage scenarios. As a result, wardrobes fill up with precarious piles of assorted belongings. Drawers become crammed with forgotten garments, and the closet rod turns into a petrified collection of neglected outfits. If you're "lucky" enough to have storage space under the bed, it inevitably becomes a giant pit full of unspecified possessions and abandoned treasures.

Again – the key to this dilemma is organization and optimization. This chapter describes several ways to make the most of your RV's bedroom including California-style closets, under-bed partitions, storage bins, and custom storage units. All of these solutions can have a profound impact on the volume and manner in which things are stored in your RV. However, one of the first rules of creating and improving storage is to design your solutions around identifiable requirements. For example, if your problem is too many books, build bookshelves. Likewise, if you have too many miscellaneous possessions, get rid of everything you don't need. Then use labeled bins and boxes to keep track of the rest. It's all here in the book…somewhere.

Additional Resources

"Bedrooms: Remodeling and Decorating" by Sunset Publishing Co.

"Bedrooms: California Design Library" by Diane Dorrans Saeks

"The Sacred Bedroom: Creating Your Personal Sanctuary" by Jon Robertson

"Pottery Barn Bedrooms" (Pottery Barn Design Library) by Sarah Lynch, Prue Ruscoe, and Clay Ide

Index